My Orchestras and Other Adventures:
The Memoirs of Boyd Neel

My Orchestras and Other Adventures

The Memoirs of Boyd Neel

Foreword by Sir Peter Pears

Edited by J. David Finch

UNIVERSITY OF TORONTO PRESS

Toronto Buffalo London

Foreword only © Sir Peter Pears 1985
© University of Toronto Press 1985
Toronto   Buffalo   London
Printed in Canada

ISBN 0-8020-5674-1

Canadian Cataloguing in Publication Data

Neel, Boyd, 1905–1981.
My orchestras and other adventures
Discography: p.
Includes index.
ISBN 0-8020-5674-1
1. Neel, Boyd, 1905–1981. 2. Conductors (Music) –
Canada – Biography. 3. Conductors (Music) –
Great Britain – Biography. I. Finch, J. David
(Jolyon David), 1932–   I. Title.
ML422.N43A4 1985   780'.92'4   C85-098928-0

Contents

Foreword

'Let us composers, too, remember what Boyd Neel has done for us ...'
These words, written by Benjamin Britten, formed part of the introduction to Boyd Neel's first book, *The Story of an Orchestra*. I am delighted to have the opportunity to repeat them and to add a few of my own, in recognition of the great respect I had for Boyd, not only as a conductor (though his name will be forever linked with that of his famous orchestra) but also as a person.

It seems appropriate to introduce these few remarks of mine with Britten's words, for his debt to Boyd Neel was considerable. It was Boyd's urgent request for a new work for the Salzburg Festival of 1937 which led to the composition of the *Variations on a Theme of Frank Bridge* and its subsequent wonderful reception at the festival. I was lucky enough to be at that first public performance, on holiday from the BBC Singers with whom I was singing at the time. I remember being very impressed, not only by the work, which was obviously the best piece in the program, but also by the orchestra's account of it – it was a work which calls for great virtuosity from the players, and it was very well received.

I attended many of Boyd's concerts, of course, as both listener and performer. He was a damn good conductor by any standards, giving the impression of entire sureness and authority. The actual beat was unusual, and, if at times it may have been rigid in places where one would have expected more rubato, at least he was clear, which an awful lot of conductors aren't. I sang many times with the orchestra and was always struck by how well prepared they were (Nadia Boulanger remarked on this too, I see) and by the marvellously interesting programs which Boyd devised.

But his real genius, I think, lay in selecting the right people. They were a very good lot – Freddy Grinke, David Martin, Max Gilbert – all first-class musicians, and devoted to him. They followed him like an eagle.

His importance in helping to transform the British music scene was well described by Rosamund Strode in a program note to a special Britten concert at Aldeburgh in 1977, the year after Ben's death. She wrote: 'Nowadays when we take chamber orchestras very much for granted, it is difficult to realise that in forming his orchestra Boyd Neel was actually breaking new ground ... [His] programmes were famous not only for introducing neglected works of the past: he also performed and commissioned important contemporary pieces.'

Readers in Canada may not have been aware just how great Boyd's achievement in Britain was. But they were lucky to have the benefit of his later years, in Toronto where he was Dean of the Royal Conservatory of Music for eighteen years. There too, it seems, he made a significant mark on the musical scene, continuing to champion new works and encourage young native composers. We have evidence of this in 1966, when he brought the Hart House Orchestra to Aldeburgh, and included in the programs works by two contemporary Canadians, Godfrey Ridout and Harry Freedman. Of course, Freddy Grinke was a Canadian too, so Boyd's links with Canada can be said to stretch back even before 1953! One impression I did have about his time in Toronto was the importance of his role in the building of the new Edward Johnson music block. Having a building as clever and smart as that changed the whole musical picture there.

But this book is not simply an account of Boyd's professional life. It is much more, and I found it difficult to put down once I started reading it. His character comes across very clearly – charming, unpretentious, aware of the value of what he was doing, but quite unconceited. I liked him very much as a person. His many records are testimony to his musical skills. These memoirs are a fascinating account of the life of Boyd Neel, the man.

Peter Pears

Preface

Before his death in Toronto on 30 September, 1981, Boyd Neel had been working on these memoirs, but problems with his eyes prevented their completion. Parts had been read, with appropriate musical selections, on the Canadian Broadcasting Corporation radio network; parts – on the founding of the Boyd Neel Orchestra and its Australian tour – are taken from *The Story of an Orchestra* (London: Vox Mundi, 1950); and the chapter on music at the Stratford Festival, Ontario, is from *Thrice the Brinded Cat Hath Mewed*, a 1955 publication of Clarke Irwin and Company Limited, reprinted by kind permission of Irwin Publications Limited. Since times and perspectives change, some omissions have been made in these two latter works. The excitement of the epoch-making trip of the Boyd Neel Orchestra to Australia and New Zealand in 1947, for example, has become less in need of being a descriptive travelogue in an airborne and television-conscious age. The permission of the CBC and the original publishers to use this material is gratefully acknowledged. The contribution of Penelope Nettlefold and Tordie Woods in helping prepare this manuscript is also gratefully acknowledged. I hope that readers will recognize the authentic voice of their author as well as enjoy the history of his and his orchestras' part in the various developments, if not revolutions, in twentieth-century music.

J. David Finch

Financial support for the publication of this book was gratefully received from:

The Canada Council
Frank Evans
Judith S. Finch
Doris Leslie-Smith
Gerald F. Mason
Ralph and Janet Marson
Doris McCarthy
Babs Messervy
Gray and Charlotte Osborn
Guy and Pauline Russel
Margaret G. Slater
Jack Taylor
Charles Wagnieres
Bill and Leah Walls
David and Valerie Walls
Marion Walker
Jade and Tordie Woods

*My Orchestras and
Other Adventures*

1

The Neels

When my name became known in connection with the Boyd Neel Orchestra I often had people remark on the unusual spelling of Neel. Strangely enough it comes from Scandinavia via Normandy and the Channel Islands. In the United Kingdom you won't find the two EEs at all unless it is a branch of the family. There you will find NEAL, NEIL, NEALE, and in Ireland, NEILL, but to see NEEL you will have to travel around the Cherbourg peninsula and Normandy, especially in towns like Bayeux, Carentant, and Avranches, this district being the part settled by Viking pirates, who supplied the necessary Scandinavian element for the name.

NEEL appears for the first time in the records of 963 AD as Viscomte de St Sauveur in the Cotentin district of Normandy. He became a governor of Normandy, repelled an invasion by Ethelred the Unready, who was evidently in one of his unready moods, and later defeated the Bretons. Later he was described as being the son of Richard the Dane and a friend of Robert the Devil. I have always been disappointed that Meyerbeer did not give a Neel a part in his opera about Robert the Devil, the libretto of which, in the words of one commentator, is 'grotesque to the point of absurdity.' There is a marvellous scene in the third act where the real devil summons from their graves the nuns who, during their lives, were unfaithful to their vows. This, of course, gave Meyerbeer his chance for his third-act ballet, obligatory in Paris at the time; it is said that the nuns were led by the famous ballerina Taglioni. They tried to seduce Robert, who was looking on, and nearly succeeded. Later in the opera Robert and the devil have a duet which, in the English translation, appears as 'our great delight is constant infidelity.' All the same, Chopin said of this opera: 'If ever magnificence was seen in the theatre, I doubt it reached the level of splendour shown in *Robert the Devil*. It is a masterpiece with which Meyerbeer has achieved immortality.'

Neel's son, Neel II, was, however, an early tarnisher of the family escutcheon because he was the leader of a revolt against the Conquerer William. He was defeated but escaped to his castle, where he held out for three years before being pardoned and restored to favour in 1054, when his confiscated estates were returned to him. Later he made full amends by joining the invasion of England in 1066, acquitting himself well at Hastings, where he was 'leader of the first army corps' in the battle. Nevertheless, he was never rewarded with a grant of land in England, as were all William's other supporters. We must assume that he returned to Normandy, having married the sister of William the Conquerer, who objected to living in England after the sophisticated court life in Normandy.

At least one branch of the family to which I belong must have emigrated to Jersey, the largest of the Channel Islands; it had, of course, been part of the Duchy of Normandy and continued as such long after the invasion of England. When King John lost Normandy more than a hundred years later, Jersey drifted along on its own, belonging officially to no one but maintaining Norman laws and language, the Norman system of feudalism, Norman money, and Norman weights and measures. All this necessitated the creation of its own constitution, which Jersey still has, and which has been defined as 'that of a principality united to another in the person of the Prince only.' In the nineteenth century England began to take an interest in the island and its inhabitants, inaugurating a regular ferry service to this beautiful place where one could live cheaply and where, *mirabile dictu*, no one paid any taxes. This was possible because a number of islanders, through devout loyalty, performed civic duties without salary. By 1840 there were fifteen thousand English residents, with the result that the French-speaking natives had to begin learning English as well, although until 1900 the official language remained French, which was used in the courts of law, the churches, and the Parliament (called the States). After 1900 English was declared optional and today the huge English population has made English the primary language, although in the country the old Norman

French can still be heard. My maternal grandmother used to switch from one language to the other, sometimes in the middle of a sentence. Since then, there have been Neels in the island continuously until recent times, when most of them seem to have drifted back to France or gone to England.

It is from Jersey that my own family came. We read of a Peter Neel being created '*Seigneur des Meaux*' there as early as 1331. My father was born in Rheims but lived for most of his boyhood at Langueville in Jersey, where the family home had been Sion House since the end of the eighteenth century. My mother was also a Jersey woman, a Le Couteur, a family which, like the Neels, had been well known in Jersey since the Middle Ages. Many Le Couteurs have been rectors of St Martin's, one of Jersey's oldest churches, mentioned as early as 1042; between 1661 and 1789 no fewer than five Le Couteurs held the position of rector. There was also a judge in the nineteenth century.

My mother showed a musical talent when quite young and, at the age of sixteen, was sent to London to the Royal College of Music to study piano and, later, singing: a remarkable enterprise for a young Victorian girl. When she left the College, Hubert Parry, who was then principal, gave her a glowing testimonial. This enabled her to get a job as accompanist to Gustave Garcia, a nephew of the two great singers Maria Malibran and Pauline Viardot, and I have a letter from Garcia thanking her for her excellent work and enclosing her pay cheque for the previous week – the sum of two pounds! Working for Garcia brought her in touch with many of the greatest singers of the day, who, in turn, invited her to play for them in their public appearances.

My mother used to tell wonderful stories about the Garcia family, and especially the visits of Pauline Viardot to her brother and nephew in London. Viardot had been the greatest Orfeo of her time. Her brother Manuel lived to be a hundred and one and will go down in history not only as an outstanding teacher of singing but also as the inventor of the laryngoscope, one of the greatest advances in clinical medicine ever made. There is no doubt that any musical talent I may have inherited came from my mother, who had given up her professional work when she married but had continued her playing. I have not been able to find any recordings of Garcia's songs, a great many of which used to be sung by his pupils at that time. We did, however, find a recording of one of the most famous of Viardot's pupils, Felia Litvinne, a Franco-Russian and one of the greatest Wagnerian sopranos of her day; she was the first

Isolde to be heard in Paris and she was the Brunnhilde of the first complete *Ring* to be given at the Monnaie in Brussels in 1903. A few years later, she sang Isolde at Covent Garden, with Nikisch conducting, and my mother, who had met her often at the Garcias, always told me it was the greatest performance of *Tristan* she had ever heard. Litvinne made a recording around 1907 of the aria 'Voi lo Sapete' from *Cavalleria Rusticana*.

Viardot was not only a great singer and teacher of singing, but also a superb pianist (a pupil of Liszt), a talented portrait painter, and no mean composer. As a singer she had few equals at that time, and her technique was so fantastic that she arranged Tartini's violin sonata, *The Devil's Trill*, for voice, and sang it at a concert! Apparently Viardot was the essence of propriety on her London visits, although the *ménage à trois* in Paris, when Turgenev joined the household, and the later even more notorious *ménage à quatre*, when Charles Gounod joined the party, had been the staple gossip of the French capital for years before the turn of the century.

Maria Malibran was even more celebrated than Viardot when, at the age of twenty-eight, she died of severe head injuries received in a fall from a horse in April 1836. It is possible she might have lived had she received the correct treatment, but she concealed her injuries so as not to interrupt her preparations for an engagement at the Manchester Festival in September. She fulfilled the engagement and died soon after, leaving a bereaved husband of only a few months, the noted Belgian violinist Charles de Bériot.

My father came to London at the turn of the century and married my mother there, starting a mass emigration of Neels and Le Couteurs from Jersey. The Neels split into two halves, one of which went to France, the other to England. We lived in a beautiful Georgian house on Maze Hill at the eastern end of Greenwich Park in south-east London, a convenient location for my father's paint business across the Thames on the Isle of Dogs.

Every weekend well-known singers and players would come down from town and, apart from being a wonderful introduction to great works, the chamber music I heard had a profound influence upon me. I used to beg to be allowed to sit up late and I can remember quite well the impact of the Schubert trios on those occasions. They have never sounded quite so magical to me since that time. They were a marvellous introduction to music for a very young child.

Boyd Neel's grandparents on his father's side,
Elias and Annie Neel (née Boyd)

Boyd Neel's grandparents on his mother's side,
Frank and Alice Le Couteur

Boyd Neel's parents, Louis and Ruby Neel,
on their wedding day, October 18th 1904

Boyd Neel at about age four dressed as Robin Hood

Boyd Neel at age seven

Three of my uncles on the French side started a small private bank in the rue Daunou, just off the Place de l'Opéra, which bore the name Boyd Neel et Cie. That is where the 'Boyd' comes from. It was the maiden name of my paternal grandmother and she was the only non-Norman element in the family, coming as she did from Cootehill, County Cavan, Ireland. It was at the time of the famines, when over a million Irish left their homeland. The Boyds probably chose Jersey because they were ardent Methodists and Jersey had always been a stronghold of that denomination. It was therefore quite natural for them to meet the Neels, who were also pillars of the Methodist Church in the Channel Islands. Annie Boyd married Elias Neel when she was only sixteen and in pictures he himself looks hardly any older! The strange thing is that none of their children were ever members of the Methodist Church, or of any church at all.

Uncle Boyd died fairly young, but the other two brothers ran the bank until the Second World War, which finished the bank and both of them. The bank was an extraordinary institution. It had just one office, which was tiny, and it was more like a club than a bank. There were armchairs and small tables at which the customers sat and discussed the day's horse-racing. Every well-known trainer and jockey banked there, as did the large number of Americans who, in those days, swarmed over Paris. The only client who was neither of the racing fraternity nor an American was James Joyce, a neighbour and great friend of my uncle Jack. I well remember seeing Joyce sitting in the bank surrounded by the strange clientele and looking quite at home. If one wanted a tip for the day's racing one didn't consult the newspapers, but either 'phoned one of the brothers at the bank or, better still, went to the bank and sat for half an hour listening to the conversations. For lunch everyone repaired to the bar of the Chatham Grill, a hundred yards away, and business was carried on there! This was as far as my uncles ever walked in their lives.

I remember going over to Paris with my family to see them just after the First World War. As we walked past the Opéra, we saw a poster on the wall outside announcing a performance of *William Tell*. The date on it was 1914, and it was then 1919. The Opéra had been closed for the duration of the war and the posters had never been removed. I remember that the name of the tenor who was to have sung the part of Arnold was John O'Sullivan, a strange name to see at the Paris Opéra.

The Second World War with the German occupation and the death of my uncles meant the end of the bank, but I still meet Americans who ask if I am related to the brothers. The bank was certainly a unique institution.

My father, one of thirteen children, was the only one of the English branch of the family who seemed to have any business sense at all; consequently, he often supported the entire family over long periods. My great-grandfather Neel, who had been a member of the *Jurat* in Jersey, part of the Royal Court of Justice, and quite a distinguished local citizen, became involved in the Joint Stock Bank, which crashed in 1873. He was tried at the assizes of 1874 and acquitted, as it was found that there was no sign of fraud or dishonesty – only 'an incomprehensible lack of business ability.' In other words, great-grandfather was a typical Neel!

My mother's parents had also come to England shortly after the Neels and lived about five minutes' walk up the hill from us. Grandfather Le Couteur had been in the wine business in Jersey and their house is today, as is that of the Neels, part of an hotel. Although the two families must have known each other fairly well, they seldom met in London. Perhaps the atmosphere of the Neel home was regarded as rather too Bohemian by the Le Couteurs, but I'm only surmising at this distance in time.

The Neel house at Maze Hill was a long one with a coach house in the middle, and almost the entire English branch of the Neel family lived there. We had the lower end, which had a walled-off garden, and my grandparents and countless uncles, cousins, and aunts lived in the upper end – the coach house dividing the two dwellings. At Christmas thirty-five of us used to sit down to dinner, after which charades of a most elaborate nature were acted in the hall. I was usually given a makeshift part which had been written for me 'to keep him quiet.' Rehearsals went on for weeks before Christmas, and some of the 'productions' were incredibly lavish. The difficulty was that, as we all lived in the same building, secrecy was virtually impossible to keep, yet essential lest a rival cast should overhear any clues during rehearsals. Our own charade was, of course, always a 'musical' with a score provided by my mother, who was never able to act, as she always had to be orchestra, conductor, and producer as well. Some of the dance numbers got very wild with the aid of Christmas champagne. How I loved those Christmas shows! I looked forward to them the whole year long!

The garden at Maze Hill was large and beautiful with a tennis court at the far end, and the weekend tennis parties were celebrated all over the neighbourhood. My parents were a powerful mixed-doubles team and won many tournaments. Tennis was not the only game at which my father excelled. He not only formed a rugby football team called Park House, which made quite a reputation in the League, but also introduced the game to France when he took a group of players over to play there. It gave him the greatest satisfaction when France finally entered a team in the International League some years later.

My mother played a strange backhand stroke, unknown at that date, which in some ways resembled the two-handed one used today. It was entirely her own invention, and I have never seen it used by anyone else. It had a most disconcerting effect on her opponents, and she won many points in this way. Sometimes there were fifty people at these tennis parties, about a dozen playing while the rest watched and awaited the climax of the afternoon: a gargantuan tea spread under the huge trees on the lawn. We kids could hardly wait for this moment, especially in the strawberry season, when the fruit was piled high on the dishes. While the grown-ups were occupied at this feast there was always a children's doubles game going on accompanied by stentorian coaching from the respective parents. These were the afternoons when my grandmother Neel left her window, where she always sat, and was escorted down the garden to a kind of throne by the tennis court, where she held court among the guests. A lovely, sweet woman, her dress was always black, buttoned right up to her neck with a small white lace frill around the collar; whatever the temperature she was always dressed in the same way. I never saw her excited or perturbed and having had children seemed not to have taken any toll of her physically. She was a victim of the great flu epidemic at the end of World War One. Of my grandfather Neel I can remember little as he died while I was still very young.

Enough, I think, of the Neels. My outstanding memory of the Le Couteurs is of being taken every Sunday morning by Grandpa Le Couteur from Greenwich Pier to Westminster and back on an old paddle steamer called the *Edmund Ironside*. This was my greatest joy of the week, and I never take that trip today in a sophisticated motor boat without thinking of those wonderful voyages among ships from all countries and climes which caught my child's imagination so vividly. Sometimes an old man played an accordion on the deck if it was fine. These river trips and the Drury Lane pantomime at Christmas were the greatest joys of my life at that time.

2

The London Scene I

I suppose I can be said to have grown up in an 'artistic atmosphere,' whatever that is exactly. The first theatre I was ever taken to was the Palace Theatre in London, which had been built by D'Oyly Carte as an opera house. He started his first season with Sullivan's *Ivanhoe*, which had quite a long run. Gilbert was not involved in that opera. A man called Sturgis wrote the libretto, basing it on the Scott novel. For some reason, D'Oyly Carte lost his new theatre, which then became a music hall, and it was to see Anna Pavlova and her partner, Michael Mordkin, that I was taken there.

These two had just left the Diaghilev company to make solo appearances and they arrived in London before the whole Diaghilev company danced there. They caused a sensation. Such dancing was unknown in Western Europe. I well remember Pavlova in her famous solo, *The Dying Swan*, danced to the familiar music from Saint-Saens' *Carnival of the Animals*. I can see it now: the pitch-dark stage, the pool of white light, and the astonishing wave-like movements which seemed to pass along Pavlova's arms from shoulder to hands. I have never seen quite the same thing since in any other dancer. The tense silence of the audience impressed me, even awed me. What a start to a life of theatre-going and, at times, working in theatres! And then, of course, came the *Bacchanale* with which she always finished the evening, often having to repeat it several times. Mordkin was also impressive, but we were to see greater male dancers when the whole Diaghilev troupe arrived. The following is from an article which appeared in the London *Times* on 18 July 1910, about the *Bacchanale* from Glazunov's *The Seasons*:

If Pavlova had never danced ... the public stock of harmless pleasure during the past theatrical season would certainly have diminished. Nothing like it has been seen before in the London of our time. There was, to be sure, the delightful Genée, with her gaiety and brilliance, and there was the seductive posturing of Isadora Duncan and Maud Allan. But Pavlova and the Russian dancers of the present moment (including not only those of Pavlova's own troop, but the beautiful Lydia Kyasht of the Empire – a rival who runs, or rather dances, her very close – and others at the Coliseum and the Hippodrome) have given us Londoners something really new; an extraordinary technical accomplishment, an unfailing sense of rhythm, and an unerring feeling for the elegant in fantasy, and what Hazlitt would have called a 'gusto,' a passionate enjoyment. The dancing of Anna Pavlova is a thing of perfect beauty. This is no case of a Mr. Pepys and his 'best legs that ever I saw.' In the presence of art of this stamp, one's pleasure is purely aesthetic. Indeed, the sex element (though, of course, necessarily somewhere in the subconsciousness) counts for very little; for a man the dancing of Michael Mordkin is almost as pleasure-giving as that of Mlle. Pavlova. The combination of the two, above all in their Bacchanalian dance, is an even choicer thing than their pas seuls.

Quite as much of a novelty to Londoners is the dancing of the troop. The freedom and swing of their limbs in the Mazurka *almost lures you from your seat to 'shake a leg' with them: but you sit quite still while they are alternately quickening up and slowing down in the* tempo rubato *of the* Rhapsodie Hongroise, *seeing clearly that here is something you couldn't do to save your life. This is a very different thing from the ballet to which Londoners used once upon a time to be mercilessly subjected – rank after rank and file after file of honest bread-winners from Camberwell and Peckham Rye performing mechanical manoeuvres with the dogged perseverance of a company of Boy Scouts. When people tell you, as they sometimes will, that ballet dancing is a bore, you recognize the trail of the honest British bread-winners. Once they have seen the Russian dancers they will hardly again be guilty of that bêtise.*

So seeing Pavlova dance was my earliest recollection of the theatre. I remember someone telling me that once, during Pavlova's the *Dying*

Swan, at the supreme moment of ecstatic hush, a woman's voice, with a strong Scottish accent, rang out, saying, 'You're right, dear; she *is* the image of Mrs Wishart!'

I always listened intently to the talk at home and the names constantly recurring were Beecham and two Russian names of which I had no idea of the spelling – Diaghilev and Chaliapin. I gathered, from what I heard, that something had hit London pretty hard, that it was Russian, and that Beecham was responsible for its coming to England. It was not long, of course, before my parents went to see this phenomenon and they talked about it so much that I insisted that, next time they went, they also take me. They said that I was too young to enjoy it and that perhaps in a few years time I could go. Then I clearly remember my mother saying: 'Well, I don't know, I think he would love the *Igor* dances.' And so I went, wondering what the *Igor* dances were, but I was soon to find out. I also discovered that 'it' was the Diaghilev Ballet.

Pavlova had been a sensation, but no one today can have any idea of the impact of the Diaghilev company on the Western world. Such an ensemble, such brilliant, exciting décor, such a galaxy of superb dancers, especially the men, and last but certainly not least, all done to wonderful music by great composers, under great conductors. Until then the music of an average ballet company seen in Western Europe had been pretty poor. True, some of the big operas of the nineteenth century had charming ballets, but these were usually performed very indifferently, with very weak dancers and dreadful choreography. When the Russians arrived with works especially commissioned from composers like Stravinsky and Ravel, as well as their own masterpieces by Borodin, Rimsky-Korsakov, Balakirev, and Tchaikovsky, and played by a full orchestra under a star conductor (Monteux, Ansermet, or Beecham), the evening became a feast for the ears as well as the eyes. In subsequent years it grew even more important because symphonic works were played *between* the ballets, and many pieces such as Saint-Saens' *Symphonic Poems*, many short pieces by Stravinsky, much Russian music, Chabrier's *Suite Pastorale*, Walton's *Portsmouth Point*, and many, many others made the intervals an exciting experience. Why can't this admirable idea be revived today? It could well be done where the orchestra is adequate, as in the larger houses, but not, of course, with the touring 'pit' orchestras of dreadful memory. Intervals in ballet performances are always of boring length but could be made part of the evening's pleasure in this way.

So it was that I went to Covent Garden for the first time in my life to see the Russian dancers. Entering the famous and beautiful old theatre was not the least part of the evening's excitement and I little knew then of the hundreds of wonderful visits I would pay there during my life, both as a listener and as an occasional performer. The program that night started with *Thamar*, with music by Balakirev, in which Karsavina danced. She was, at that time, the 'prima ballerina assoluta' of the company. I recall very well the Bakst setting and my feeling of being wafted into another world of fairy tales and mystery. Of the actual ballet, I only remember the Prince disappearing through the secret panel as Thamar stabbed him. What a thrill for an eight-year-old! Then came *Petrouchka*, with Nijinsky and Karsavina and, I think, Pierre Monteux conducting. I have seen this ballet many, many times since, but it has never had the same effect on me again. I have not seen anyone to compare with Nijinsky. When he beat on the door and finally fell, he really did appear to be made of cloth and filled with sawdust. Of a human being there appeared to be no trace.

That evening with Diaghilev's *Ballet Russe* ended with the *Prince Igor* dances, but I can't remember much about them. For me, *Petrouchka* had been the highlight of the evening and, after all these years, I still think it is the supreme masterpiece of ballet. It has everything a great work of art should have. The 'first time' is nearly always the best and, in matters of art, one seldom recaptures the 'first fine careless rapture,' although through the years a greater understanding and a deeper appreciation can result. It is the initial impact of suddenly becoming aware which is so unforgettable, especially on a very young and receptive imagination. Nijinsky became my hero, although I had only seen him as the puppet. In the last scene when he was struck down by the Moor, his head seemed detached from his body. He remains by far the greatest male dancer I have ever seen, and I always regret that I was not fortunate enough to see him make his famous leap through the window in *Le Spectre de la Rose*. When the scandal of *L'Après-midi* was raging, I begged to be taken to see it, but I was told I 'wouldn't understand!' It is amusing that such things could have caused scandals in 1913 when we witness what is said and done in our theatres today!

But what about that other Russian name which I kept on hearing discussed – Chaliapin? I had no idea if this was a dancer, actor, singer, or conductor. Whatever he was he seemed to have caused as much of a sensation as Nijinsky. Finally, some months after the visit to Covent

Garden, I was told we were going to Drury Lane to hear, this time, a wonderful company of Russian *singers*. I had already been once to Drury Lane for the Christmas pantomime and this started an annual event to which I always looked forward. My Paris uncles (with the bank) knew Arthur Collins very well; Collins was the general manager at the Lane and we got free stalls every Christmas. This was the only time I ever sat lower than the upper circle, anyway until I was much older. Dan Leno I never saw, alas, but George Graves, Will Evans, Florence Smithson, and Marie Blanche made up the 'team' until the pantomime was looked upon by me as 'childish and stupid.'

The Russian Opera Company which Beecham brought to England, complete with chorus, caused almost as much excitement as the ballet. The London theatres had never seen such a spectacle, and, towering over it all, the astonishing Feodor Chaliapin, who was making his first London Appearance. He had, however, sung in Paris some years before and had been famous in his native Russia since 1896. We saw him as Boris in Moussorgsky's *Boris Godounov*, his most famous role. All I can remember was his terrifying appearance at the door of the nursery, when he breaks in on the children at play, and the final death scene. As a child I really had no idea of what *Boris Godounov* was all about, and you are probably thinking how unsuitable an opera it was for a child of eight. However, a few years ago, in Toronto, the opera chosen for the school performances of the Canadian Opera Company was *Salome* – and it was an outstanding success! Children are far more sophisticated than most parents realize or, rather want to realize.

After that *Boris* I saw Chaliapin many, many times throughout the years – in *Boris*, when he sang in Russian and sometimes everyone else sang in Italian; in *Prince Igor*, where he loved to double the parts of Galitsky and Khan Kontchak (a marvellous feat of characterization); as the mad miller in Dargomyzhsky's *Russalka*; as Don Basilio in *The Barber of Seville*; as Salieri in Rimsky-Korsakov's *Mozart and Salieri*; and as Mephistopheles in both the Gounod *Faust* and the Boito *Mefistofele*. What an artist he was! Certainly by far the greatest opera singer I have ever heard, and I would say, music apart, he was probably the geatest *actor* I ever saw. But he was the despair of conductors and directors and thought nothing of doing a bit of improvisation if it suited him. I shall always remember him years later in *Faust* at Covent Garden with Eugene Goossens conducting: Chaliapin came right down to the footlights in the garden scene, to beat the tempo he wanted, then returned to the deserted Martha left waiting for him upstage! Could any other artist get away with this kind of thing without a murmur of disapproval in the theatre today? So overwhelming was his personality that Chaliapin performances tended to be just that, and it is hard to recollect who else shared the stage with him. Yet he could, when he wanted, take his part in an ensemble better than most people. In *The Barber*, for instance, he was the perfect Basilio, and I shall never forget the 'Calunnia' aria with its almost terrifying crescendo, starting in an actual singing *whisper*, Chaliapin crouching low and gradually rising to his enormous height, with Bartolo motionless in front of him, held by the piercing eyes as if he were the prey of a snake. Chaliapin's versatility was extraordinary and he could excel in so many different kinds of music, even that of the church. There is an extraordinary recording (made in the late 1920s by Chaliapin and the Choir of the Russian Metropolitan Church in Paris, of 'Glory to Thee, O Lord' from Gretcha-ninov's setting of the liturgy of St John Chrysostom) which gives some idea of Chaliapin's hypnotic vocal art. There will never be anyone like him again. Thank goodness we have the records, which give some idea of the amazing subtlety of his singing. He could vary the colours of his voice like no one else. The first Russian companies always used the Korsakov version of Boris, and I believe they are still doing so. This is the version which ends with the Death Scene. I know I am a heretic in preferring the Korsakov version to all others, but I find the original too stark. The trouble is perhaps that I heard only the Korsakov until I was about thirty years old and got so used to it I just can't make the neces-sary adjustment.

By 1914 I was a staunch balletomane (after one performance, unless we count Pavlova) and a rather mystified opera-goer (also on one performance). I heard my parents discussing a ballet all about tennis, which, of course, appealed to them, but I wasn't taken to see it. I imagine this must have been Debussy's *Jeux*. Nor was I taken to the *Sacré* which everyone thought would cause a riot similar to that of the Paris première the previous year, but it all passed off quietly. I was, however, taken again to the Diaghilev ballet, this time at Drury Lane. I saw *Thamar* once more and *Schéhérazade* for the first time. Being already an ardent reader of the *Arabian Nights*, I found this the biggest thrill of all. Even today, if well done, it never fails to excite me. I remember vividly the blazing colours of the Bakst scenery and the negro slave who was painted a kind of blue colour all over. When he was released at Zobeida's command, he shot out on to the stage in a great leap, and seemed to be made of rubber. His convulsions when he was finally killed were dreadful to behold. I can't remember who danced this part – originally it had been Nijinsky, but by this time Nijinsky had formed his own company and broken away from Diaghilev. I never saw him again. They say that in *Schéhérazade*, when struck with the sword, he spun on his neck before falling flat on the stage; and, later on, the crazy idea was circulated that, in performing this astonishing feat, he might have undergone some brain damage, which could have accounted for his subsequent mental collapse. A good story, but medically, I think, rather questionable.

The third ballet that night was a première in England and I, of course, had no idea what an important event it was in the musical world. It wasn't until I was much older that I realized that I had been present at a rather historic occasion. Maybe that was also the mood of the majority of the audience, because the composer concerned was certainly not as famous then as he later became, nor was anyone to guess that the work we heard that night for the first time was to become one of the most popular pieces of the orchestral repertoire. This was the *Daphnis and Chloë* of Maurice Ravel, which had been commissioned by Diaghilev. I can't remember much about it on that occasion because I had been so carried away by *Schéhérazade*, but I think Karsavina was in it and a new name, Michael Fokine, had appeared. Bakst did the scenery and the newcomer the choreography. Apparently, as I was to realize years later, there were all sorts of undercurrents in progress, and on the morning of that performance the following letter had appeared in the *Times*:

Sir,
My most important work Daphnis and Chloë *is to be produced at Drury Lane Theatre on June 9th. I was overjoyed, and, fully appreciating the great honour done to me, considered the event as one of the weightiest in my artistic career.*

Now I learn that what will be produced before the London Public is not my work in its original form, but a makeshift arrangement which I had agreed to write at M. Diaghilev's special request in order to facilitate production in certain minor centres. M. Diaghilev probably considers London as one of the 'minor centres' since he is about to produce at Drury Lane, in spite of his positive word, the new version without chorus.

I am deeply surprised and grieved and I consider the proceeding is disrespectful towards the London public as well as towards the composer. I shall therefore be extremely thankful to you if you will kindly print this letter. Offering you thanks in anticipation,
 I remain, dear sir,
  faithfully yours,
   Maurice Ravel

Diaghilev replied as follows:

Two months ago I produced Daphnis and Chloë *with great success at the Théâtre de l'Opéra, Monte Carlo, and I presented there the second version of that work, that is to say, without chorus. After the first performance, I received a most gratifying telegram of congratulation from M. Ravel's publisher, and the composer, until yesterday, never seems to have had any idea of protesting against the manner in which his work was presented, the production, in fact, meeting with unanimous approval. The second version, without chorus, is not a haphazard affair and was very far from being written with a view to production in small theatres. The experiment of giving* Daphnis and Chloë *with chorus was tried two years ago, and it was clearly proved that the participation of the chorus was not only useless, but actually detrimental. I was, therefore, obliged to beg M. Ravel to write the second version which was successfully accomplished by the distinguished composer. I had the pleasure of asking M. Ravel to write* Daphnis and Chloë *for my ballet; more, the composer did me the honour to dedicate this remarkable work to me, and it would be very extraordinary in view of this if I had not made every effort to present it in the most perfect manner to the London public to whom I owe a very great debt of admiration and gratitude.**

I always feel that it is, in a way, a pity that these great ballet scores have become what their composers never dreamed they would – that is, virtuoso pieces to be played at symphony concerts. *Le Sacré du Printemps, Daphnis and Chloë, Petrouchka, La Péri, La Tragédie de Salome*, etc., were conceived as ballets and lose an enormous amount when played on their own. This was brought to my mind very forcibly in 1929 when I heard and saw *Sacré* in the theatre for the first time,

---

* Cyril W. Beaumont, *The Diaghilev Ballet in London* (Putnam, 1940)

having heard it for years as a concert piece. In that year Diaghilev revived it at Covent Garden in a new choreography by Massine, and the whole thing took on a completely new meaning, gaining enormously in power and excitement. Of course, the trouble is that a great number of quite well-known ballet companies simply haven't got an orchestra which can cope with the score, especially when on tour. It is a difficult and, in these days of financial stringency, an almost insoluble problem, but there is no doubt that much is lost when these scores are just played as concert pieces.

August 4th, 1914, and we still lived in the big house on Maze Hill. This meant that we were right in the track of any German raiders which followed the Thames on their way to London. First the Zeppelins came by night, and I saw two shot down in flames. Then, one day, I was cycling home from school and saw people staring at the sky. Lo and behold, fifteen German aeroplanes in the first daylight air raid in history, coming up the Thames at what seemed no great height. They were in close formation, and were being shot at by what anti-aircraft guns we had in those days. Another day, on my way to school, I saw that the front lawn of some friends of ours, who lived about half a mile away, had, during the night, become a large crater, but their house wasn't damaged. That was the nearest bomb we had in the first war. By the time the second war came along, we were quite seasoned air raid subjects, and we agreed that, in some ways, although the damage in the second war was, of course, far, far greater, we had found that having a Zeppelin hovering over you for an hour or so was a greater strain than a stick of bombs from a fast plane, which was all over in a few seconds. The flying bombs, of course, were another matter.

My father was put on to some hush-hush job which entailed him making frequent trips to the front lines in France although he was not in any of the services, and I have a 'laisser-passer' issued by the War Office, and written in French, with which he was issued for one of these trips. We discovered later that he had to deal with polluted water, which apparently the troops had been drinking. Just before the war he had left the paint business and had started a water-softening firm, which eventually did pretty well, and he was awarded the royal coat of arms on its stationery, following the installation of a water softener at Buckingham Palace. About a week after it had been in use he got an urgent phone call from the palace, asking him to come over at once. When he arrived he was greeted by the king's (George V) private secretary, who told him that a few days after the king had started bathing in soft water his nails had begun to fall off. My father asked to see the bathroom, and found a shelf of bath salts of varying colours over the bath. He asked if the king always used these, and was told that, as he had to have perfumed bath water, a spoonful was always added. The soda added to the already softened water caused a softening of all the nails, and my father said that must stop at once. General consternation, as the king had to have a perfumed bath. 'All right,' said my dad, 'add Eau de Cologne,' and the crisis was averted.

One night during the winter of 1917 I was playing with my cousins, in their section of the Maze Hill house, and we were rehearsing a little play we had written ourselves. Suddenly the lights faded out and I, with some annoyance, shouted 'Don't turn them off now, it's too soon!' to the lighting controller, my cousin Patricia. I had no sooner shouted when an eerie light lit up the sky – the sort of light you see surrounding UFOs in science fiction films – followed by the loudest noise I have heard in my seventy-five years on this earth. Every window in the house blew in and the floor heaved under our feet. We stumbled and crawled down the stairs and I ran into our part of the house to find every window shattered and my mother with her hands badly cut by the flying glass. Outside, the orange light had changed to a ruby red glow which seemed to come from the direction of the river. From our house, during the daytime, we could see the ships passing up and down the Thames from the docks to the sea. None of us had any idea of what could have happened, but we imagined it must have been some sort of bomb. When my father came home from his office, he said he had been standing on the platform at London Bridge railway station and that the station shivered even at that distance, which must have been at least ten miles. The huge fire burnt for several days and an enormous column of black smoke rose from the spot. Still nobody knew what it was, or what had happened to 'it.' Security saw to that. Rumours were rife, and we set about patching our windows. After a week or so we learnt that it was a munitions factory at Silvertown, just across the Thames from us, but, as far as I know, the *real* cause of it was never divulged to the public. Naturally everyone suspected sabotage. W. MacDonnagh later recalled this event in *In London during the Great War* (London, 1935):

I was sent to Silvertown today to write about the disaster. What a scene of devastation and sorrow. Silvertown is a sordid district of factories and of streets of one-storied houses lying about the riverside and the docks. A huge crater marks the site of the chemical works of Brunner, Mond & Co. It is the centre of a square mile within which many hundreds of the little dwellings have been razed to the ground. Close on two thousand people have been made homeless. The casualties are officially stated to be sixty-nine killed and four hundred injured. But by common report they are really far greater. The locality is made a prohibited area, and is enclosed and guarded by military and police. Admittance is allowed only on an order issued by the Ministry of Munitions or the War Office.

The authorities are satisfied that the disaster was accidental. The fire broke out on the top floor of the factory. Some minutes elapsed before the explosives and chemicals were reached by the flames, and the time was availed of by Dr. Andrea Angell, the chief chemist, to get the work people out. He perished with the factory. The kaleidoscopic sky was caused by the blowing up of the chemicals and the explosion of the firing of five tons of T.N.T. – the most terrible of explosives. I was told that a tongue of crimson flame darted right across the river to the Woolwich side, setting a gasometer near the Royal Arsenal ablaze. For a time it was feared that the Arsenal was in danger.

Stories are being circulated of people in the East End running about the streets almost crazy with fear during that half minute of dreadful uncertainty last night. But for a war being on it would, I believe, have been assumed that the awful and mysterious appearance in the heavens presaged the Doom. The prevailing desire for the end of the war leaves no room for concern about the End of the World.

My mother worked in a canteen in Woolwich Arsenal, and on nights when the Zeppelins hovered over us that was not a pleasant place to be. I was going to day school, which I didn't like at all. The headmaster drank terribly, and when on a bout, would thrash us mercilessly. I learned very little there, maybe a bit of maths from a master called Ferry, who played a hymn on a harmonium every morning in the hall, but that was all.

Our house on the hill was in a mess after the explosion, and it was impossible in wartime to get the windows mended for the rest of the winter, so my father took a small house at Ashtead in Surrey, from where I went to another school near Ewell. This time I liked the place; it was a boarding school which had a very civilized headmaster, and we actually had a bit of music now and then. I learned Rubinstein's *Melody in F* and something by Heller on the piano, which I played with the utmost virtuosity at a school concert. I was eleven years old and from that date my playing steadily deteriorated until an operation on a finger in 1957 put paid to it altogether.

Apart from the keyboard, I used to practise later on an old viola which I had bought in the Portobello Road and also had lessons on the clarinet from a member of one of the crack bands of the Brigade of Guards. He only knew me as 'Dr Neil' spelt in any of its many ways, and never connected me with the 'Boyd Neel' he often heard on the radio. I only learnt with him for about a year and was a fair pupil, I believe. Many years later, I was asked to conduct an orchestra – I can't remember where – and there was my teacher sitting in the wind section. I can see his face now when he looked up and saw who the conductor was!

I had read somewhere that all conductors should be able to sing, however terribly, and I agree one hundred per cent with this. But of my singing exploits more anon.

3

Not on the Ocean Wave

By the time I had become a pupil at the school near Ewell, I had decided to join the navy. Patriotism was the fashion. It was 1918 and the war was nearing its close, although nobody seemed to realize it. In those days, even during the war, to become a regular naval officer one had to enter at the age of 'more than thirteen plus four months and less than thirteen plus eight months, and to pass a written examination in general subjects.' This was not very difficult, but it was important in that you entered the service in a certain order with your fellow cadets, and it was well-nigh impossible to improve your status during the whole four years of your training. This one was never told on entering – which, I realized much later on, was very unfair. The written exam, however, was not by any means the largest hurdle one had to face. There was also the famous and dreaded 'interview' at the Admiralty. This ordeal had become legendary and the questions asked of candidates were said to be bizarre in the extreme. One of the favourites was: 'What was the number of the taxi you came in?' And I was warned to notice every detail of my day before I had the interview, which was conducted in what I imagined to be the First Sea Lord's panelled room, hung around with portraits of great British admirals. There were some half dozen high-ranking officers around the table at which I took the one vacant chair. After some initial pleasantries, one of them suddenly said: 'Are you ever seasick?' I said 'Yes, sir, very often.' 'Then why do you want to join the navy?' Greatly daring, I replied: 'Because I thought it might cure my seasickness, sir.' This produced a roar of laughter and I felt my rather impertinent answer had not offended the great ones around the table. 'I wish it had cured mine' came from the head of the table in a gruff voice. This, I learnt many years later, was the voice of Admiral Sir Reginald Tupper, who chaired the meeting on this occasion.

A spirit of bonhomie and camaraderie having been established, I felt on safer ground, but I was still trembling with terror and trying to recall the number of the bus (no taxi for me) that I had come on. This was quite unnecessary, however, because from now on seasickness was to be the main topic of the meeting.

'How many ships have you been in?'

'Several times crossing the Channel before the war to see my uncle in Paris, and in a dinghy which I sailed whilst on holiday in Dorset last summer.'

'Whereabouts in Dorset?'

'Lulworth Cove, sir.'

'I know Lulworth Cove very well. Did you eat lobsters?'

'Yes, sir, very often. They were so easy to catch and we had several pots we put down.'

'Lucky people, we never had any luck.'

And that finished it. There was some more conversation as to how to cure recurrent seasickness, which at least half the committee confessed they still suffered from, even after many years in the service. During this I was forgotten, but finally the chairman said: 'Well, Mr Neel, I don't think we need keep you any longer. Mind the step as you go out. Good afternoon!'

I stumbled out and felt I had made an appalling mess of the whole thing. I would be dismissed as an impertinent little wretch and that would be that. But no, I heard in about a week's time that I had been accepted and would report to Osborne in January 1919 as a member of the Grenville term. Much astonishment at my school, because the captain of the school, who had also tried for the navy, had been turned down. This was rather sad, because we were good friends and had hoped to enter the service together. I heard later that he had got into the army successfully and distinguished himself as a good soldier.

In 1919 Osborne College was the place where you commenced your training to become a naval officer. Originally the stables of Osborne House, it consisted of some half-dozen dormitories constructed of something called 'Uralite' and connected together by long covered ways. Each 'term' was admitted and named after a famous admiral; everyone on joining was between the ages of thirteen and four months and thirteen and eight months. From this early age, the customs and traditions of H M Navy were drilled into us for four years. Its modern counterpart is the assembly line of a giant motor factory. Many succumbed to this treatment, but others kicked against the pricks of the overpowering 'total immersion' atmosphere and either got out, or were asked to go quietly. The advantage was that you got a first-class public school education, with many added subjects in the engineering and scientific fields, for an absurdly low fee, which mightily pleased my father. Besides the usual academic subjects we learned such things as foundry technique, including the making of patterns and actual casting and worked in the copper smithy on everything to do with steam and internal combustion engines as they were then. Even so, there was time left for sports (always encouraged a great deal) and a few sidelines such as drama and even music!

The discipline was formidable in the extreme. Reveille was at 6:00 a.m. and each dormitory had a small swimming pool at its end. This contained unheated sea water, and even in midwinter, the cadets had to leap out of bed and run into a so-called 'plunge' while watched by a cadet captain who was there to see you totally immersed yourself. If you didn't you were made to go through again. You kept all your clothes and worldly possessions in a sea chest at the foot of your bed, and you had to get dressed in five minutes, and then run (always run) to the dining hall for breakfast. Everything had to be done at the double, even when you had half an hour to spare between classes. The result was that you were always waiting for something, but you had to put up with this stupidity as being all 'part of the training.' The cadet captains were martinets of the most lurid description and, if you offended in any way, you were thrashed. In the course of time you yourself had the chance of becoming a cadet captain, when you had the pleasure of savage retribution on an incoming term. It all sounds very cruel treatment of a thirteen-year-old, but it certainly did not do me any harm; in fact, I feel that a bit more of this kind of thing would do a lot of good in today's so-called 'permissive society,' which has been the curse of our time. Far from being crushed and the victims of 'traumatic psychoses,' we were a very high-spirited crowd who managed to enjoy ourselves enormously. The officers were a splendid bunch and, far from being stand-offish gods, they were our friends and counsellors and always ready to help.

Every Sunday we were taken on wonderful picnics in steam pinnaces along the Solent and Spithead, but we were never allowed out of the grounds on our own. The grounds of Osborne House are so extensive that this was really no hardship, but it was a curious experience to return to the outside world at the end of each term.

The scheme at that time was two years at Osborne, followed by two at Dartmouth. We were almost the last term to go to Osborne, which was closed for good in 1919 and all the training was then transferred to Dartmouth, where one led much the same sort of life, except that there was perhaps a slight loosening of the discipline, especially at weekends, when we could go and have Devonshire cream teas at 'Mother Crocker's.' Mrs Crocker was a dear old lady who had a cottage at Dittisham and who had given teas on Sundays to generations of naval officers during their training. She was known throughout the navy at that time. We also had much more sailing and, every now and then, a destroyer would look in and take us down the Channel when we were made to act as the ship's crew for the trip.

One thing that had been criticized many times was that, for four years, except during school holidays, we were completely cut off from feminine society of any kind. We even danced together every night to the college band on the 'quarterdeck,' as the big hall was called. This did not seem in the least strange to any of us cadets, but as I look back on it now, it must have appeared so to outsiders.

At Dartmouth our masters in the various subjects were an amusing and varied crowd. One of the physics professors had loose false teeth and used to demonstrate a 'scherynge with a schepherical nozzhle.' This, when pushed, squirted water all over the room and showed us how pressure was equal in all directions. We loved this one and made him do it over and over again until he and the cadets sitting in front were soaked.

Then there was a master known as 'Mossy Bags' because he had worn the same pair of trousers as long as anyone could remember and they had turned green with age. Whenever he made a joke or mistake, in fact whenever he gave us any excuse whatever, there ensued what was known as 'Mossy-Bang,' which consisted of everyone banging on desks and floor as hard as they could. This was heard all over the college, and if one was three floors away the eruption of a 'Mossy-Bang' could be plainly heard and the result was a chain reaction of similar 'bangs' in every classroom, triggered off by the initial 'Mossy-Bang,' and ending with the entire college in an uproar. This was eventually put to an end by the captain, who delivered a speech on the 'dignity of a naval officer,' which went down very badly.

It was about halfway through my time at Dartmouth that I began to feel unsure of myself. I had hitherto accepted the navy as my career, but other factors began to assert themselves. For one thing, I began to get interested in the arts and each vacation (or 'leave' as it was called) I began going to concerts, plays, art exhibitions, etc. My parents had moved to London during my time at Osborne and I had every chance to broaden my knowledge of things artistic. I realized then how this side of my life had been neglected during my naval training. Strangely enough, it was my mathematics master at Dartmouth who played a major part in this change of attitude. I have to thank Henry Piggott for awakening for the first time in me the realization of what music can mean to one's life. He was an inspiring teacher of music. I don't mean a pianist or string player who imparts his technical knowledge to a student, but a man who revealed to a teenager of seventeen the joys of listening to great music. This, as far as I am concerned, is just as important as the production of a virtuoso on any instrument. Very few people are blessed with the gift of giving insight and imparting enthusiasm to one whose musical enlightenment is just beginning. Piggott was one of these, and in no time I was 'hooked' on good music, which nowadays for some reason is known as 'classical' music – which is ridiculous, as much of it is certainly not that. This meant Covent Garden and Queen's Hall on my 'leaves.' The British National Opera Company, the remnants of Beecham's wonderful company, were giving splendid performances of operas in English at Covent Garden and we had a complete *Ring* in English in 1923. Albert Coates conducted and singers like Florence Austral, Agnes Nicholls, the loveliest Sieglinde of her time, Edna Thornton, Robert Radford, and Robert Parker made a formidable Wagnerian team. We also had *Meistersinger* and, in 1925, a *Tristan* benefit performance for the Wagner family, who were destitute in Bayreuth owing to the war and subsequent German inflation having cut off their royalties for eleven years.

I was rather amused to read reports in the late 1960s from London of an 'English *Ring*,' as though it had been just thought of as a good idea.

In the early 1920s it was all we had, until the Germans came back in 1924. Even then it was somewhat 'old hat,' because Richter did an English *Ring* at Covent Garden way back in 1908. As a matter of fact, in those days the 'English *Ring*' among musicians also meant *The Lily of Killarney, Maritana,* and *The Bohemian Girl*!

All these things were having an insidious effect on me and I found I was becoming less and less interested in my work at Dartmouth. I began to realize how much I had missed through not having gone to university. I would now pass out from Dartmouth, go off to sea in one of H M ships, and, apart from the odd course on shore now and then, spend many years at sea out of reach of the things which were beginning to occupy my thoughts continuously.

Just at this time I got something similar to the dreadful 'flu which swept over Europe just after the first war and from which so many people, including my grandmother, died. This left me in a very weak condition, and I had to miss one term at Dartmouth, which meant that I had more time than ever to think about my future. The thing which finally influenced my decision to leave the navy had nothing to do with any of these matters. The war was over, demobilization was the order of the day, the armed forces were being reduced in size, and economy was the key word everywhere. The famous 'axe' of Eric Geddes was being applied ruthlessly, not least to the navy. We all received an offer of three hundred pounds to resign from the service. This offer, if I remember correctly, held for six months, and, coming as it did at that psychological moment for me, proved too attractive to resist. I also guessed that if I didn't take it, many of us would probably be discharged anyway, at some later date, without compensation. As it turned out, I was right.

Three hundred pounds was a considerable sum in those days, and I decided to go to university and, on the advice of my mother, get myself a profession of some sort, for, as she said, if I did this I need never be out of a job in the future. Excellent advice, but what profession? One of my father's good friends was Sir Alfred Fripp, who was then senior surgeon at Guy's Hospital. He suggested that I should consider medicine. We all thought it a good idea, so medicine it was – just like that! I always had Cambridge in mind as to where I wanted to go, I don't know why, so I entered my name at Gonville and Caius College which had a reputation of being rather medically oriented, and was to 'go up' in the following October. It was then Christmas, and I discovered to my dismay that in order to get into Cambridge, I would have to do an exam in Latin or Greek, all other subjects being covered by my passing-out exams at Dartmouth. I hadn't done any Latin for five years. Could I do it in the time available? The headmaster of my old preparatory school at Ewell had retired and was living with his stepfather, who was vicar of a church at Kingsdown near Deal. He was now 'cramming' a few boys for various exams, so off I went to the vicarage, where I lived for six months, and where I read Latin, thought Latin, and conversed in Latin. The vicarage was without any means of heating other than fireplaces, and no fire was ever lit in any room. The grates all had bulrushes standing in them, and the chairs and sofas were covered in a velvet-like material, thick with dust. There was a very ancient maid, with a mask-like face, known as 'Jane.' There were two other boys cramming for different exams and we slept in an attic which was so cold that the oil in the door hinges sometimes solidified and the door would not open. The east coast of England in winter is colder than anywhere else in the world. I have lived through many Canadian winters that have been positively tropical compared to it. The only way we could exist and do any work was by going out jogging every few hours to warm up. The Rev. Jones, a widower, seemed not to notice the cold at all. He had white hair and a bright red, very shiny, face which looked like a Mackintosh apple. His face never moved, nor had it any lines or wrinkles on it. It was like a mask inset with two tiny boot-button eyes. When he spoke, he barely moved his mouth. We had to go to all the services every Sunday in the village church, which was heated no more than the house. My old schoolmaster seemed to be resigned to living in this inhospitable house, but ventured one morning to suggest that we might have a fire among the bulrushes. This was received very coldly, and nothing happened. How I existed through that winter I shall never know, but I got through the Latin exam by learning a speech of Cicero's by heart, and spent the summer at Guy's Hospital doing as much 'pre-med' as possible.

At Lulworth Cove in 1920

A naval cadet at Dartmouth in 1922

A Cambridge undergraduate

A young doctor at twenty-three at St George's Hospital

4

The London Scene II

It was about the end of 1922 that the BBC started broadcasting in a pretty crude way, and in my home we had one of the first sets. The quality was good, but one had to wear earphones, as there were no such things as loudspeakers, and I can well remember the large hooks on either side of the fireplace on which hung the earphones – one for each member of the family. They were an awful curse, as the leads were always getting caught in the furniture and in people's hair.

Many interesting things were going on in the musical world, but, of course, at that stage of my life I didn't realize a lot of what was happening – the première of Roussel's *Padmavati* for instance; Stravinsky's *Les Noces*, which I *did* go to when it was done in London in 1926; and the Ravel orchestrations of Moussorgsky's *Pictures*, which Koussevitzky paid ten thousand pounds for, in order that he might have the exclusive rights for five years, and ten thousand pounds in those days was a vast sum of money. *Les Noces* I remember well, especially the pianos with a keyboard at each end which were specially constructed for it. They were on either side of the stage, and the action took place between them.

Another piece of exciting news which went around in 1919 was that Toscanini would come and conduct the London première of *Trittico*. Puccini got wind of this and asked Ricordi's, the publishers, to stop the performances. Nor did he mince his words. He wrote to a friend in England: 'I've heard about Covent Garden and I protested to Ricordi because I don't want that pig of a Toscanini to conduct. He has said all sorts of nasty things about my operas, and has tried to inspire critics to run them down.' The result was that Covent Garden got neither Toscanini nor the *Trittico* that year, but in 1920 it arrived with a little-known Italian conductor and Puccini, who took a bow.

While that never-to-be-forgotten return of the Germans to Covent Garden was taking place, Diaghilev was gathering his forces again after the disaster of 1922, when he went bankrupt over the *Sleeping Beauty* season. He had put the famous ballet on for a run at the Alhambra Theatre. This was an experiment and had never been tried with ballet before. Repertory had always been the order of the day. *The Sleeping Beauty* ran for three months over the Christmas season, and I remember going twice when Eugene Goossens conducted. I think that, in many ways, this was the most sumptuous theatrical production of any kind that I have ever seen. No wonder Diaghilev and his backer Oswald Stoll lost their shirts over it. It must have cost several fortunes to mount. Lopokova was the Lilac Fairy and, later, when she married Maynard Keynes, she became the life and soul of Cambridge society. *All* the stars were in the cast and Stravinsky was said to have 'edited' the score. I've never been able to find out what he did to it, or what 'editing' it can possibly have needed. After all, if anyone has ever been able to orchestrate it was surely Tchaikovsky! I asked Goossens just before he died about this, and, as far as he could remember, Stravinsky *did* touch things up here and there, but not as he did in *Baiser de la Fée*. Apparently Tchaikovsky's score had suffered during the course of time, due to publishing errors, etc., and what Stravinsky did was merely to clean out the errors and restore the original. Bakst did the sets and they turned out to be his finest creations. The mystery, and it will always remain a mystery, is why the public never turned up in its thousands. At the time, none of us realized what was happening, but later, when it was forced to close, it transpired that Oswald Stoll, the owner of the theatre, had financed the production for as long as he could, and then had to give up when he found that Diaghilev had overspent his budget by many thousands of pounds. Diaghilev disappeared to France and the ballet seemed to be wrecked for ever. The creditors seized the props and costumes and locked them up in a store. About three years later when Diaghilev got going again he asked Stoll if he could use them for *Aurora's Wedding*, but when they opened the store, they found the whole lot had fallen to pieces. This ending seems symbolic of the whole tragic story. Anyhow, Diaghilev was not the sort of person to be down and out for long and he soon revived himself and the company. He was now, however, at His Majesty's Theatre, which was much better for his purposes than the Coliseum, which he had had to use the year he returned after the war, and which is now the home of the English National Opera.

His company was now far from being entirely Russian. Two of the leading dancers were Irish and another English. The Irish girl was Edris Stannus from County Wicklow, and the stage name she used was Nina Devalois, later to become Ninette de Valois. She it was who later founded the Sadler's Wells troupe which eventually became the Royal Ballet. The Irish boy was Patrick Healey-Kay, who adopted the name of Anton Dolin and became one of the greatest dancers of his day. The English girl, Hilda Munnings, danced as Lydia Sokolova, and was one of the leading stars of the company for many years. She was the daughter of Sir Alfred Munnings, the famous painter of horses.

The company was now a very mixed cosmopolitan crowd, but in 1925 a new Russian appeared among the men: George Balanchine, who created his first ballet that year to music by Rieti. It was called *Barabau*, and it had a chorus. I remember it very well and it wasn't very good. We were not impressed with the new choreographer, and we little knew how famous he would become.

It is so interesting to have seen all these people start their careers. I don't know why we in London never saw *Les Noces* until 1926, because it had been performed in Paris in 1923. It triumphed when it did arrive, and we were lost in admiration of Nijinska, who had done the choreography. Trained as a classicist, she took Stravinsky's music in her stride. The setting was utterly crude and the music violently powerful. I think we all liked *Les Biches* better, and Poulenc's delightful music was whistled everywhere. There were, however, a few raised eyebrows at the sexual implications of the choreography. Today, of course, they would hardly be noticed. *Les Biches* has always seemed to me one of the best of all ballet scores and the whole work, with the exquisite Laurencin décor, was a great favourite for some years. What riches there were! In one season we had *Les Noces*, *Les Biches*, *Les Fâcheux*, *Les Matelots*, and Constant Lambert's *Romeo and Juliet*, all for the first time. *Les Fâcheux* had music by Auric, and he, with Poulenc, Dukelsky, and Rieti, all famous composers of the day, were the four pianists in *Les Noces*. The public didn't take easily to *Les Noces*, as Diaghilev had prophesied, and I remember H.G. Wells writing a letter to *The Times*, telling everyone to go and see it. I can't think why he suddenly became its champion, because I never remember seeing him at any ballet performance.

In the Lambert ballet, I remember one scene where you only saw the feet of the dancers under the curtain. The ballet was called *A Rehearsal without Scenery in Two Parts*. The music seems to have vanished and it was never revived in England as far as I know. That same season, we also saw another new ballet, *La Pastorale*, for which Auric did the music and Balanchine the choreography. All I can remember about this is that the leading male dancer, who, *I think*, was Lifar, took the part of a telegraph boy and had to ride a bicycle most of the time and did little dancing.

Georges Auric was very much part of the Ballet's life at that time and 'Les Six' were all connected with it at one time or another. The only member of 'Les Six' whom I never met was Durey. Incidentally, 'Les Six' were never voluntarily 'Les Six.' They – Auric, Durey, Honegger, Milhaud, Poulenc, and Tailleferre – were really forced into being 'Les Six' by the public and Jean Cocteau. There was never any conscious effort to be a group. They were all friends, but one could hardly say they all shared the same artistic ideals. It was Cocteau who really made them into an imaginary group to please himself, along with Erik Satie, who appointed himself as arch high priest. Honegger didn't like this and could never stand Satie's music, and Durey hardly belonged the group at all. Incidentally, we should hear Durey's *Robinson Crusoe* songs more often. These are songs expressing Crusoe's disillusionment when he returns to civilization from his island. Later on in my life a very dramatic incident connected me with Honegger. But more of that when we come to the Second World War.

Cocteau's dictum that, if there was anything the group could be said to have had in common, it was 'saving the melodic line from oblivion' may make us smile, but we should remember that people had been a bit shaken at that time, firstly by the iconoclastic *Le Sacré du Printemps*, then by the first twelve-tone works of Schönberg, and lastly by an opera, produced in Berlin in 1925, which required 137 rehearsals! This was Alban Berg's *Wozzeck*. Cocteau may well have thought melody had been banished by these revolutionary works. The idea of 'Les Six' being reactionary is certainly rather comic, because they were always considered most avant-garde and daring. The Schönberg and Berg works had no tradition, and could not be judged by any then-existing standards.

There was so much going on around 1924. I can hardly remember any period in my artistic life which was more exciting. 'Les Six' were very busy. We have already discussed Auric's great share in the Diaghilev successes of the twenties. Salzburg and Donaueschingen were getting into their stride as festivals of avant-garde music (it was later that Salzburg gave up this policy and went 'straight,' so to speak). Bayreuth reopened after the war. Flecker's *Hassan* had just been produced in London with Delius' incidental music and had caused quite a stir. Richard Strauss produced a ballet – a *jeu d'esprit* called *Schlagobers*, which never cut much ice with either musicians or balletomanes. Sibelius produced his *Seventh Symphony*, Honegger *Pacific 231*; and three astoundingly different operas made their appearance almost simultaneously – Schönberg's *Erwartung*, Vaughan Williams' *Hugh the Drover*, and, what is to my mind a masterpiece of the first order, Boito's *Nerone*. Regarding *Nerone*, it had its première at the Scala under Toscanini and the publicity was unbelievable. I have always thought that this was its undoing because this première proved a disappointment, although the production apparently was worthy of Cecil B. de Mille. We heard what we could over the Italian radio, but in those days that wasn't very good, so we studied the score and got quite excited over much of the music. I never got a chance to see it on the stage until just before the Second World War at the Scala, and I was very impressed. I regard it as one of the operatic masterpieces of this century. Boito spent the latter half of his life working on it, but he never heard it before he died. It was not until six years after his death that it was finally performed. I do hope that *Nerone* will be heard one day in North America. It is so much finer than his *Méfistofele*, which we hear comparatively often.

I mentioned Flecker's *Hassan*. This play had a most lavish production and Delius was just the right composer for the incidental music. Flecker's standing as a dramatist of the twentieth century is negligible, but as a poet he is to be reckoned with. He was, incidentally, an alumnus of my college at Cambridge. Delius was a bit nervous at taking on this commission, because the only previous attempt he had made at incidental music was for a Norwegian play by Heiberg, at the first night of which, in Oslo, there was a riot in the theatre staged by the university students, and Delius, who was conducting, had to run for it. This was worse than the famous *Sacré du Printemps* riot in Paris, because there Monteux at least retained some sort of control in the pit. Beecham in his memoirs tells us Delius fled into the hotel next door where he found Ibsen at the bar chuckling over his rival Heiberg's discomfiture!

Anyhow, nothing like this occurred with Flecker's *Hassan*, which had a long run in the West End, and for which Delius wrote at least one tune which almost became a pop number in the 1920s, the *Intermezzo*.

Delius wrote the music in 1920, when *Hassan* was originally going to be produced, but there was a financial crisis in England (no rarity in that country even then!) and it had to be postponed. Beecham's description of all this is so amusing. He writes: 'Frederick by this time had completed the score of *Hassan* and was looking forward to the production in the autumn. Unluckily the economic position in England had been changing for the worse during the past six months. The Treasury and the Bank of England having taken alarm at the general prosperity of the country, had decided that measures should be taken to curtail it substantially. A policy of pressure known in these latter days as "credit squeeze" was applied with ruthless vigour, with the consequence that a slump descended upon the whole community.' Poor Sir Thomas wrote with feeling, because he was one of the victims of this squeeze.

What is the position of Delius in the musical hierarchy? Would he ever have made his mark without Beecham? I think we are inclined to forget that Beecham was not by any means his only champion. Delius was well known in Germany at the turn of the century. It was in his native England that he was hardly known – indeed he was better known in Virginia, where he taught violin after leaving his orange farm in Florida. It was Beecham who made him known in England, but that was not until just before the First World War. I feel he would have made his mark without Beecham, but I doubt if that mark would have been perpetuated, as it has by the Beecham records and broadcasts.

I always think Beecham's finest work with Delius was in the operas, and I shall never forget the performances of *The Village Romeo and Juliet* which he gave with the students of the Royal College in London. The best description ever of Delius' music was Roger Quilter's, who said it was 'the music of distance.'

When Beecham returned to England in 1929, he organized his Delius Festival. The blind and paralysed composer came over from France, where he lived, and attended all the concerts. I can well remember the final one when the *Mass of Life* was given under Beecham. Delius sat in his wheelchair with his masklike face lifted up to the music, a most moving sight.

North America had its own avant-garde in the early thirties, and it was Varese and Antheil who were the particular *enfants terribles* of that time. The *Ballet Mécanique* of Antheil had actually been written some few years before this, but I had never heard it. This is the work you may remember which includes in its score a Large and Small Airplane Propeller and a Large and Small Electric Bell! Antheil stated that this was an effort to escape from the 'iron grip of the tonal principle,' as he put it. The tone clusters on the pianos were banged with the palm of the hand. So you see, our young bloods today are not as 'advanced' as they think they are!

The Varese *Arcana* had just caused an audience riot in Berlin and everyone was talking about it. One of the Berlin critics put it thus: 'This is the maddest thing heard in Berlin for a decade, an abortion of sounding madness so unendurable to many of the listeners that they fled.' In this piece Varese uses a *tambour à corde*, which is a single-headed drum with a piece of string attached to the centre of the membrane on which a sound approximating to a lion's roar is produced by drawing a piece of leather along the string. And so it goes. 'Plus ça change ...'

The summer spent doing pre-med at Guy's Hospital gave me a chance to do some serious opera- and concert-going for the first time in my life. I only worked at the hospital for what is known as 'office hours,' and I was then free in the evenings for anything that took my fancy. The only trouble was that perennial one of the student – I had hardly any money, just pocket money from my father – so things had to be organized carefully. The summer of 1923 saw me in the gallery of Covent Garden for the summer season of the British National Opera Company, that heroic group of singers from the Beecham company who tried, and to a large extent succeeded, in keeping the operatic flag flying in London after the war. It had been a tragic time for opera in England because the immediate post-war seasons with Beecham had looked so promising. The spring season of 1920 ended in triumph, and Beecham, at the last performance, made a speech in which he stated: 'Opera in English is now the rule, that in a foreign tongue is an exception.' Everything looked rosy indeed, but by the end of that summer a receiving order in bankruptcy had been made against Sir Thomas. This resulted in his disappearance from the English music scene for twelve years – one of the greatest tragedies of English musical history.

The gallant remains, saved from the ruins, gave me my first taste of what opera could be, and I was in the gallery at the dear old house every evening I could get in. The gallery in those days had no seats. It was really a hole in the roof with steps rising steeply from front to back. You sat on the steps and the knees of the person behind dug into your back all the evening. There was no ventilation, and the heat rising from the auditorium proper was intense. But to the regular galleryite there was a known way of escape from this purgatory. This was the part of the gallery known as the 'slips.' I think it is still there today. The 'slips' are two clefts in the roof which run either side of the theatre from the top of the proscenium to the front of the main gallery. If one could get into the slips (and it could be achieved only by those at the head of the queue), Shangri-la was yours. There was room for your legs and you had a fairly comfortable shelf to sit on. The only snag was that, except from about half a dozen seats, you could hardly see the stage at all. But what did that matter? You heard superbly, because you were in the main auditorium, and not in a hole in the roof. The occupants of the 'slips' were a friendly and eccentric crowd. Besides myself there was David Harris, later to become Opera Director of the BBC; Walter Legge, then general factotum at HMV but later to become famous in the recording world; Joan Cross, just about to start her great career in opera; sometimes Lawrance Collingwood the conductor, score under arm, and later to play such a vital part in the Sadler's Wells opera; many students from the Royal College and Royal Academy. It cost one shilling and sixpence to get in. In today's money that would be about seven and a half pence, or fifteen cents. Of course, one didn't just sail in and take one's seat. Getting through the doors was the end of a long, and sometimes tedious, vigil, which often began on the previous evening. Many are the times I came out of a performance around 11:00 p.m. and immediately staked my claim for the following evening. This was done by putting a camp stool down outside with one's name pinned on to the seat. Many people had stools in constant use with their name woven into the seat to frustrate any funny business, of which there was quite a bit. On the whole, however, we were a happy band of musical pilgrims all of whom loved opera, and the camaraderie of the queue was unique.

Across the street, where the box office is today, there was a small tailor's shop, outside which sat a man whom we called 'The Spider.' He had a little table in front of him, and would be known today as a 'scalper.' On the table were arranged tickets for that evening's performance, and the hungry eyes of the people in the queue devoured these sweetmeats throughout their long wait. In this battle of wits, the Spider was known to have achieved quite a few victories when some patient member of the queue, unable to stand the strain any longer, would rush across and buy a ticket. On days when there was something very special such as a Chaliapin appearance or a Kleiber *Rosenkavalier*, the Mayfair crowd would pay messenger boys to stand in the queue for them, much to the disgust of the regular patrons. What with the 'buskers' (street performers) and the men from the fruit and vegetable market around the corner, Floral Street was a hive of activity around the clock. But the privilege of hearing singers like Lotte Lehmann, Elisabeth Schumann, and Maria Olzewska made all these tedious preliminaries worthwhile.

Those summer seasons at Covent Garden were always interesting, especially from 1924 onward. That was the year the German singers came back after the war. The year before, I had been lucky enough to hear Melba in *Faust*. This was the only time I heard her on the stage. Faust was sung by the Canadian Edward Johnson, who was to play a large part in my life thirty years later. I also remember *The Perfect Fool*, by Holst, with its amusing Wagnerian parodies, and also Ethel Smythe's *Boatswain's Mate*, in which I once sang the part of Travers, *not* at Covent Garden, I may add, but it *was* with Dame Ethel helping to direct, and I had the pleasure of meeting that fantastic character. Why is Holst's *The Perfect Fool* never done now? One hears only the ballet music.

The Covent Garden summer season usually ended about the middle of July and sometimes there was a week of performances tacked on to the regular series, with cheaper admission prices. These were wonderful nights for the regular gallery crowd! We could get front orchestra stalls for ten shillings and we felt like the prisoners in *Fidelio* being let out into the sunshine and fresh air for a few hours. The casts and conductors were the same as those of the main season, and I always had the front row seat right behind the conductor. I heard Eva Turner in *Turandot* for the first time during a cheap week, a few years later.

The end of the summer meant a move to Queen's Hall for the start of the Proms. Many of the gallery crowd turned up in the promenade, especially on Mondays (Wagner night). I think that, for me, the greatest disaster of the war was the loss of Queen's Hall. It was the perfect concert hall in every way. Its acoustics have never been approached by any other hall since, and the almost cozy size of the promenade was perfect. The wonderful part was that, despite its intimate appearance, it held twenty-two hundred people. The whole stalls area was cleared for the Proms and, in the middle, was placed a fountain, round which were a few seats. There were also seats around the whole periphery of the hall, but these were despised by the true promenaders because you couldn't see the orchestra owing to the standing crowd. I had been taken to one or two Proms when I was a boy, and it was my first experience of seeing an orchestra and a conductor on a platform. Until then my music-going had involved only theatres where the musicians were half hidden. When I became a serious promenader, Henry Wood was already a national institution, having started the concerts in 1895. Most young English musicians for the following forty years were to gain their first experience of orchestral music at the Proms. And they *were* Proms; that is, you did walk about if you wished. You paid two shillings for the promenade and, if you were early, you could get one of the chairs, which you kept for a rest in the interval. And what an astonishing musical education those concerts were! Eight weeks – a concert every night except Sunday, and all the famous soloists of the day. Monday was, for years, Wagner night; Tuesday, Mozart and Haydn; Wednesday, Bach; Thursday, a mixed bag; Friday, Beethoven; and Saturday, rather more 'pop' stuff, but all good – nothing trivial. Wood had a rehearsal every morning from ten until one, and some of the time he sat in the circle while the leader, who was Charles Woodhouse for many years, conducted. Wood had a large bell and a huge stop-watch. Every now and then the bell would ring with a loud clang, and the orchestra had to stop. Wood then shouted out what was wrong, and on they went. After some weeks of the season the orchestra began to get jittery over the bell, as they were always expecting it to ring, and, by the end of the season, they could hardly bear the strain. How on earth they got through this gruelling experience I never could understand. Today, when many orchestras share the concerts, there is no problem, but these players had a long concert every night, at which often large, complex, and difficult works had to be played. Of course, there was only time to rehearse the tricky passages, but the players had all done many seasons with Wood and knew the repertoire. It was amazing that, working under such impossible conditions, they were able to produce fairly respectable performances of most things. Of course, Wood had a marvellous library of his own, and all his parts were marked in minute detail. His scores even had the jokes he made at rehearsals written in the margin. Through the years the orchestra members got to know where the jokes were coming and used to shout them out before he could tell them himself. What a character! Certainly not by miles a great conductor, but an astonishing technician with the baton and a man from whom we all learned a very great deal. There will never be anyone quite like him again.

The Queen's Hall had a reverberation period, when empty, of 3.7, and when full of 1.7, and in the days of World War One it had a Venetian red colour scheme which was not very beautiful. In later years the scheme was altered to a lightish blue with gold outlines. In May 1942 I was to see it actually burning. It was like witnessing the death of a beloved friend.

Another feature of the music scene in London around this time was the return of the D'Oyly Carte Opera Company. This may sound rather extraordinary but, after a season at the Savoy Theatre in 1909, the company was not seen again in London until 1919. It continued to tour the provinces all through the war, but in London a whole new generation of theatre-goers had grown up knowing the Gilbert and Sullivan operas only from amateur performances. The company had relinquished its management of the Savoy in 1909, so had to go to the Princes Theatre for its triumphant return. Triumphant it was too. The company was as strong as it had ever been, and, led by Henry Lytton, Bertha Lewis, Derek Oldham, and Leo Sheffield, it played the famous works in superb style. Geoffrey Toye conducted, and Londoners in their thousands rediscovered the brilliant, satirical wit and fascinating music. The season had to be extended to a great length and it became the first of a series of revivals over the following years. In 1922 *Ruddigore* had its first revival since its original production in 1887, and caused unbelievable enthusiasm. People could not understand its long neglect, and, as we all know, it has continued to be one of the most popular of the series ever since. I saw all the revivals and little thought that I should be conducting them myself one day.

5

Into Medicine

In October 1923 I began my first term at Cambridge. For a medical student in those days the process was that you did your first and second Bachelor of Medicine courses while you were at university, and then went to a teaching hospital to complete your medical training and take your final exams. You also took some other arts subjects which, combined with your medical work, gave you an ordinary B A. I chose psychology, and would have become really interested had not the main medical subjects taken up so much time.

We had some great teachers; for instance, Gowland Hopkins, whose work on vitamins was already world-famous, although he did not get his Nobel prize until 1929. At one of his lectures he brought in his celebrated rats to show us graphically the effects of vitamin deficiencies. Then there was Professor Adrian, later Lord Adrian and Master of Trinity, whose lectures on the nervous system were a world of wonders to a young and enquiring mind. I used to look forward to each one with intense anticipation, and was delighted when he received his Nobel prize soon after Hopkins. And I remember Professor Duckworth, who, in his anatomy lectures, could draw in colour on a blackboard the most perfect pictures – far better than those in any textbook. For zoology I had Brindley of St John's as my coach. He had played a prominent part in the Erskine Childers affair and appeared as one of the characters in *The Riddle of the Sands*. At that time he had rooms over the main gate of St John's, where the twin sons of Childers were then undergraduates.

Brindley was famous in the dissecting room for demonstrating things on specimens with the mouthpiece of his pipe, which he smoked incessantly all day. Sometimes one could hardly watch when he thrust the pipe into the innards of a dogfish and then replaced it in his mouth! His knowledge was fantastic and all his students did well.

Cambridge was idyllic in the twenties. Madrigals at dawn in punts on the river under the bridge at King's, and then breakfast in the rooms of a friend just above the bridge, who had papered the walls of his living room with miniature scores carefully cut, and each work stuck on the wall in the proper sequence. He used then to put on a record of whatever it was, and walk slowly round the room following the score on the wall. I remember the fugue from the third Rasoumovsky *Quartet* brought you exactly from the door to the fireplace. Then the *Tristan Prelude* took you from the fireplace into the bathroom, and I will draw a veil over what happened in the bathroom! Let me just say that, among other things, the toilet roll played Bach's *Forty-eight* when rotated! What a crazy lot we were! Then the May Week balls, with the trip down the river for breakfast in the orchard at Grantchester with Rupert Brooke's clock looking down on us, but *not* stopped at ten to three, although I believe it had been kept like that in his memory for some years after the First World War.

There is a venerable institution in England known as The Three Choirs Festival. It is given by the combined choirs of Hereford, Worcester, and Gloucester Cathedrals and always starts on the first Sunday in September and runs for a week in one of the cathedrals. Many works which have later become famous have had their first performances at this festival, and many famous composers and performers have taken part through the years. It has been criticized for its conservatism and its parochial self-satisfied attitude to things, but it certainly has had a considerable influence on English musical life. It dates from 1724, so it has had a good long innings. Handel and Boyce both wrote for it and, eventually, in the late eighteenth century, it tended to become a Handel festival. Nowadays its music program is quite ambitious and contemporary works are interspersed with the classics. Certain composers became associated with one or another of the festival's three locales – Parry with Gloucester for instance, and Elgar with Worcester, which was, of course, his home town.

I paid my first visit to the Festival in 1922 and heard the première of the *Colour Symphony* of Arthur Bliss. This was a daring choice for the

hitherto rather staid festival and the venerable old cathedral at Gloucester took quite a beating with music which sounds charmingly harmless
today, but was considered very avant-garde at the time. Apparently, it
was Elgar who asked Bliss to write a work for Three Choirs and the title
was suggested by a recent study of heraldry which Bliss had been
making. The symbolic meanings associated with the various colours
gave each movement of the work its character. You can judge how the
austere and ancient nave of Gloucester Cathedral must have shed a
cobweb or two that day! I remember Bliss conducting and it was very
well received. It is a stimulating work and should be played far more
often than it is. Bliss was, in those days, regarded as somewhat of an
enfant terrible, having shocked the Salzburg audience in 1919 with his
Rout.

One of the great things about concerts in churches used to be that
there was no applause. What a relief this was. It was one of the reasons
why, given good acoustics, I would rather play in a church than anywhere else. This applause business is becoming one of the major
curses of our contemporary scene. It is certainly far worse than it was
when I was a student, and, if something drastic isn't done about it soon,
musical people, that is people who like listening to music, will cease
going to operas and ballets altogether. Opera, of course, is the hardest
hit of all. I haven't yet heard applause during the music in a concert
hall, but it is becoming quite common at the opera and the ballet. This
applies, of course, mostly to North America. You would seldom hear it
in any European country, although I have heard disturbing rumours
recently. The Italians are wild applauders, but they will always wait until
the end of the piece. It has got to the pitch now where we reckon we
will hear about two-thirds of any performance we go to. The curtain has
only to rise disclosing a bare stage and maybe one chair in a corner, for
a tumult of clapping to break out – very often during some exquisite
music from the pit. What is the applause for? And it is quite evident that
its perpetrators haven't come to hear the opera because they do all they
can to make it inaudible, not only for other people, but also for themselves. I have actually heard clapping *during Tristan*, and also *during
Elektra* and *Salome!* I could hardly believe my ears. In fifty years of
opera-going I have never heard anything like it. Surely our newspaper
critics could do more than they do? I have seldom seen a complaint in
their writings, yet it must annoy them as much as it does us. One of the
critics in Toronto, to do him justice, was finally roused to fury in a very

good attack on the clapping fraternity, but it seems to have had little effect. Some scenes in operas end with the most beautiful music of the score, which is seldom heard for the noise.

What else can we do about it? Couldn't someone come on to the stage before the opera and *ask* people not to applaud *during* the music? I have seen it in very small print on the program, but nobody ever reads it. It's strange, but when anyone is *actually* singing, there is never any clapping. Couldn't it be arranged that someone stand up and clap loudly during the quietest part of some aria and see what would happen? I have had spies out among the audience in order that they may observe this phenomenon at close quarters, because another strange thing about it is that the clapping never starts near to where one is sitting, but some way off! The results of my investigations were devastating in the extreme. Once, when the curtain rose, it was the wife of the conductor who started the uproar, effectively drowning out her husband's music!

The Greek plays at Cambridge had a great tradition which went back to the beginning of the century, and in my time they were done every year in the translations of either John Shepherd or Gilbert Murray. Vaughan Williams had made his contribution in 1909 when they did the *Wasps* of Aristophanes. He produced some incidental music which has become quite a classic of its kind. That was a vintage period for Vaughan Williams, as it also produced the *Tallis Fantasia*, the *Sea Symphony*, and *On Wenlock Edge*.

During the twenties many well-known musicians came and performed in Cambridge. The one who remains most vividly in my memory is Elena Gerhardt, the most famous lieder singer of the day. I seem to remember Rachmaninov, who wore his heavy overcoat even in summer so he wouldn't crease his evening clothes on his way to a concert. Then there was Landowska, who left the town in a shambles from her temperamental outbursts. At the 'Informal Music Club,' where you could stand, sit, or lie on the floor, you heard great music-making, from chamber concerts by the Cortot-Thibaud-Casals trio to the eccentric recitals of Vladimir de Pachmann with his running commentaries on music, usually Chopin. From what I hear about the Cambridge musical scene today, it is nothing like as exciting as it was in the old days, when pretty well all the great soloists of the day came and gave recitals, and the Beethoven Quartet Cycle, by some renowned ensemble, was an annual event. This may be because of the motor car: everyone commutes to London. But we never visited London at all in term time because we couldn't afford it (and as for students having cars, well such a thing was unknown). But there was always King's College Choir – and that was free! And certainly no theatrical producer has ever had a setting which could compare with the marvellous chapel in which it sang (and still does sing).

Cambridge was over for me in 1926, and I got my BA in psychology while working in the medical program. Next it was London, and medical work at St George's Hospital. The position of this hospital, right at the busiest traffic point of the whole city, made it an emergency hospital first and foremost. Accidents came in by the score, morning, noon, and night, and one soon gained wonderful experience with fractures, concussions, and injuries of all kinds. Although I was now in the heart of London, and only a few minutes from Covent Garden and the concert halls, I became so interested in my hospital work that I began to hear *less* music than I had at Cambridge. The hospital became my whole life. Each student was assigned to the firm of someone on the staff. You started doing a year in a surgical ward. You did all the chores, and, on the rounds with your chief, twice a week, you hung on his words of wisdom as each bed was visited. Each surgeon had his houseman, who lived in, and who ruled our lives completely. Later when you had passed all the exams and had become a qualified doctor, you became a houseman yourself and held all the house appointments as an intern, and this was a fascinating and busy life. We lived in a house which adjoined the hospital. It was extremely high and narrow, and was known as the 'cottage.' There was no elevator and, if you had a room on the ninth or tenth floor (which, incidentally gave you a wonderful view over Hyde Park) and if you happened to be on duty, you got a lot of exercise! Each of us was on duty for four days and nights in turn, which meant that during your shift you couldn't emerge from the building at all, and every emergency admitted during those four days and nights was your patient. Very often you would be called from your bed in the middle of the night. You would descend nine floors, deal with the case, climb the nine floors again, and usually, just as you got back to bed, the phone would ring again. You often ended by stealing a nap on the operating table in the emergency wing.

St George's was (and probably still is) a neighbourhood hospital, but it has lost a great many of its most colourful patients since the laws were changed after the Second World War when it moved to its new situation in Balham. I refer to the Piccadilly 'ladies,' a great many of whom were regulars at the VD clinic. One knew them all by name and sight after working there for a few months, and to walk at night from the hospital to Piccadilly Circus was extremely amusing. Occasionally one would accost you and retire covered in confusion when she saw who it was – someone who had only just told her that on no account was she to ply her trade until passed as fit.

All that has changed now, of course, and Piccadilly is completely deserted after dark these days. London has lost a lot of colour and zest, I'm afraid. I always thought it so strange that Paris was the 'wicked city' about which all the music-hall jokes were made. Paris could never compare in those days with London in this respect, nor could any other city. I can remember when one had literally to push one's way through the crowds of prostitutes along the sidewalk in Piccadilly.

Opposite the south side of St George's was a row of large houses in Grosvenor Crescent, some of which had been converted into a hospital. This was 'King Edward VII's Hospital for Officers' – to give it its full title. It had been founded, and was run by, one of the most astonishing characters I have ever met. Known as 'Sister Agnes,' she was a Miss Agnes Keyser, and had been in her youth a great beauty and a girl-friend of Edward VII. Her father was a South African diamond merchant, and she must have been very wealthy. She ran this hospital in memory of the late king and called herself 'Sister' Agnes, but she was not a trained nurse at all. She wore a nurse's uniform with a huge red cross on her chest. When I was resident doctor there she was a very old lady indeed, and her walnut-like wrinkled face was surmounted by a flaming blonde wig. She usually had a St George's man as her resident, and it was well known that no one had lasted in the job for more than six months. I was determined I would and did – and for seven! The resident doctor lived in a small hut on the roof overlooking Belgrave Square, and had his meals with Sister Agnes, who lived in the adjoining house, with which a communicating door had been made in the wall.

This job was a fascinating one in many ways. Firstly, all the most famous doctors of the day had patients there from time to time, so, for a young doctor, the contacts he made were invaluable. Secondly, the variety of cases encountered was fantastic, as there was no specialization as far as the hospital was concerned. Lastly, and by far the most exciting, was the fact that one met, not only the top ranks of the medical profession, but also some of the other important people of the day.

Sister Agnes and the resident doctor usually had lunch together, just the two of them; but tea was a ritual and was open house. People dropped in ranging from the prime minister to ex-King Alfonso of Spain, a famous actor, or the Aga Khan. The young doctor had to help entertain all these people.

Every morning at eleven Sister's ancient Rolls would pick her up with her dogs, drive round the traffic circle at Hyde Park Corner, and deposit her, with the dogs, at the small back door in the wall of Buckingham Palace garden, which was across the road. She had a key to the door, and for an hour she would walk her dogs round the lake in the garden. She would then return to lunch and one awaited the news. If you asked, she shut up like a clam and that was that. Usually over coffee it came out.

'Oh yes, Sister?'

'He came and walked with me round the lake.'

And then one heard *all* the latest news, the scandals, the politics – the state of the nation in fact! The job was worth it for those sessions alone. When Sister was in a good mood it became even more interesting. Then one might be asked in to her home next door for coffee after dinner. Out would come the old albums of snapshots, and one lived again through the naughty nineties and the escapades of the then Prince of Wales.

Yes, being Sister Agnes' house doctor was a stimulating experience in many ways, and I had two bouts of it, one of seven months, and another, later, of three. What a character! There has never been, and never will be, another Sister Agnes. The hospital goes on, and has now moved to the other side of Hyde Park, and I imagine is now run on much more professional lines following the death of its founder. Strange things used to go on during the night, and the visiting doctors were well aware of them, but could do nothing. Many's the time I have seen Sister Agnes do a round of the wards in the small hours with a hypodermic in her hand. If any patient showed signs of being noisy and keeping everyone awake there was a simple remedy to hand, no matter from what trouble – some one suffered.

I soon began to realize that I could drift on indefinitely in this way, and that it was not getting me anywhere. I wanted experience and, above all, responsibility. Sister Agnes had never allowed the young doctor to make any decisions on his own and the doctor whose case it was always had to be consulted about everything. This was slightly ironic considering the sort of thing that went on during the small hours, which I have already mentioned. I remember thinking at times that the resident doctor seemed almost redundant, although I suppose that, if a real emergency had arisen, it would have looked bad if there had been nobody on call. I can remember how, at times, I envied the interns across the road in St George's and wished that I was still one of them. There, the never-ending stream of accidents and emergencies of all kinds was a wonderful experience for a young doctor. In fact, on many evenings, I used to steal across the road after dinner and join my colleagues in the Casualty Department. One of the great drawbacks at No. 17 was that the resident, being the only doctor on the staff, was, theoretically, permanently on duty. Sister Agnes was well aware of this, yet she made no attempt to solve the problem. One had, therefore, to resort to all sorts of subterfuge to get any time off at all. Luckily, there was usually someone over at the hospital willing to stand by if one wanted to get away for a few hours.

As far as music went, there was never a mention of it in the King Edward VII Hospital and it played no part in the life of Sister Agnes. Following my sessions there, I held appointments at various provincial hospitals, gaining much experience all the time. I had an offer to join my ex-chief, Claude Franks, at St George's in his excellent practice, but evidently in the back of my mind there was always this hankering after music, because I turned it down and started looking for a job that might give me time for more music study.

I think I was the only one of her resident doctors with whom Sister Agnes had never clashed, although we had one or two periods of armed truce during my time there. My predecessor had been deposited on the pavement in Grosvenor Crescent, with all his belongings, and told he was never to darken the threshold again. Both my departures were, however, quite touching leave-takings; but then I hadn't allowed myself to stay too long! On leaving the second time, I was given a long lecture by Sister Agnes on how a young doctor should behave, and how she hoped I would always remember all that I had learnt at No. 17. She looked exactly the same as always until I finally shook hands, when her face altered completely, and I saw something there I had never seen before. I could have sworn that there was a slight glistening in the corners of her eyes.

So ended my association with one of the most remarkable characters I have ever met. I never saw her again. The hospital was badly damaged during the war, and for some years No. 17 stood there derelict and the ruins of the little chalet could be seen from Belgrave Square. I never pass there today without thinking of that unique experience.

6

Bavarian Revelations

It was around 1927 that I started going to the continent for my holidays whenever I could get time off from the hospital. This meant, of course, hearing all the music I could, wherever I could. Wagner was my passion at that time, and the old Bayreuth wizard has never really lost his hold on me, although there have been periods of greater or lesser allegiance through the years. Sometimes I think I have had it all, and don't want to hear it again, and then I find myself at Bayreuth or Munich, having been persuaded by somebody to go to a *Tristan* or *Ring*, and when those first notes of the *Tristan Prelude* creep out of the darkness at Bayreuth, or the deep E flat sounds from the bottom of the Rhine, I am completely enslaved once more and resistance is hopeless. The strange thing is that the weaknesses are probably more obvious than with any other composer, but one is so completely carried away by the beauty of much of the music and also immersed in the extraordinary atmosphere of each work that criticism is of no use. I can't think of any other works of art, except maybe some of the French Impressionist paintings, which have this amazing power of atmosphere.

During the *Ring* one is right there living in that strange world of gods and dwarfs and sub-humans. The music creates this world for you and it all becomes plausible. One finds oneself taking a childish delight in the gigantic fairy tale. Then *Tristan* – another world completely; the very sound of the music is different. And, again, with *Parsifal* and *Meistersinger*, all different realms of sound, each one creating a com-

pletely new world within which the story unfolds. This amazing al-
chemy, which I don't know in any other composer, is part of the eternal
fascination of these works. It is commonly said that the chromaticism of
Tristan explains the difference there. Maybe, but how does one explain
the chromaticism of *Parsifal* which differs completely from that of
Tristan? There, you again have two utterly different sound worlds. Even
within the same work we have it: the radiance of the mountain-top at
the beginning of *Götterdämmerung* gradually becomes the stark
ominous primitive brooding of the Gibichung's hall. At what point in
the music this actually happens we can't tell. The change is brought
about with consummate subtlety. We then have a completely different
sounding music for the Gibichung scene – a music which could only
be the music of Hagen and Gunther – and so it goes on.

Mozart is always Mozart, and Beethoven is always Beethoven, which-
ever work of theirs we are hearing. But there are a dozen different
Wagners, according to whatever scene he is setting, and this is part of
his endless fascination.

My first visit to Bayreuth was in 1928, and the Festival was then under
Siegfried Wagner's direction. Cosima was still alive, of course, and I
shall never forget seeing her one day in her wheelchair, coming out of
Wahnfried, Wagner's home. In those days, some of the rooms of Wahnfried were open to visitors, and fascinating they were, filled with
Wagner's own things. Cosima came out just as I was going in, and I
passed right by her. I'm afraid I was very rude and could not help
staring at this link with the past. To think that this woman had known
Chopin, Schumann, Berlioz, and all the famous composers of the nineteenth century, and to think that her father had been Franz Liszt, her
mother the Comtesse d'Agoult, and her husband Richard Wagner was
too much for me, so I just – stared! And she stared back. Nobody said
anything. In another moment, I'd have said something, but her attendant, who I think was one of her daughters, came out and pushed the
chair down the drive. I stood rooted there, having had one of the
unforgettable experiences of my life.

By 1928 the Bayreuth Festival was going strong once more, and I saw
the *Ring* with Siegfried Wagner's décor. I believe it was one of the first
times projections had been used in the theatre, and the underwater
scene in *Rheingold* was startling in the extreme with wave projections.
Siegfried Wagner was a great producer and should have stuck to it.
Unfortunately he insisted on conducting and composing, at neither of

which was he much good. Anyway, he did a fine job of keeping the Festival alive during those years and his productions were magnificent.

I suppose one of the great thrills of a musician's life is the first sound he hears in the *Festspielhaus* at Bayreuth. I had, of course, read and heard about the fantastic acoustics, but until you have heard it in that theatre I maintain that you have never really heard Wagner properly. I started with *Rheingold*, which I already knew by heart, having heard it at Covent Garden and having studied the score for years, but I never dreamed it could sound as it did at Bayreuth. I was carried away on the Rhine flood, and only came to two and a half hours later with the final chords. The first time is, of course, the best, but every time I have been there again through the years I have been thrilled.

That first Bayreuth *Ring* was a landmark in my musical life. Unfortunately, the next year, 1929, was a blank year at Bayreuth (in those days they had a blank year every fourth year), so I went to Munich instead to hear the local Wagner Festival in the Prince Regent Theatre, which is a copy of Wagner's *Festspielhaus*. Some of the performances were good, but nothing could take the place of the theatre on the hill among the corn fields, with the wonderful views in every direction. At Munich in 1929, however, I underwent another conversion which was almost greater than my Wagner revelation of the previous year.

I was back at Bayreuth in 1930, of course, for in the spring of 1930 Toscanini arrived in London with the New York Philharmonic orchestra and caused the greatest sensation I ever remember in a London concert hall. London orchestral playing had sunk to abysmal depths and the deputy system was rampant. This was a system whereby you could send a deputy to any rehearsal if you wished, or even to the concert after you had done all the rehearsals! You can imagine the standard of the performances. That visit of the New York Philharmonic woke us all up and, almost at once, the situation began to improve. I remember especially a wonderful *Enigma Variations* – and also *La Mer*. I then heard that Toscanini would conduct at Bayreuth later that summer and was determined to go. I arrived there by car on August 5th and found all the flags at half-mast, and the town deathly quiet. The clerk in my hotel told me that Siegfried Wagner had died the day before, but the show would go on. And on the show went with Toscanini's *Tannhäuser*. This performance, and that of *Tristan* a couple of days later, were the two greatest, as far as the orchestral playing went, that I heard at Bayreuth until Karl

Böhm's *Ring* in 1965. The whole thing was charged with much more emotion than usual owing to Siegfried's death, and I felt that all the singers gave just a little bit more on that occasion. It is a great pity that we don't have any recording of a complete Wagner opera under Toscanini. The *Tristan* especially would be a fascinating study. The whole score sounded amazingly transparent. All the lines were clearly defined and perfectly balanced, so that the ever-shifting chromatics took on a strangely incandescent glow. I suppose, in a way, it was a very Latin performance, but it seemed to fit *Tristan*, and certainly *Tannhäuser*. I never heard Toscanini's *Parsifal* which, to the astonishment of everyone at Bayreuth, took about twenty-five minutes longer than that of Karl Muck, and yet apparently sounded much faster. Of course, anything would have sounded faster than Muck's *Parsifal*! I always thought it was dreadfully boring.

Karl Muck was the only conductor of *Parsifal* at Bayreuth for thirty years. I think I must have heard his last performance in 1930. Toscanini was sitting right behind me, and was making hissing noises all the time and sticking his feet into my back. The next year he conducted *Parsifal*.

Mozart, I knew, was being performed in 1929 at the Residenz Theatre in Munich, but I was not interested; I could think of nothing but Wagner. On this occasion, however, I noticed that the great Richard Strauss himself would conduct several of the Mozart operas, and that my favourite soprano, Elisabeth Schumann, would sing in them. I was looking forward to both rehearsals and performances with such artists, but, remembering previous disappointing experiences, the fact that the operas were Mozart's thrilled me not at all. I arrived in Munich on the day when *Così fan Tutte* was to be performed there and had no chance to attend any rehearsal.

Those who remember the Residenz Theatre in Munich (it was completely destroyed in the Second World War) will agree that there has never been a more perfect setting for eighteenth-century opera. The tiny baroque auditorium, holding only six hundred people, had been perfectly preserved, but the stage had been modernized. It has now been completely restored to its original state. Strauss entered, looking quite bored, as he always did when he conducted. He appeared hardly to move the entire evening. From the first notes of the overture I sat transfixed. I can remember no interval. At the end, I still sat unable to move until an old attendant came and politely reminded me that the audience had departed. For days I could think of nothing else and realized that I had at last heard and seen Mozart performed in the correct style, with the result that the composer's real greatness was suddenly made apparent to me. The intimacy of the performance was a great factor in the overall effect; Mozart cannot be performed effectively in large auditoriums. This has been one of the chief reasons why the Glyndebourne Opera House has become world-famous. In that Mozartean shrine, holding fewer than a thousand people, you can today hear and see operas performed in the correct traditional style. Size of performance is all-important with Mozart; he is the most intimate of all great composers; that is why he will never be a popular composer in the sense that Beethoven and Handel are. Mass worship of Mozart is inconceivable. A Mozartean Bayreuth would be ludicrous. I can never understand why the large opera houses persist in giving his operas in their huge auditoriums where they can never make any effect.

What is this fascination he holds for musicians? In the first place, we have been given no key to the inner personality of the man himself. This may seem a startling statement concerning a composer who has hitherto always been regarded as one who revealed himself completely to posterity in the letters to his family. A superficial reading of the letters may give that impression, but, except in perhaps four or five instances, he has done no such thing. In fact, perusal of the letters will only heighten the mystery to a musician. As a documentary commentary on the life of the eighteenth century, and as a contemporary musician's view of the idiosyncrasies and failings of his colleagues, the letters are unsurpassed; but we are no nearer the secret of the music when we have read them. We are offered a few glimpses, but these really only serve to confuse us all the more – for instance, the famous passage in the letter to his father: 'Since death, when we come to consider it, is seen to be the true goal of life, I have made acquaintance during these last few years with this best and truest friend of mankind, so that his image not only no longer has any terrors for me, but suggests, on the contrary, much that is reassuring and consoling.' Then, later in the same letter: 'I never lie down upon my bed without reflecting that – young as I am – I may perhaps never see another day – and yet not one of those who know me can say I am morose or sad among my fellows.' In these few sentences a corner of the veil is lifted for a second, but he is soon telling his cousin, in another letter, that he would love to be pinching a certain portion of her anatomy! Have we here a clue to the man? This extraordinary preoccupation with death in a young and vigorous man of thirty-one? Is this the drama underlying the music? This would explain the riddle of such works as *Così*, *The Magic Flute*, and the many instrumental movements which, although gay enough on the surface, keep reminding us of the depth of emotion which lies beneath. Is this music one long struggle to conceal?

We have no doubts about what kind of man Beethoven or Wagner was: we feel we know them almost as intimate friends, and their music is completely descriptive of their characters. If their personalities had not been revealed to us by contemporary observers and their own writings, we should still know them through their music. But we cannot say the same about Mozart. Not only has Mozart's inner man never been revealed by any historian; it also can be only guessed at from a study of his music.

To this day *Così fan Tutte* remains the supreme enigma of music; hence its endless fascination. On that evening in Munich, fifty years ago, I understood properly for the first time the oft-used phrase about great art being universal. What had, hitherto, seemed a trivial pantomime with some pleasant tunes attached became, in the light of a perfect performance, all things combined: at one moment, apparently the wildest farce, set to music which plumbed the depths of human emotions; at another, seemingly serious drama, wedded to music of scintillating wit and flippancy. So varied are the emotions to which we are subjected by this extraordinary opera that, by the end of a good performance, it seems that we have been through a lifetime of experience in a few hours. We may take one instance as an example. In the first act there is a scene of farewell as the two young men, ostensibly en route for military service, take leave of their sweethearts. In the background the old cynic, Don Alfonso, mutters to himself. The dramatic situation is one of the highest farce – the mock anguish at leaving on the part of the men, the swooning of the two girls, and the biting comments of the old roué all combine to produce something which should be uproariously funny. It is here, however, that Mozart upsets all our calculations. An ordinary composer would probably have set da Ponte's scene to music as slight and amusing as the dramatic situation seems to demand, but instead Mozart writes a quintet of indescribable beauty, touching the very profundities of human emotion, and so, where we had been prepared to chuckle, we find ourselves ready to weep at the bitter-sweetness of the music. I suppose that it might be perfectly legitimate criticism to say that, in this case, the composer has set the scene badly. But this opera is full of similar situations and so are his other operas. When we have experienced this and accepted it, we perceive that we have here an art which is, as far as I know, unique, and of which we can never tire because its ultimate secret always eludes us.

I suppose that nine out of ten musicians, on being asked whom they consider to be the greatest genius in the history of music, would answer 'Mozart.' Yet, if a random observer were to ask ten people on the street whom they considered to be the greatest, I doubt whether one would give that composer's name. The answer would probably be Handel, Bach, Beethoven, or Schubert. Can we draw any significant conclusion from this? Perhaps a personal experience may be of help. During my youth in England I heard all kinds of music – good, bad, and indifferent. Gradually I acquired discrimination, and began to realize who, among composers, were the giants, and who the smaller fry. The only famous composer about whom I could not make up my mind was Mozart. It was difficult to hear much of his music in England in those days and, apart from the last symphonies and a few performances of *Figaro*, his music was seldom performed. He was virtually unknown until Sir Thomas Beecham started reviving the operas and playing some of the earlier symphonies. Not that Mozart's eclipse can be compared in any way with that of Bach, who was quite forgotten until the middle of the nineteenth century. But the greater part of his work remained unplayed, and the feeling was that here we had a composer whom children could appreciate easily and who wrote charming little tunes which were easy to whistle.

To describe aesthetic experience, especially musical experience, in words is well-nigh impossible, as the time-honoured dictum 'music begins where words leave off' always reminds us. It is, however, necessary in discussing Mozart to make some sort of effort to analyse, because the very real difficulty of the analysis in his case helps us to be more aware of the enigma which the man was himself.

What kind of man was Mozart? Could it have been that, in attempting to avoid wearing his heart on one sleeve, he inadvertently wore it on the other? There is always, as I see it, a fear of letting himself go, but, at the same time, a futile endeavour to prevent us seeing through the attempt to dissemble. Beethoven, as we all know, had his 'unbuttoned moods' and they were frequent. Mozart never has even one button out of place. Everything has the perfection of form of classical architecture. Yet, just as the Elgin Marbles teem with life, so Mozart's music is filled with an inner warmth and vital urge, despite its formal perfection. After all, there is no reason why classical art should always be considered 'cold.' The well-known definition of architecture as 'frozen music' reflects this attitude and the two ideas have become indissolubly linked. The fact is that composers since Mozart have lost the power of condensing their inspirations into formal moulds. The romantic era broke out from the confines of what is regarded as its prison and swept all before it in a glamorous flood. Men were carried away with its excess and unbridled subjectivity, and did not realize that, in the cataclysm, much had been lost. It is the rigid discipline of the classics which is their eternal attraction for us. When Mozart takes the great nuggets of his theme in the development of the finale of his *G Minor Symphony* and crushes them together in the crucible of his imagination, the effect is overwhelming. Such a combination of intellect and passion has never been witnessed in music, either before or since. With Mozart, the balance between the emotion and the form is always perfect and we have the most complete satisfaction possible in listening to music.

It is often stated that a mathematician undergoes a real aesthetic experience in the solving of a complex equation. A reasonably well-trained musician can write a complex fugue and, in so doing, give us a certain satisfaction as we follow the working-out of the feat; but if the content of his music is without spark of genius, the total effect will never amount to very much. A Mozart can take the strictest of classical forms and give it a vivid emotional life apart from its formal construction; he can not only display his creation in all its formal beauty, but touch our hearts with its content, and the two effects, accomplished simultaneously, produce something far greater than either factor on its own. This combination has seldom been achieved by composers in musical history, although it can be discerned in the works of the greatest of them. Mozart, who achieved it to a far greater extent than anyone else, thus plied a far more specialized and subtle kind of art than that of the ordinary run of composers, and this is one of the reasons why musicians agree regarding his greatness. This facet of the composer, unlike others, is not an enigmatic one.

There has always been speculation as to the connection between great genius and precocity. There is no doubt that Mozart was the most startling example in all musical history of the child prodigy. He 'knew' and was 'aware' at a far earlier age than any other musician before or since. There was little sign here of the 'infinite capacity for taking pains'; apparently there was no need. He has told us that he often had two or three completed compositions in his head simultaneously. The only 'pains' to be taken were those of getting the notes down on paper. This would seem to indicate a visual memory far, far greater than that possessed by an ordinary person. It also indicates a concentration of thought quite out of the ordinary. Without any great conscious effort, it was all there and just had to be shaped, and then photographed in the memory for future use. We all talk loosely of the 'act of creation' as though it were a clearly definable entity, but if we study the way various great artists have worked we are soon convinced that the phrase means nothing. Certainly with Mozart there was no such 'act.' Beethoven's entire life was a continuous 'act' of this kind, and we can witness it all in his sketch-books. Mozart's composition was no simple 'act,' but an endless transmutation of ideas. An interesting and not too well-known fact is that there is also a sketch-book of Mozart's dating from his eighth year, which shows that he was not, by any means, a genius in composition at that early age. The fashionable and cloying picture of him drawn by many writers who should know better is one of a child who wrote masterpieces as soon as he could hold a pen.

It is also interesting to observe how, at the end of his life, he writes music of an almost childlike simplicity, a music purged of all earthy emotion. Much of the mystery of *The Magic Flute* lies in this divinely innocent-sounding music; again, as in the case of *Così*, the casual listener has almost the feeling of triviality, but, when the opera is really understood, it transmits a message of noble serenity rarely achieved in any art at any time. A well-known English critic has recently put it very well. In reviewing a performance of *The Magic Flute*, he writes of 'those lost souls who pathetically believe that music which sounds simple can be performed by simpletons. It is notoriously difficult to stage this fairy tale without either giving audiences the giggles, or sending them to sleep; notoriously difficult to reconcile the sublime truths and ridiculous trappings, until the laughter provoked by the comedy becomes as the laughter of children, and therefore meet to enter the Kingdom of Heaven.' Here we have, once more, this extraordinary 'borderline' in Mozart's music very well described.

Psychologists never cease to tell us how close love is to hate, or that we laugh really because we are frightened. These emotions are related in the most complex ways, and I feel that such a relationship applies to Mozart's music. Not that I would suggest that this music should be connected with the couch and the consulting room; far from it, for there was never saner music written, but the seemingly contradictory components might seem to be illuminated by the kind of reference made here.

I have hitherto mentioned the operas almost exclusively because I feel that they best illustrate the mystery of Mozart's make-up. He has set producers almost insoluble problems. For instance, no one has ever yet decided whether to treat *Don Giovanni* as a comic opera or a tragedy. As in *Cosi*, the emotional temperature is constantly changing through-out the work, and we are never quite sure how far the composer's tongue is into his cheek. Scenes of the highest dramatic grandeur jostle with others of the lowest comedy. Throughout the superlative music we do not know whether to laugh or cry at its sheer beauty. Many writers have pointed out that the final sextet gives us the clue to the entire work, and yet for many years it was omitted altogether, as producers could not see how it fitted into the scheme. Again the insoluble enigma of Mozart's attitude mystified his hearers.

Any work of art which eternally intrigues mankind must be of the highest quality. Leonardo's painting of Gioconda is one of these, and is in many ways comparable to Mozart's music. The inscrutable Mona Lisa looks at us as Mozart looks at us through his masterpieces. What fearful grief inspired the *String Quartet in G Minor*? Even in a seemingly cheerful work, such as the *Symphonie Concertante for Violin and Viola*, we have a slow movement of which the resigned nobility is without a parallel in all music. There is nothing even in the romantic period of the nineteenth century to approach it. It was neither of its time, nor before its time. It stands apart as possibly the most perfectly beautiful creation in the world of sound. But the emotion which inspired it will never be known. There is no such thing as 'absolute' music. Since completely objective music is impossible, the mere writing down of the notes must entail some kind of subjective emotion in the composer. One cannot imagine of a state of mind which is uninfluenced by any sensory impression. Great artists have attempted to describe such a state. Goethe attempted it in the second part of *Faust*, but was not successful. Mozart used to be regarded as a writer par excellence of 'absolute' music, but this only illustrates how utterly he was misunder-stood. There has never been music so highly charged with subjectivity, but of what kind we cannot ascertain. The mystery remains as profound as that of the ultimate structure of the universe, and just as that mystery will always intrigue mankind, so will the music of Mozart.

It was just before this Munich period that I paid my first visit to North America and Toronto. We had an invitation from the universities there to visit their medical schools and hospitals, so seventy-eight of us medicos from Cambridge did the tour and, the following year, we asked them back. I remember Toronto, as it was then, very well; the Union Station had recently been opened and was the showpiece of the city. The Royal York Hotel wasn't built, but there was an old hotel called the Queen's, covered in creeper, where we were entertained. When in Montreal I remember staying in a residence at McGill and, knowing no better, some of the boys put their shoes outside their doors in European fashion, hoping for a shine during the night. In the morning, of course, not a shoe was to be seen, and lots of people were walking around in their socks! The sight of the shoes had been too much for the students in residence, and they had removed them during the night to a tank on the roof, where they were finally discovered!

We were, of course, extremely interested in meeting Banting and Best, who had recently become world-famous through the discovery of insulin. I also recall being taken for a long drive into the country to dine at, believe it or not, the Old Mill! I little thought, in those far-off days, what a large part Toronto would eventually play in my life. One of the things I remember most vividly about that trip was hearing the Philadelphia Orchestra for the first time in its home town. Frederick Stock, the conductor of the Chicago Symphony, was the guest conductor, and they played a *Hungarian Rhapsody* of Liszt. Until then I had never heard such virtuosity in an orchestra. That, remember, was at a time in England when orchestral playing had reached an all-time low and a performance such as we heard in Philadelphia was something we had only read about.

Once I had discovered the delights of Munich as a musical centre, that city became my second home. Whenever I could get time off, I would go over and study music there, and it was about now that I really began to do some serious work in conducting. I got to know the regular Munich crowd and sat at the feet of people like Bruno Walter, Hans Knappertsbusch, Leo Blech, and Richard Strauss. I attended all their rehearsals and was allowed to sit in the pit for performances. I also kept on studying singing, which is so important for a conductor. A great personality whom I met and worked with there was Hans Pfitzner. He came to direct his opera *Palestrina*, which I still think is one of the greatest post-Wagnerian music dramas. The preludes are sometimes heard at concerts and the opera is still performed occasionally, but since the great performance of Julius Patzak in the title role, Munich has tended to leave it alone.

The Munich repertoire was a wonderful grounding for a young musician who was still, remember, a doctor, now holding hospital appointments. Gradually medicine got the upper hand, however, and as I got more and more involved in my hospital work I began to lose contact with music to a great extent. This lasted for about four years in the early thirties. After my appointment at St George's I took one of the most entertaining jobs of my whole career.

7

London Practices

When I left St George's I went to see the Secretary of the Medical School, as he usually heard of any jobs which might be going. He said that one had come in that very day – a doctor at Sheerness urgently wanted help. I rang up and agreed to go down the next day. This was to be my first experience of general practice. The winter of 1930-1 was a bad one in England – very cold and a lot of snow – and I shall always remember setting out in my tiny Austin sports car, muffled up to the eyes against the icy wind. First impressions of Sheerness were pretty awful. Situated on an island in the bleakest part of the Thames Estuary and, at that time, a large naval dockyard, it was hardly a health resort or a beauty spot. I found the house and discovered a most tragic situation. The doctor who had sent for me was in partnership with his brother-in-law, a younger man, whose wife, the doctor's sister, had died three days previously while giving birth to her first child. To make matters worse, the two partners had themselves attended her at the confinement, and had found they could do nothing to save the situation, with the result that the younger man had experienced the horror of seeing his wife die before his very eyes.

As can be imagined, the general atmosphere was hardly one to give a young and very raw doctor confidence in his first attempt at general practice. The winter was so severe that on several occasions the more isolated places we had to visit were cut off by snowdrifts. The doctor told me that, a year or so previously, a barge had fouled and damaged the only bridge connecting the island to the mainland, with the result that Sheerness was quite cut off from the outside world. If they had an emergency case needing an immediate operation, they had to do it themselves instead of sending it to Chatham, as was the custom. But this man revelled in this sort of thing. He worked harder than any doctor I have ever met before or since, and he was a man who loved his profession passionately. I don't think he ever took a day off, and I remember thinking that if this was general practice, then I didn't like general practice! It was, however, hardly fair to form any opinion on the strength of this experience, because the combination of family tragedy, dreadful winter, uncomfortable lodgings, and 'first time' nerves all went to make an unpleasant mixture to be suddenly digested by a young and very green doctor.

I helped them at Sheerness until the younger man returned to work and then heard of a vacancy at the old Tunbridge Wells hospital, which has long since been supplanted by a fine modern building. The work here was just what I wanted. There were only two of us in residence and we had to cope with all the emergencies ourselves. All this time I was extremely keen on my medical work, especially the surgical side of it, and music was kept more or less in the background. It seems strange now that music can ever have taken second place in my life but it certainly did at this time, although I had no set plan of a medical career in my mind. I suppose that somewhere deep in my subconscious, a process of marking time had been decreed until I could get going with music again. A lot of my colleagues went on trips as ship's doctors and saw a lot of the world. I rather wished later that I had done the same, although a ship is not the place to gain much medical experience.

The man I was relieving at Tunbridge Wells came back and I returned to London. One day I got a call from an old friend who had done a turn as ship's doctor, and was now assisting in a general practice near the Elephant and Castle. In those days 'The Elephant' was one of London's worst slum areas, but, during the Second World War, the Germans devastated the region, so that much of it has, luckily, had to be rebuilt. This practice had a typical 'shop front' surgery, of which one used to see hundreds in those days. It belonged to a doctor who lived in the salubrious air of Kensington, and who came down every day for a few hours. One might describe it as 'Practice without Tears.' The assistant, who had to cope with the tears, lived over the surgery and dealt with all the emergencies and night calls. My friend had enjoyed working there, and, as he had to leave to do a course somewhere, asked me if I would like to try it for a while. I was introduced to the senior doctor and promptly was taken on. Thus began one of the most interesting periods of my life. Here was not only medical experience of all kinds, but also an insight into human nature which I don't think could have been gained in any other way.

For five years I lived and worked among an assortment of characters, many of whom seemed to have stepped straight out of a novel by Dickens. Most of the patients were what was then known as 'on the panel.' The panel was the precursor of the National Health Service and it seemed to me to work perfectly well. The only things wrong with it, according to our friends at Westminster, were that: (a) it was voluntary and (b) it was run by private insurance companies and (c) it didn't cover the entire population. It has always seemed to me that, with some modifications, it could have continued to work well and we should have been spared the frightful upheaval of the National Health Service, which was introduced in a violent hurry, long before anyone was really ready for it. The resulting repercussions are still to be felt thirty-five years later, and although I am now far away from it all, I cannot help feeling that something is wrong when millions of people in Great Britain still prefer to join private hospital and health schemes at their own expense, although they are, of course, forced to belong to the National scheme as well.

The sob stuff that poured forth from Westminster when the National Health Service was being pushed through was revolting in the extreme. I had lived and worked for five years among what were known as the 'poor,' so I felt I could speak with some authority about the situation. I am willing to swear on oath that, during all those five years that I worked in that practice, I never knew of anyone who did not receive adequate medical treatment because of his or her inability to pay the bills. In hospital the patients either paid as much as they could afford, or, if they couldn't afford anything, they just didn't pay. The rich man paid through the nose for his operation; the poor man got his for nothing; in other words the rich man paid for the poor man's operation as well. What could be more democratic?

I suppose it all boils down to a question of education. It should not be necessary to have a compulsory health service. Surely the first thing a prudent man should do is to insure himself and his family against sickness? But human nature works differently. The average man of little education will buy a motor car or television set long before he will consider buying health insurance; therefore he has to be forced into it. Yet I wonder if the nation's health is statistically any the better for it? It is a hard thing to evaluate, because so many new 'wonder drugs' have come into use during the last twenty years, and these have completely transformed the practice of medicine. The whole picture would have changed anyway.

When I started to work at the Elephant I was paid four pounds a week and my keep! This was the only money I had in the world. I had never asked my parents for help and, anyway, I doubt whether they would have been able to assist me. They had their own problems during the Great Depression and my father had to sell the house he had so lovingly built for his retirement at Lulworth Cove in Dorset, which must have broken his heart.

My apartment over the surgery was pretty dingy, and I started to clean it up and redecorate it myself. Eventually, it didn't look too bad. There was a couple who lived upstairs, and who acted as caretakers. Mr Row was an old soldier with a walrus moustache, rather given to boasting of his military exploits, and Mrs Row was a wizened little lady with a hair-do which was, in those days, known as an 'Eton Crop.' In the next house lived a Danish couple who made a precarious living on the music hall circuit with two performing seals. The beasts were kept in a garage off the Old Kent Road, where a small tank had been installed for them. One day, the lady came in to see me and broke into floods of tears, announcing that, during the night, one of the seals had died. What were they to do? It would take months to train a new one and they were not insured against this happening, which struck me as rather short-sighted, but I sympathized. Eventually they continued the act with the remaining seal while training the other, and some years later, I noticed on a playbill that they were performing somewhere with their *seals*, plural, from which I gathered that they had weathered the awkward period successfully. I was glad, as they were worthy and hardworking folk.

The characters one encountered in a practice of this kind would be enough to fill a very large volume. Any practice doubtless encounters its share of eccentrics, but this one seemed to breed some very special varieties. There was the man who kept coming in and imploring us to go and see his 'show.' He would never explain exactly what this was. One day we promised to go. He lived at the top of a house which was

let out in separate rooms and we found a rather dirty place with a few
rickety chairs. We were bidden to sit down, the lights were turned out,
and we saw a skull illuminated against a dark background. Imagining
this to be the prelude to some macabre spectacle, we waited breath-
lessly for more, whereupon our friend turned on the lights and announced that the 'show' was over! To this day, I have never discovered
what it was all about, but he evidently thought it was full of some deep
significance, and seemed highly satisfied with the proceedings.

I remember well a young bricklayer's assistant of fifteen coming in to
see me about an injured wrist. It struck me then that he was an un-
commonly intelligent lad and we often used to discuss books and
music. Years later I heard he had had a commission in the Indian Army,
and, after a splendid war record, became an important person in the
British film world and eventually a director of the Boyd Neel Orchestra!
Knowing a background such as this makes life very interesting, and I
have always been one who believes that 'talent will out' whatever the
circumstances. I have never had any sympathy with the 'if only I had
had a chance' school of thought because it is all too often a weak
excuse for incompetence. I have so often seen real talent make its way
when its possessor had the right determination, and when the odds
had looked pretty hopeless.

The Elephant and Castle was a pleasant place in which to live during
those years. The old streets were mostly wide, some tree-lined, and
there were many beautiful and peaceful squares which consisted of
magnificent houses that must at one time have been the homes of
prosperous merchants of the nineteenth century. Theirs was a slightly
faded glory, and most of them had been made into apartments or let
out as single rooms. Most of our patients lived in this sort of house.
Some were sanitary, others were anything but. Each was a little self-
contained community, usually ruled over by some sort of 'dragon.'
Endless feuds went on regarding the doctors. Mrs Jones on the ground
floor went to Dr Smith, whereas Mrs Brown on the first (two knocks)
patronized (and that is the word) the black doctor in the High Street
because he gave her 'that there red mixture,' which Dr Smith had
refused to repeat any more. It was quite extraordinary how the colour
of the medicine mattered – almost as much as the colour of the doctor
– and endless permutations of this colour complex were always in
evidence. If the black doctor would give the red mixture, he was to be
preferred to the Indian doctor down the road who gave the green,

although 'they say them Indians are very clever.' We poor white doctors had to think out new colour combinations almost weekly in order to keep in the running at all. It was amazing how many different races were in practice around that district.

In case it may be thought that I took this medicine business too flippantly, I must make it clear that all these idiosyncrasies of the various patients merely emphasized how potent a factor in treatment psychosomatics really are. My chief at the hospital never ceased impressing on us that, as he put it, 'There are only two kinds of medicine, those which do no good and those which do no harm.' It is those which do no harm which happen to do an enormous amount of good, so that his advice was really extremely sound and not as facetious as it might appear. Of course, he was not quite right in a technical sense because, even in those days, there were certain drugs which we knew had a very definite effect on living tissue and could do a great deal of good – digitalis for example – and, nowadays, there are many new 'wonder' compounds which perform miracles. I can't help feeling that a lot of a doctor's skill must have gone out of medicine these days, when certain afflictions, which we once looked upon as extremely serious, with perhaps a fifty-fifty survival rate among their victims, have become no more dangerous than the common cold. Psychosomatic troubles, however, are still and probably always will be with us, so that the 'red' and the 'green' medicines will have their curative powers for a long time to come.

One of our doctor neighbours at the Elephant was a White Russian who had set up practice in the Walworth Road and changed his name to Swann. We used to help each other out if one of us wanted to be away at any time. Mrs Swann, an Englishwoman, was a very fine violinist and the whole family were keen musicians. In later years it was a great pleasure to watch one of their children, Donald, blossom into a world celebrity in his famous collaboration with Michael Flanders. Many years later, Donald became a good friend of mine and took me down to Richmond to see his parents. We had a session of reminiscences of the old Elephant days amid much hilarious laughter.

Strange things can happen in even the quietest of practices. I always recall a Sunday morning when a choir boy appeared at the door, arrayed in cassock and surplice, and very out of breath. Would I please go round at once to a neighbouring church? I entered at the west door and found the usual morning service in progress. The *Te Deum* was being sung and everything appeared to be quite normal. I stood there for a few minutes, wondering why I had been called, and then something in the aisle, down by the chancel steps, caught my eye. I walked the whole length of the church and, sure enough, it was a human body – an elderly man, who was quite dead. Nobody took the slightest notice of either me or the corpse while I made a quick examination to see if I could diagnose the cause of death. There I was, kneeling in the aisle examining the corpse while the *Te Deum* went on majestically around me. I remember thinking: 'What a scene for an opera!' Finally I asked a man in a nearby pew if he would help me move the body down to the west door, which he did with some reluctance, and, as we bore our grim burden down the aisle, not a single soul took the slightest notice. From that day to this I have never understood the reason for the strange behaviour of all concerned.

There was a woman who would persist in calling me out whenever her dog was ill, even when he merely had a warm nose. The first few times I went expecting to find a human patient, but after several visits and subsequent expostulations on my part, I was wary of any more calls from her home. She would insist that the dog refused to go to the vet, but always got better when I saw him. One day, the usual call came, but, this time, a weeping voice announced over the telephone that it thought the dog was dead and would I come round to see 'how peaceful he lay.' I couldn't resist this terrible *cri de coeur* and, sure enough, the dog was dead. She was happy in the thought that his soul would rest in peace owing to my having seen him at the end. All very touching. I would probably have shown more enthusiasm if it had not been a horrid, bad-tempered little mongrel.

All these diversions helped to enliven the sometimes rather boring routine of the day-to-day work. I shall never forget answering the door to a frantic banging and finding a woman with a small boy on whose head was wedged a certain piece of bedroom crockery. The child was howling under this novel helmet, while the mother poured forth a stream of invective. 'That'll teach yer to play at being Napoleon again, yer little wretch!' seemed to be the refrain. Having calmed the boy by talking to him as best I could under the rim of the offending article, I began to try and prise it off, which only had the effect of renewing the shrieks from underneath. In the end, I had to crack it gently with a hammer in order to remove it. I asked her how she had come, as she lived some way away, and she replied: 'In the bus.' I have often wondered what the other passengers thought of this strange headgear!

Then there was the endless battle between the doctor and the patient over certificates. It must be far worse these days, when people have to produce certificates for almost everything except living! Doctors I used to work with tell me that today most of their time is taken up with writing out the accursed things. One had always to be on guard, of course, against the malingerers. It was extraordinary how demands for certificates (or 'sustificates' as they were always called – I never heard the word correctly pronounced in five years) would increase near Derby Day or the hop-picking season! But the battle of wits was conducted in the best of good humour and caused a great deal of amusement on both sides.

The old South London Music Hall was just behind our house, and I often used to drop in to see the show. I shall never forget the first time I went in there. It was like walking on Brighton beach. The thick carpet of nut shells left over from the first house crunched under foot exactly like shingle, and the aroma of oranges was quite overpowering. When the show began, the noise of nuts cracking quite often drowned anything from the stage. One night I was called in there to see a patient. I found an enormously fat lady trapeze artist sitting, practically naked, on a red plush armchair in one of the dressing rooms. She was covered in a rash, and it was an obvious case of smallpox – the only case I ever saw in general practice.

The Old Vic Theatre was only a few minutes' walk away, and I became a sort of 'unofficial' doctor to that famous institution. So well known was I to the staff that I was allowed to drop in any time I was passing to watch from the back of the circle. Those who never went to the Old Vic during the time of Lilian Bayliss certainly missed some experiences, especially when operas were performed. The conductor was an astonishing man called Charles Corri, who once, believe it or not, arranged the whole of *Tristan* for seventeen instruments and performed it there. I suppose we should be thankful that nobody has to do such things any more, but, all the same, I can't help secretly wishing sometimes for a few Corris to be still around to enliven and astonish us. The 'English *Ring*' was quite often to be seen at the Old Vic and complete cycles were fairly common. Where is it seen today? Beecham did revive *The Bohemian Girl* at Covent Garden after the war, but I can't remember any performances of either *Maritana* or *The Lily of Killarney* since the Bayliss days.

Although most of my waking moments were devoted to medical practice, quite a lot of music went on over the surgery in off-duty hours. I was studying at the time with Dinh Gilly, who had been a famous Scarpia at Covent Garden and the Met at the beginning of the century. A Rif from Algiers, he was an impressive man to meet and needed little make-up when he played Amonasro. Emmy Destinn, with whom he had had a celebrated love affair, once told my mother that, at his entrance in the *Aida* triumph scene, he would always slip a shilling into her palm as he whispered 'Non mir tradir.'

I think I could have been a fair singer if I had had the time to practise. Adrian Boult told me once that he remembered me singing the solo part in Somervell's *The Forsaken Merman* with him at Tunbridge Wells festival and wondering who on earth I was!

Ethel Smyth had also heard me sing somewhere and wrote that she wanted me for the part of Travers in her opera, *The Boatswain's Mate*, which was being done at Guildford under Claude Powell's direction. I had always wanted to meet this legendary figure and looked forward to the rehearsals, to which she came on her bicycle, and where she sat in the front row just behind the conductor with a large shopping bag, which contained her lunch of a ham sandwich and a bottle of stout. These were consumed while we were working, and she would try to sing bits with us, despite her mouth being full of sandwich; this so infuriated Claude Powell that he would call a ten-minute break when he could bear it no longer. *The Boatswain's Mate* is certainly no masterpiece, but the W.W. Jacobs story is very amusing and we all enjoyed doing it. I wish I had known Ethel in her militant suffragette days when she is said to have conducted *March of the Women* with her toothbrush through the bars of her cell window in Holloway Gaol. A great character and probably the supreme exponent of Women's Lib in history.

For years I had conducted amateur orchestras and choirs of all kinds, and had had some success at competition festivals with my choral and orchestral entries. Someone said: 'Why don't you have a go with a professional group sometime? You seem to have a talent for conducting.' Well, that was all very well, but I earned four pounds a week and my keep, so just how this was to be accomplished I had no idea. I had absolutely no money other than what I earned, and I had twenty pounds saved in the bank. Later, when the Boyd Neel Orchestra became well known, it was amusing to read and hear stories, which had begun to circulate, of my vast personal fortune. Up until then it had always been considered quite impossible to start such a venture without heavy financial backing. The possibility of its succeeding on its own merits had never entered anyone's head.

When the suggestion was made that I should start something, I began to turn the idea over in my mind and I realized that it was a waste of time to try and start yet another large symphony orchestra, of which there were already many in existence, and, anyway, the cost would have been quite prohibitive. The only alternative would seem to be a smaller orchestra of some kind which might be an economic possibility. The question was, how many players were there to be and what sort of combination were we to have? But before deciding these things I felt it was necessary to get hold of some players who might be interested and discuss it with them.

Keeping to the principle that this orchestra, if it were to succeed, had to be different from others, I realized that it was no good approaching the usual run of orchestral players; they were all busy with their own work, and could not be expected to bother about a completely un-known amateur (as I then was) with no money. I therefore hit on the idea of going to two of the great teaching institutions, the Royal Academy and the Royal College of Music, putting up notices asking any students who might be interested to communicate with me. The re-sponse was most encouraging, and when I had enough names I decided to hold an audition.

Now, one of the major problems of musical performance on a fairly large scale is to find a place where people can play. This may sound trite, but it is an ever-present problem of orchestras. Luckily, I knew a music club in Holland Park which had a large basement we could use. Our first audition produced about twenty students, mostly string play-ers (today it would have been winds). There were one or two winds and, as far as I can remember, a trumpet. At this stage of the proceed-ings, the final composition of the orchestra, if it were ever to come into existence at all, was still quite undecided in my mind; all I knew was that it would have to be small in numbers. How well I remember that first evening! Twenty rather shy young people, some of them just out of high school, and me, equally shy, wondering what I had let myself in for. The memory is vivid of how good the general standard was. I explained my idea to each one, that we could all benefit by starting a small ensemble of some kind, which would work regularly and try to attain as high a standard as it could under these conditions. They all wanted practice in ensemble playing, and I wanted practice in directing. I think we had three such auditions, and from these I picked seventeen of the most likely players.

It was now that the final composition of the group began to take shape. The idea occurred to me that one very seldom heard music for strings alone. This may sound unbelievable today, but in 1932 it was true; and it was the formation and subsequent history of this little group of mine that was responsible for the change. The large orchestras seldom played string works, as it was uneconomical to have half their personnel doing nothing, and there were any number of these orchestras, all playing roughly the same repertoire. But there were no small combinations, consisting of strings only, working permanently together, with the consequence that the repertoire for this combination was seldom heard at all.

I remember that the Berlin Philharmonic under Furtwängler used to give a concert in London every year, and sometimes began with a Handel *Concerto Grosso*. These performances were given by the whole body of strings, and I had always felt how much better it would have sounded with fewer players. Anyway, having mentioned my idea to one or two people, I was told, more or less politely, that I was mad, and that even if I did form a string group, there were only some five pieces that such a combination could play. It certainly did seem at first that the repertoire would be very small, but nevertheless I was determined to give it a trial.

I think the results of all this are now well known. We discovered a vast repertoire of music which was virtually unknown in the concert halls of the nineteenth and early twentieth centuries. Apparently nobody had ever bothered to explore it and the large orchestras had certainly never bothered to play it. The baroque period alone came as a revelation and the concerti of Handel and his contemporaries once more took their place in the concert repertoire. I like to feel that it was our pioneer efforts in the 1930s which opened up the whole treasure house of this music, and sparked the fantastic baroque revival which we have today. And if imitation is the sincerest form of flattery, then we should indeed have felt flattered by the number of groups similar to ours which have appeared through the years, and are still appearing. In fact, the chamber orchestra has come into its own, and has now a large following.

We rehearsed every Sunday morning, and loved every minute of it. We felt it was quite good, but no thought of ever doing anything with it, apart from enjoying ourselves, ever crossed our minds. After we had worked for a few months, someone suggested that we should take a hall somewhere and invite our friends to come and hear us and get some candid criticism. For this we would need a special program, and we looked around for a première of some sort. Respighi had just written his *Third Suite of Ancient Airs and Dances*, and we decided to give its first performance in England at our concert. As to a hall, we took the old Aeolian Hall in Bond Street, which is now a BBC studio. Looking back on it now I realize what a nerve we had, because someone invited some BBC people, and another asked someone from the Decca Record Company. Then it was decided to go the whole hog and invite the press! I was, remember, running a medical practice all this time, so the concert had to take place on my night off. We added the Tchaikovsky *Serenade* and John Hunt, a young pianist starting his career, played Haydn's *D Major Concerto*. Also, greatly daring, we did the *Adagietto* from Mahler's *Fifth Symphony*. In those days Mahler was seldom heard in England.

Our ensemble had, by the time of the concert, achieved some kind of character, and the enthusiasm of the group was extraordinary. There was a great *esprit de corps*, and everyone felt he, or she, was part of it. It was really an adventure of a group of people, all intensely interested in their instruments and the music which they played. So casual now does the whole thing seem in my memory that the wonder is that the concert ever took place at all, as we had no organization and were eyed askance by both agents and hall staff. Yet this extraordinary evening was to change the whole course of my life.

I am grateful that I was privileged to have taken part in the English orchestral renaissance of the 1930s; it was an exciting time. The finest orchestra in England then was the Hallé in Manchester, which was the only one on a permanent basis, and it had a great tradition from Charles Hallé himself, through Richter, Beecham, and Hamilton Harty. But London had nothing but ad hoc groups which bore names such as the London Symphony, the Royal Philharmonic, etc., but these names basically meant nothing. 1930, however, was a vital year of change. The

Toscanini visit in the spring had shown us what things might be. The BBC formed its symphony orchestra, the first permanent one London had had for some thirty years. Then, in 1932, Beecham formed the London Philharmonic, the same year as our modest little group also started rehearsing, although our first concert was not until 1933. So in the short space of three years London had two first-class symphony orchestras and one chamber orchestra to remedy the situation. It was indeed an exciting time, and we had some lively music-making.

8

The Boyd Neel Orchestra

The story of the Boyd Neel Orchestra begins in the first person singular, but soon becomes the first person plural. That is to say, in the very first place the idea of such an orchestra as the Boyd Neel was my own, but once I got it going it rapidly became a communal effort.

Our first leader was Louis Willoughby, with whom I had been associated in a few concerts with different combinations in the past, and who was very keen to help me get things going. The Willoughby family had long been well known in London orchestral circles, Louis' father, Philip, being renowned for his arrangement of all kinds of music for small ensembles. It was a sad loss to music when he was killed in the Blitz. Willoughby and I decided that we would have eleven violins (six first and five seconds), two violas, two cellos, and two double-basses. This was a complete shot in the dark, and we had little idea of what the exact balance would be like, and also how many instruments would be necessary in each part for musical requirements. We soon found that at least three violas and three cellos were necessary, not only from the balance point of view but also because the music often demanded the division of these instruments into at least three parts and sometimes even four. The constitution of the orchestra at the very first concert, however, was:

Violins	*Violas*
Louis Willoughby (Leader)	Max Gilbert
Gordon Mutter	Nora Wilson
Beatrice Marr	
Esmé Haynes	*Cellos*
Jacqueline Townshend	
Samuel Rosenheim	Eileen McCarthy
Doris Langham-Smith	Megan Lloyd
Edward Silverman	
Noreen O'Sullivan	*Basses*
Valda Oswald	
Hilda Pereira	Nora Mukle
	R. Tildesley

The audience at the first concert gave us quite an ovation at the end of the evening, and I can distinctly recollect some BBC people coming round afterwards and making detailed enquiries about the combination and its composition. I felt that this was a good sign, as it showed more than an ordinary interest in the proceedings. At its first appearance, the orchestra had the cumbersome title of 'Boyd Neel London String Orchestra.' The inclusion of the 'London' was Willoughby's idea, as he said that it gave the thing a 'cachet,' and would impress people. We soon found, of course, that it was far too unwieldy and the 'London' was dropped shortly afterwards.

After the concert I went straight back to my office on the South Bank, and found a call to a house built pretty well exactly on the spot where Shakespeare's Globe Theatre had stood. It was a woman in labour, and I duly delivered the child at about 2:00 a.m. and went home exhausted. I'm sure I'm the only person who has ever conducted a major concert in a capital city and delivered a child on one and the same evening.

It has been said that the reputation of this orchestra was made in an evening. That is probably more or less true, and it put the conductor in the very critical position of having to decide almost immediately whether he was going to continue his medical career or stake everything on this new venture. Was anybody ever faced with so difficult a decision? I had practically no money, and I knew if I stayed in my job I would at least have a reasonable living. On the other hand, if I launched forth into the professional music world with hardly a contact therein, who was to say what would happen?

I must pay tribute to someone whose sympathy at this vital moment really meant everything to me, and who was instrumental in forming my final decision. This was Dr Fairbairn, for whose practice I worked, at the time, as assistant. He was an enthusiastic amateur pianist, and extremely keen on music. I discussed my dilemma with him, and he said he was quite willing for me to work a kind of half-time arrangement for the next few months, until I could see more distinctly which way the wind was blowing. This was a great help to me because it meant that I could go on living at the surgery, in return for which I would do a certain amount of work, and at the same time would have sufficient free hours to devote to the orchestra. If I had not had such a sympathetic employer at this time, I very much doubt that the orchestra would ever have continued on its successful course.

It was in this way, then, that the next few months were spent. Rather as a snake sheds its skin, I found myself gradually shedding my connections with the medical world and becoming more and more involved with the musical, and I soon saw that it was only a matter of time before the final break took place. A few days after the first concert we had a meeting which took the form of a post-mortem and also turned out to be the point of emergence of the members of the orchestra themselves as co-partners in the enterprise. For, at this meeting, when I asked for a show of hands as to whether they thought it worthwhile continuing or not, they rose as one man, and said that they were determined to keep together whatever might befall, so much had they enjoyed the last six months. The general attitude seemed to be that even if the orchestra did not get much work, it provided a great stimulus to the players themselves. I at once saw that they were in earnest, and I felt that my fate had been decided for me. We then and there resolved to continue our weekly rehearsal and take whatever jobs happened to come along, and eventually we gave our second concert – again at the Aeolian Hall, on 24th November 1933. This time we were more ambitious and played the *Introduction and Allegro* of Elgar with André Mangeot's International String Quartet as the soloists. The remainder of the program consisted of a *Concerto Grosso* by Geminiani and a *Serenade* by Wolf-Ferrari, which had never been played in England before, although written in 1899. The performance of this work, which proved to be a delightful piece of cleverly written light music, marked the start of our exploration of the hitherto completely neglected repertoire for strings. As I mentioned earlier, people had tried to deter us from starting, harping on the assumption that no repertoire existed for strings alone, and that we were working along a cul-de-sac. I, however, somehow had an intuition that this was not so, and a very cursory glance at a few catalogues confirmed my suspicion. Later visits to the British Museum revealed the hidden treasure of the eighteenth century, which will, of course, always be the backbone of any string repertoire. The golden age of Vivaldi, Pergolesi, Geminiani, and their eighteenth-century Italian contemporaries has never been surpassed for this kind of music.

The solo pianist at our second concert was Kathleen Long, who thus started a long and happy association with the orchestra. Her style of playing and readiness to learn new works was always a perpetual source of delight to us, and her intensely musical performances have been the highlights of many concerts given by the orchestra. At this concert she played the Mozart *Concerto in A* (K.414) and the *D Minor Concerto* of Bach.

By this time word had gone round that something rather extraordinary was to be heard – extraordinary because of the extreme youth of the participants, and the out-of-the-way pieces which they played. We found, therefore, that there was a great demand for tickets, and the musical world turned up in force. The press was again enthusiastic. *The Times* described the Elgar as a 'dignified and noble performance, only needing rather more solidity of tone to make it first-rate.' The *Daily Telegraph* stated that: 'The conductor had obviously taken pains to ensure the careful observance of all dynamic and expression marks; the gift he possesses for the right tempo gave to their performances a freshness and alertness that are far from common.' The *Evening Standard* voiced my own idea when it said: 'London at present has an unusual number of symphony orchestras, and there is every reason why the example should be followed on a smaller scale.' The *Morning Post*, which in those days had an independent existence, said that the orchestra was composed of 'exceedingly competent young players under a conductor who has undoubtedly the right stuff in him. He did wonders with the material at his disposal in the Aeolian Hall last night. One long crescendo was really wonderfully handled. More will be heard of this young conductor.'

After this concert, the BBC invited us to give our first broadcast, which took place on 18th December 1933. I can remember that evening very vividly. I am not usually given to nerves, but on that particular night I can remember being really frightened at what seemed then such a great responsibility. The thought that millions of the public were about to hear and judge us for the first time was very awe-inspiring. Since that day, although I have broadcast many hundreds of times, I have never again been afflicted with such a bad attack of nerves. The broadcast took place in the sub-basement of Broadcasting House, which is now the Control Room. It was not a good studio for sound, and we were all rather depressed at the quality of tone which we produced in there, but nothing could be done about it, and we were assured that over the air it sounded well. At this first broadcast we played pieces which we had already performed at the public concerts. John Hunt again joined the orchestra in Mozart's *Piano Concerto No. 14 in E Flat* (K.449). As far as I can remember all went quite according to plan, and the broadcast was well received by the critics, for in those days nearly all the daily papers had their regular radio criticisms, a feature which might well be revived. The *Daily Express* commented that the hour-and-a-quarter-long broadcast 'was an exceptionally long session for a new combination.' Evidently the BBC were pleased with the results, for it was not long before we were asked to go on the air again, and we had our second broadcast on 18th February 1934.

Two days before this, the orchestra had been honoured by being chosen to play under the famous composer Ernest Bloch, in a concert of his own works, again at the Aeolian Hall. I had long admired the work of this very original artist, and I looked forward very much to making his acquaintance. As he was only to arrive a couple of days before the concert, I was entrusted with the task of preparing the orchestra in the various pieces, which disturbed me not a little, as I was quite unaware of how he would perform them. I need not have worried, however, because Bloch turned out to be the most charming and easy-going person one could hope to meet. He expressed himself as delighted with the orchestra's work, and the concert was a great success.

My first meeting with the composer was rather unusual. When he arrived in London, he took to his bed at the Langham Hotel (now part of the BBC) with a chill, and I had to visit him in his room. I found him propped up in bed, smiling benignly on various satellites who were waiting on him. As soon as I was introduced, he proceeded to give me a long dissertation on the harmonization of Bach's *Chorales*, telling me that everything a student wanted to know about harmony was to be found in these masterpieces. Apart from an afternoon spent many years later with Sir Donald Tovey, I have never had such an illuminating music lesson.

As soon as we started to broadcast regularly we became known all over Europe, and soon, when the first records were made, the whole world knew of our work. With the music clubs and odd concerts in large private houses, we managed to keep going until another milestone was reached in the orchestra's career. This was the offer of a contract from the Decca Record Company to record, over a number of years, all the major masterpieces of string music. My long and happy association with Decca-London records started with a recording of Holst's *St. Paul's Suite*. Records were still, of course, 78 r.p.m. speed. We recorded a large part of our repertoire in those years before the war. Our early '78s' became known all over the world and contained many works which had never been recorded before. These all received glowing tributes as they were produced, the *Daily Telegraph* devoting a whole column one Saturday to the venture. I am not one of those optimists who believe there has been a great increase of general interest in music. I agree that more people go to hear music of a certain *type* (usually connected with the films) but is the interest a really *musical* one? Musical people *went* to concerts far more than they do now. Some of the most truly musical people I know today are the gramophone record collectors, very few of whom ever go near a concert hall.

When we started making records, Decca were using, as a studio, an old warehouse high up above Cannon Street Station in the City. One reached it through a graveyard, and up many flights of narrow, rickety stairs – the last place in the world where one could expect to find a gramophone studio. It was quite good acoustically, in fact sometimes rather too good, because you not only heard the music in the studio, but also the trains going in and out of Cannon Street Station! There was one record of mine, on the market for many years, on which, in the middle of the slow movement, you could hear the 3:15 train leaving the station; I believe it was regarded as a 'collector's item' at one time.

The Holst work had a large sale, and a press cutting from the *Yorkshire Post* of March 1935 had as a heading: 'A Holst Work for Three Shillings – Welcome Issue by Decca.' The success of this issue started a long series of records of mostly eighteenth-century music, including the *Concertos* of Handel. These wonderful works were very little known in those days and only about three of them were ever played. When we started to play all twelve of *Opus 6*, the public and critics were astounded that this lovely music could have been neglected for so long. The *Opus 6* of Handel is the greatest contribution of any composer to the string orchestral repertoire. The variety and invention in these masterpieces is a never-ending source of amazement. All are written for the same combination of soloists – two violins and a cello. This group is contrasted with the main body of the strings, and a harpsichord should, of course, be used in performance on every possible occasion. Towards the beginning of 1936 we started recording the whole series, and this great undertaking remained the only complete recording of these works for many years. For the records my old friend Arnold Goldsborough performed the continuo part on the harpsichord in splendid style. It needs a musician of real learning to discharge this task adequately. An interesting thing is to compare the opening of our 1952 record of Handel's *Opus 6, No. 12* with that on our 1934 one. The 1952 version shows the advance of my musicological studies in the interim! The double dots are the key to the difference.

We also recorded several Mozart piano concertos with that fine artist Kathleen Long. These were all 'first time on record' works; in fact I don't think we ever recorded more than three or four works which were already on disc in twenty years of work in the studio. The K. 503, especially in those days, was never played at all.

This pioneering was an interesting musical life for me and, if it hadn't been for the Second World War, I think we would have still been in the vanguard of the chamber orchestra movement, and my life might have been very different. As it was, we retained our lead, if such a situation can be so described, until 1953, when so many competitors arrived on the scene, all subsidized by their respective governments, that we had to reassess the whole position.

Following the Holst *Suite*, we recorded, in quick succession, the Respighi *Dances* which we had played at our first concert, the Elgar *Introduction and Allegro*, two *Divertimenti* by Mozart, Handel's *Faramondo* Overture, and some Grieg pieces. About this time Decca leased the Chenil Galleries in King's Road, Chelsea, and it was here that the first records were made of Vaughan Williams' *Fantasia on a Theme of Tallis* and a *Romance* of Sibelius. For the recording of the *Fantasia*, we had the invaluable help and advice of the composer himself, who was present the whole time, and said afterwards that he was completely satisfied with the results. Some days before the recording was made, the four boys who played the solo quartet visited the composer at his Dorking home, where he went through the music with them. I often feel that this wonderful work is perhaps the greatest of all achievements in string composition. Problems of recording it were immense, because we had to strive for the impression of the music being played in a vast cathedral nave, preserving at the same time the wonderful effect of the echo orchestra, which in a church or concert performance should be at some distance from the main body. We also had to give the solo quartet its rightful proportions in the whole scheme.

Radio programs about this time contained two new works by the Swedish composers Lars Erik Larsson – the *Little Serenade* and a *Sinfonietta*. These are both original and excellent compositions. We also gave one of the first performances of Benjamin Britten's *Simple Symphony* in May 1935. At that time Britten was known only to a small circle of music-lovers, but had already made a profound impression with his choral work, *A Boy Was Born*. I had not yet had the pleasure of meeting the composer, and it was not until two years later that he started his long and close association with our orchestra. The *Simple Symphony* is a *tour de force* for one so young to have composed, for the original pieces date from when he was aged between nine and twelve. They were for solo piano, and he made them into this delightfully humorous orchestral composition during his late teens. In the *Sentimental Sarabande*, he achieves a lyrical warmth which he has rarely attained since.

The composer later wrote to me about the *Simple Symphony* as follows:

As you probably know, starting at a hideously early age, I poured out reams and reams of music – songs, piano works, chamber music, orchestral works, oratorios (not opera) only slowing down when I reached the age of wisdom, or rather, when I left the age of innocence. Bits of these works were used as the basis of the Simple Symphony *which I organized in 1934 (I think). The themes come mostly from piano sonatas (I wrote twelve before I left my private school!) or songs. The development of these is sometimes quite new, but often left as it was – except for the re-scoring for strings; – as far as I can remember most of the pizzicato movement, the scherzo, i.e., is 'echt.' Mrs. L. Sutton used to teach me the viola in Norwich – she was, maybe still is, one of the leading lights of music in Norfolk. Used to run a string quartet led by our old friend, Mangeot! I feel particularly grateful to her because it was she who introduced me to Frank Bridge and Harold Samuel, with whom she had been at college. Her son, by the way, now music master at Lancing (John Alston) was my early music – boy – rival in the Eastern Counties.*

That's all I can think of about that 'early masterpiece' –
Hope it'll do.

> *Yours ever,*
> *Ben*

Other works which we broadcast in the mid-thirties included a Pergolesi *Concertino*, a *Sinfonia* by Torelli, a *Fugue for Nine Violins* by Dubensky, a *Suite* by Frank Bridge, and a *Concerto for Flute, Cello and Piano* by d'Indy, which has since become a favourite.

One of the stalwarts of those early days was David Martin, who led our second violin section for many years. David was one of the many Canadians who at one time or another were in the orchestra. There was a period when we had no fewer than five violins, all of whom came from Canada – four from Winnipeg, and all pupils of the remarkable Mr Waterhouse. Frederick Grinke, our leader for ten years, was, of course, the most brilliant of these bright lights. Our violas were led by Max Gilbert, who appeared at the very first audition at Holland Park. Other personalities who had so much to do with forming the orchestra's style were Peter Beavan and Eileen McCarthy, the cellists. Many famous players were with us from time to time, such as Watson Forbes, Frederick Riddle, and John Walton. At one time our viola section consisted of Gilbert, Forbes, and Riddle, surely the strongest combination of its kind that can ever have existed. John Walton was our principal double-bass for many years, and is a member of that famous family of musicians who were the mainstay of most of the orchestras in London. All these players had much to do with the establishing of a *tradition*; a tradition which lasted.

Our method of working had always been rather unorthodox, and people coming to a Boyd Neel rehearsal for the first time were some-times quite mystified at our procedure. The principle established many years ago was that we were essentially democratic in a musical sense. When we studied a new work, we would go through it without stop-ping, playing it as best we could. We would then take the obviously difficult pieces and get the notes right; when we felt we had the actual playing more or less fixed, the discussions would then begin. It was these debates that astonished any strangers. First, I rehearsed the piece according to my idea, but as we went along, the playing would be stopped by any member getting up and making suggestions, either regarding my ideas, or the playing of his own or any other section of the orchestra. This might be thought rather tiresome in practice and not productive of anything worthwhile, but we found that it had extraordinary results. Each player feels that he or she is much more than a cog in a machine, and has the satisfaction of knowing that he or she has contributed something more than mere obedience towards the final result. I acted as a kind of chairman, and, of course, the final decision was always left to me. In this way, we built up performances which were the result of the combined deliberations of everybody. In a large orchestra this would be quite impossible, but in a small group it creates a unique atmosphere. Everyone is keen about his instrument and the music he plays. The players can *hear* themselves and they can regard the whole thing as a more or less glorified string quartet. People who heard the orchestra for the first time said that they often got that same impression, the sound and the general style of playing being far more like a chamber music group than an orchestra. As a help toward this type of performance, I would quite often sit in the hall and let them carry on without a beat. In this way they had to learn to listen intently – a very good discipline. It also helped me to consider matters of balance more detachedly. I mention this point in order to bring home the very different type of work which we did in this orchestra, and how our general procedure differed from the usual run of orchestral practice. The evolution of this spirit of communal striving for an ideal was not consciously cultivated at any one time. It is a thing which seemed to grow with the years into a tradition.

The start of the long recording program with Decca gave us the feeling that we were at last launched on our future career in earnest, and small jobs began coming in from all sorts of unexpected sources. My rift with the medical world was now complete, and I commenced a precarious living, always wondering where the next job was coming from. The position of any musician without private means is forever uncertain, and the constant anxiety of wondering where I was going to get jobs for eighteen other people as well as myself began to weigh rather heavily after a time. All through the orchestra's existence the right person managed to turn up at the right moment.

At the time of the orchestra's formation I had done some amateur operatic work with a soprano, Marjory Scott, who was very interested in the idea of the orchestra. She had just moved into a magnificent studio and suggested that the orchestra make its headquarters there. This was a gesture indeed – half our worries banished in an instant. But that was not all. Marjory volunteered to do all the secretarial work until such time as the orchestra was secure financially. It was the extraordinary self-sacrifice of people such as this that really made the whole thing possible. We used the studio for our necessary rehearsals as concerts came along, but also continued the weekly rehearsals in order to re-hearse repertoire. In this way, we kept all our now-extensive list of works in the library well rehearsed, and could produce a performance of anything at a moment's notice. I well remember an instance where this policy proved to be of the utmost help. On the day King George V died, the BBC had hurriedly to change its programs for the national mourning. We were asked to do quite a long broadcast of appropriate music at a few hours' notice. There was just time to collect the players and go straight on the air, which we could never have done had we not been quite ready with a program. It was seldom we had the whole orchestra present at any one of these rehearsals; they were quite infor-mal and optional. People just came if they happened to be free. It usually happened that we had about two-thirds present, and there were always enough to have a proper rehearsal of any works we wished to do.

I do not think we realized at the time what an enormous advantage it was to have this centre of operations where we could rehearse undis-turbed and in comfort. Conditions of work mean more than the average member of the public could ever dream of where music-making is concerned. Nobody will ever know how many poor performances have been due entirely to the artist having been reduced to a state of musical impotence before he comes onto the platform. I could write a whole volume on the iniquities of artists' rooms.

I remember one year playing the musical background for the BBC's Christmas Day *Round Europe* program. This was one of my first expe-riences of this sort of thing, and I found it very nerveracking. We played in a studio which was connected with the rest of the program only by a pair of earphones, which I wore on my head while conducting. As each capital came through, I could hear what was happening, but the orches-tra could hear nothing, and just had to follow me. Everything depended on me bringing in the correct background music at the right moment. It all went well, but I was not sorry when we had finished! I believe this was the first of its kind and quite an experiment at that time.

So far we had only appeared in London and on the radio, and we felt that it was time the rest of Britain heard the orchestra. We had gained a good reputation on the air, so the moment seemed propitious, but how were we to find the funds for such a costly undertaking? A new, and only partially known, orchestra could not hope to draw audiences in sufficient numbers to make ends meet, and it must be remembered that these were still days of crippling entertainment tax and no state subsidies. However, as usual, the right person appeared at the right time. Louden Greenlees, a fine Scottish baritone, was contemplating a tour, and wished to make it rather more interesting than his usual round of recitals. He asked us if we would join him; he was to sing at each concert, and we were to play one of our usual programs. Any losses were to be guaranteed by him. What a chance for a young orchestra! A tour of the provinces guaranteed, and at such an early stage in our existence! Lucky strokes such as this have constantly occurred, but we like to feel that if the people concerned had not had faith in the orchestra they would not have risked so much for it. The tour started at Newcastle, where Sydney Newman, later Tovey's successor at Edinburgh, was the moving spirit. From Newcastle we moved to Dundee, thence to St Andrews, Edinburgh, Glasgow, Manchester, Sheffield, and Liverpool. The notices were uniformly good, and the critics all remarked firstly on the extreme youth of the players and secondly on the novelty of the programs, which included the *Introduction and Allegro* of Elgar, a symphony by the eighteenth-century composer Carl Friedrich Abel, *Two Spanish Pieces* by Rodrigo, and a Mozart divertimento.

The *Liverpool Post* remarked: 'This orchestra is by way of being famous. It has created quite a distinctive position in a field that bears cultivation – string chamber music. Its ensemble is excellent, and because it is so obviously well rehearsed and so studious in its methods, it confronts our rather impoverished local efforts with a new standard. For that we can only be grateful. Mr. Boyd Neel himself is something of a genius, and in an unostentatious way he handles his little ensemble with the most perfect skill. He gave us performances which for neatness and precision it would be hard to excel. One might be tempted to say that there was a note of preciosity here and there, but I would discount that as being the reaction we inevitably feel to anything that is so polished and exact, so dainty and fine, as were these performances.'

Quite good for beginners, which was really all we were. At other concerts on this tour, we added Britten's *Simple Symphony* to our program.

Concerts followed at Wigmore Hall in London, at Stowe School, Harrow, Wellington, and various other places near London. At the Wigmore Hall we revived Stravinsky's *Apollon musagètes*. This ballet had been one of Balanchine's first great successes, being commissioned for a festival in Washington in 1928. Diaghilev brought it to London the next year, and I was fascinated by it. I still think the music is one of Stravinsky's finest scores. When I was thinking in 1934 that we should not overdo Handel, I suddenly realized that *Apollo*, which, by the way, is what Stravinsky liked to call it, was scored for strings only and would be an ideal piece. This strange work has a kind of indefinable classic beauty which becomes extremely haunting when one has studied it a great deal. We first played it at a concert; the recording then followed. Now, there is a story attached to this. There are some bars towards the end which have always mystified me. The time is 6/8 and there occur five bars in 2/4 during the movement. It had not been played since the Diaghilev season five years previously, and I could get no help from any of my colleagues. I could not remember how the bars were played originally and I had to go entirely by what was written in the score. Stravinsky was not available as he was in the United States and we had to play the piece the following week. If you play these bars exactly as they are written, they sound awkward and unnatural. I always felt that Stravinsky had left out an indication in the score which would have given us his intention. I was right, because years later, when he conducted it, he did *not* play it as it is written in the score. The matter concerns the time values of notes. If the eighth note is to remain constant throughout, the 2/4 bars are very quick indeed. If the quarter note of the 2/4 bars equals the dotted quarter note of the 6/8, then it sounds as Stravinsky and others now play it. When we made the recording in 1934, I was convinced that there was an error in the score, and I decided, with much trepidation, to play it as I thought it should be. Luckily all was well, and I had done the right thing, but even to this day the score has not been corrected.

When Hindemith started his *Gebrauchsmusik* series we seized eagerly on the *Five Pieces for Strings*, which we must have played hundreds of times. We also started reviving works for strings which had been almost forgotten, like Dvořák's *Serenade* and the *Serenade* of Josef Suk, one of the masterpieces of string writing. This came as a complete novelty to English audiences and I well remember the Czech Philharmonic coming to London years later and playing it. To my astonishment, at the end of the slow movement two solo violins began to play some music which was not in my score. After the concert, I went round and introduced myself to Vaclav Talich, who was conducting. I told him of my amazement, and he said Suk had added these parts later, but they appeared in no score. He very kindly said he would send me the extra parts when he got home, and they duly arrived. After that we always played it in this version and then I, in my turn, used to get asked by conductors what had happened at the end of the slow movement!

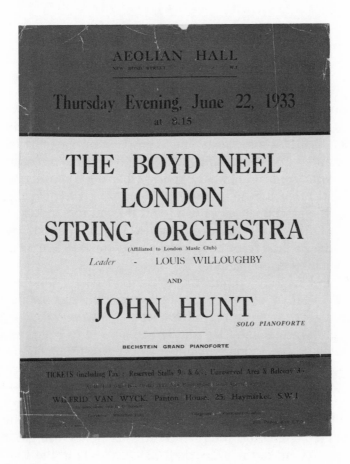

The first concert of the Boyd Neel Orchestra in London at the Aeolian Hall

9

Pre-war Adventures

In the autumn of 1935, Rutland Boughton was arranging a festival of his works at Bath, the plan being to revive *The Immortal Hour*, which had not been heard for some years, and to produce a work he had recently written, called *The Ever Young*. I had long been a devoted admirer of *The Immortal Hour*, and I was delighted when the composer asked me if I would bring the orchestra in an augmented form to Bath and conduct the performances of it myself. He was to conduct the new work, and the festival was to run for a week. The performance took place in the Pavilion (erected originally, I believe, as a temporary structure, but it became permanent).

That week in Bath was a memorable experience for all of us, and it was here that there occurred one of the most amusing episodes of our performing life. At the end of the first act of *The Immortal Hour*, two of the chief characters, the King and Dalua, have to recede through the forest, their voices getting ever fainter and fainter. The Pavilion was not deep enough on stage to get the proper effect, but we found that if they went outside the artists' door and walked down the side of the hall, the effect was perfect. All was well at the evening performances throughout the week, but at the Saturday matinée, the fun began. Those who know Bath will remember that the Pavilion adjoins the football ground – in fact you step out of the stage door practically on to the touch-line. Nobody had thought of the hideous possibilities. The time came for Dalua and the King to take their walk through the forest; the stage door was flung open and out stepped the two made-up figures, in their fantastic costumes, among the crowd lining the touch-line. They then proceeded to walk the length of the field singing their forest calls to each other. So astonished was the crowd and the players that the match came to a standstill, and this grotesque pantomime was watched by hundreds of people on the field. It must have been a shattering experience for the singers, but it gave us all one of the best laughs we had ever had.

The Bath Festival was not, however, our first operatic engagement. That summer a friend of mine had said he wanted to take me down to the country and introduce me to someone who he thought would interest me. This man had just built a theatre adjoining his house in which he wanted to produce operas so that his wife, who was a professional singer, could take part. We took the train to Lewes, about sixty miles from London, where we were met by car and driven into the depths of some of England's loveliest countryside. We arrived at an old manor-house and were greeted by a bald man with a limp. This was John Christie; the house was Glyndebourne. We had lunch and his captivating wife Audrey joined us. I had seen her in operas with the Carl Rosa Company, and had always admired her vivacity and beautiful voice. She had spent all her childhood in British Columbia, where her father, the Reverend Mildmay, was a minister in Penticton. After lunch we were taken to see the theatre which was built on to the house. Suddenly Christie said: 'I want to give a Mozart Festival this summer [it was then March] and I have no idea how the acoustics will turn out. Would you do a performance of something with your orchestra and some singers so that we can test the theatre?' I replied that I would be delighted but we would have to think quickly as there was little time to lose. I immediately thought of a little company of three, who called themselves the 'Intimate Opera Company', because I knew they performed eighteenth-century operas which would suit our orchestra, and, in a month's time, having rehearsed in London, we all went down for the weekend. Christie had invited friends to fill the theatre, and so many turned up that we had to give *two* performances. I had expected that the whole thing would be makeshift in the extreme, done probably in front of curtains – but nothing of the kind. Christie had hired a well-known scenic designer and had built the most beautiful sets in the local workshops of his construction business. The program we decided upon was a triple bill – the *Coffee Cantata* of Bach, which they did very charmingly in dramatic form, Mozart's *Bastien and Bastienne*, and Pergolesi's *La Serva Padrona*. The company already had costumes for these, and round them Hamish Wilson designed the first of his famous Glyndebourne settings. No expense was spared, and for these two performances he built some of the loveliest stage sets I have ever seen. I shall never forget the green and gold bedroom of the Pergolesi setting. It had a rich Rembrandtesque effect that even Wilson himself never surpassed when Glyndebourne had become world-famous. As far as I know, neither this set nor the one for the Mozart opera was ever used again, but the Bach scene was later used for the second act of *Figaro* in the Glyndebourne performance of that year. The performances were attended by private invitation only. Christie insisted on the theatre being full, so that the test should be correct. We played two shows in the one day, and the results were valuable in the extreme, one of them being that the floor of the orchestra pit was later raised considerably and the proscenium surround blackened to stop light reflection. The Mr Woodhouse who sang in these performances was also the Dalua of Bath football fame.

Later that year the great series of festivals had its beginning with Carl Ebert and Fritz Busch in charge. On the second night there were seven people in the theatre, but it didn't take long for the news to spread, and after the first week it never looked back, and is now probably one of the three most famous opera festivals in the world. The theatre has been altered very much from those early days and many other buildings have been added.

During the next summer, Mr Christie very kindly allowed us to camp in his grounds and use the opera house to rehearse in. It was quite a new experiment for an orchestra to go away for fourteen days living under canvas for intensive work. We pitched our tents in a field down by the lake behind the opera house. The season was over and we had the ground entirely to ourselves with the theatre as a rehearsal room. We were washed out of our tents one night, but we had a dry barn where we took our meals. In the end we found that the great music room in the house was a better rehearsal location than the theatre itself as it was warmer and contained a magnificent organ. We worked extremely hard preparing our repertoire for the coming season. Working under such ideal conditions one had an idea of how great composers such as Haydn and Wagner must have felt when given princely patronage for their labours.

1937 was an exciting year. We were getting better and better known and inquiries began to come in from all parts of the country, and also from abroad. The guest artist on our United Kingdom tour was the very famous Scottish soprano Isobel Baillie. The provincial tour was by now an annual event, and we visited new places each year. Towns like Chelmsford, Ipswich, Colchester, and all the chief Scottish centres were visited. The scheme in the pre-war years was usually to make an out-of-London tour in one period of a few weeks, and to spend the rest of the year in and around London. We continued to give our London concerts at the Wigmore Hall, always reviving some old music virtually unknown to the audience, and also trying to produce some interesting new contemporary works. It was very exciting to observe that the formation of our orchestra had provided a stimulus for composers to write music for it, and we began to receive scores from well-known contemporary musicians, to many of which we gave the first performance. Among these were an *Essex Suite* by Armstrong Gibbs, a *Divertimento* by Geza Frid, an *Oboe Concerto* by Rutland Boughton, a *Suite* by Stöhr, and a *Piano Concerto* by Anis Fuleihan.

The great event of 1937 was to take place in August of that year. In May, Sir George Frankenstein, then Austrian Ambassador in London, asked me to go and see him, to discuss an idea which he had in mind. He told me that he had heard the orchestra and considered his fellow countrymen should know something of its work, which he thought unique and of a kind which would appeal to them, because of its association with so much eighteenth-century Viennese music. He suggested that he should propose to the Festival Committee at Salzburg that the Boyd Neel Orchestra should play at the 1937 festival, preferably a concert of English music, with a well-known English soloist.

You can imagine my emotions on hearing of this idea. That we should have been asked to play at the most famous music festival in the world, the sacred ground of the Vienna Philharmonic, where, as far as I knew, no other foreign orchestra had ever been invited to play. The Ambassador told me he would give me fuller details in a few days' time. Off I went to tell the others this wonderful piece of news and the excitement was intense. Two days later, there arrived a formal invitation for us to give a concert of English music in the large hall of the Mozarteum, with a celebrated soloist, to be chosen by us. There was only one condition attached to all this – that we should give the first performance of some composition written especially for the event by an

Englishman. Here was a blow indeed. It was now the first week in June, and the concert was to be on August 27th. How was I to get any composer to write a completely new work in such a short space of time? I started to think of all the possible composers that I might ask and it didn't seem that any of them would be able to get the work done in the time.

A month or so previously, we had been doing some music for a film down at Shepperton. The composer was shown so many feet of film in the evening and had to go home and produce some music to fit it to be recorded on the following day. I had asked a young man who was making a name for himself as a composer to write some music for this particular film. The young man in question was Benjamin Britten and I rang him up and told him of our situation. He was not in the least dismayed and said he would be delighted to take it on. I was very interested in his work and had been astonished at the speed and quality of his compositions. (Film music at that time very often had literally to be written overnight and Britten could achieve this with great ease.)

In ten days' time he appeared on my doorstep with the now famous *Variations on a Theme of Frank Bridge* fully sketched out, and played it through to me on the piano. I realized at once that the battle was won and that the Salzburg concert would take place with a contemporary masterpiece as its main attraction. Frank Bridge was there also and the excitement of everyone was intense. The astonishing virtuosity of the whole piece was immediately apparent, and after such works as the *Aria Italiana*, the *Moto Perpetuo*, and the *Funeral March*, we all burst into spontaneous applause. Here was obviously one of the finest string works of the last fifty or sixty years, and it was written by a young Englishman for a young English orchestra. The work has, of course, since become world-famous, and was the first sign of Britten's astonishing facility for string writing, which progressed triumphantly through *Les Illuminations* and *Prelude and Fugue* to the *Serenade*.

As to the choice of a soloist for this important concert, it all rather depended on the concerto which was to be played. I had always liked the idea of having a wind player as our soloist, because the different sound colour gave a pleasing contrast to the prevailing string tone throughout the evening. We had played frequently with Leon Goossens, and I felt that he was the ideal person to take with us. We had recently given the first performance of Rutland Boughton's *Oboe Concerto No. 1*, and we felt this would be a good work for him to play on this occasion. In the second half of that program, Goossens played the Bax *Oboe Quintet* with four of the principals in the orchestra. We thought this would be a contrasting interlude during the evening's proceedings.

We left London on the 24th of August and gave a broadcast from Hilversum in Holland on our way through. This was the start of my long and happy association with the Dutch radio. We arrived in Salzburg on the day before the concert, and the orchestra, hardly any of whom had seen the famous town before, indulged in an orgy of sightseeing, so much so, in fact, that I was a little anxious as to whether we should get them all back into the hall for the rehearsal on the following morning. Many parties were given for us, and we found that an intense interest had been created in the concert. On the actual night we were all very nervous, and the sight of so many players from the Vienna Philharmonic Orchestra sitting in the front row did nothing to make our nerves any better. The program was: *Chaconne in G Minor* by Purcell, the Boughton *Oboe Concerto*, the Britten *Variations*, two *Aquarelles* by Delius, the Bax *Oboe Quintet*, and Elgar's *Introduction and Allegro*. Applause after the Purcell was polite, and we felt that at least we were holding our own. Goossens played magnificently and created a sensation with the concerto. Then came the Britten. The composer had entitled one of his variations *Viennese Waltz*, no doubt thinking of the audience at the first performance. Anybody who has heard this parody of the Viennese waltz will realize it might annoy the ardent disciples of Johann Strauss, Lehár, etc. The Viennese on this occasion, however, took the joke very well, and this particular variation was one of the successes of the evening. At the close of the work there was a real ovation from the audience. I realized that we had been a success and had conquered this most discriminating of all audiences. The second half went as well as the first, and at the end we received applause such as I have never heard before or since. I was recalled to the platform time and time again, and from then until exactly ten years later, at our farewell concert in the Sydney Town Hall, it remained the most exciting experience of our career. At the reception given to us afterwards, I remember vividly the excited praise of the members of the great Viennese orchestra, especially Buxbaum, the leader of the cellos, who was loud and effusive in his congratulations. Appreciation from such a distinguished musician, with so much traditional background, was the sort of thing which we treasured more than anything. The news of the

Salzburg triumph spread all round the world like wildfire, and we began receiving inquiries from every quarter. Britten was made an international figure in one evening and he never looked back. After-wards we recorded the *Variations* three times in all – twice on 78s and once on LP. Later on, Britten wrote us a work for our tenth birthday – the *Prelude and Fugue for Strings* – and the orchestra also recorded the *Serenade for Tenor and Horn* which we have played countless times all over the world with many different singers and horn players. Dennis Brain and Peter Pears performed at the première.

Apart from our visit to Salzburg, we were playing consistently in London in the summer of 1937, quite often in superb surroundings such as Hertford House (Wallace Collection), the ballroom of London-derry House, and other beautiful concert halls. In Londonderry House we gave an interesting dramatic performance, in costume, of Debussy's *Blessed Damozel*. Maggie Teyte sang the chief part.

A recording we made about this time was Peter Warlock's *Capriol Suite*. This was made a year or two after his tragic death. We made a second recording of this later on, and also one of his *Serenade to Delius*. Philip Heseltine, his real name, was a strange individual with a split personality. His output as a composer was small, but his few songs will go down in history as some of the finest by any Englishman. He was aware of this dichotomy in his nature, and his adoption of the name Warlock, which means sorcerer, was exactly right for that side of his nature. Warlock it was who made history at the old Queen's Hall by shouting out 'Thank goodness that's over' at the end of a piano con-certo by Herbert Howells. His *Serenade to Delius* is unashamedly writ-ten in the full Delius idiom and is as hard to bring off in performance as any work of Delius himself. It is very rarely performed.

The life of a musician is nothing if not varied, and at this same time I was also arranging and recording the music used by Cecilia Colledge for her skating exhibitions. She was then World, European, and British Amateur champion and the music she used for her displays was a very important part of the proceedings. I used to go down to the rink when she was practising and carefully note every movement she made, tim-ing it with a stop-watch. I then had to fit the music she had chosen on to a gramophone record, making sure that certain notes came at each split second. If we were so much as a second over or under time, her whole display was thrown out of joint, so marvellously timed were all her movements. It was particularly pleasant for me to do this work, as I was an old friend of her father's, having been taught by him as a student when he was ear, nose, and throat surgeon at St George's Hospital.

During 1937 we changed our leader from Louis Willoughby to Frederick Grinke. I think that the Salzburg concert was almost Grinke's first appearance with the orchestra. His ten years' leadership was one of the most outstanding things of the orchestra's history, and there is little doubt that he was largely instrumental in forming the style and creating the spirit of its performances. To have only three different leaders in seventeen years of existence is, I think, a fairly good record for any orchestra.

Among the events of 1938 which stand out in my memory are the Canterbury Festival and the Charity Concert arranged by Princess Helena Victoria, which had by then become an annual event in our calendar. The scheme of this concert was always the same. It took place during the Covent Garden Opera Season, and two or three of the leading singers used to give their services, so that we had the pleasure of working with artists such as Lauritz Melchior, Kerstin Thorborg, Freda Leider, and John Brownlee. The 1938 concert was specially memorable, as it was the first occasion on which the Queen had heard the orchestra, and we treasure a letter saying how much she had enjoyed the evening's performance. (That would have been Queen Elizabeth, the Queen Mother.)

The Canterbury Festival was another of our favourite events. The concert in the cloisters always had bad luck with the weather, and one year we had to hold the music on to the stands with clothes-pegs. We were giving the first performance of John Ireland's *Concertino Pastorale*, which he had recently written for us, and he sat in the front row, shivering, with a rug round his legs. The concert was broadcast, and friends who were listening at home told us they could hear the music flapping in the wind. Sir Adrian Boult used to come and conduct the orchestra, usually in a choral work, and I recall a very moving performance of the Fauré *Requiem*. I have never heard it sound more beautiful than it did from the west end of that wonderful building.

The ISCM (International Society of Contemporary Music) met in London that year, and the orchestra was asked to take part. We played, among other contemporary works, the Britten *Variations*, and they were one of the hits of the festival. This was the first time I met Béla Bartók. He and his wife played the *Sonata for Two Pianos and Percussion* in the same program in which we played the Britten, and they gave an electrifying rendering of that amazing piece. Bartók was very taken with the Britten work, and I well remember him bursting out laughing during the 'Aria Italiana.' He was very complimentary about our group and was altogether a most delightful person to be with. It was a good festival, and there were some exciting performances, especially one of Webern's *Augenlicht*, conducted by Hermann Scherchen.

At this time I was living in a tiny mews apartment very near the BBC main building. In those days, unless one did this, it was almost impossible to work for the Corporation as a performer. This was because the short-wave, the so-called 'Empire' service, broadcast live twenty-four hours a day, and programs were beamed to various parts of the world around the clock. It therefore happened quite often that one had to conduct a concert at 3:00 a.m. Living where I did, it was possible to work in this way. It was also convenient to the Queen's Hall and this was the reason I became involved in a rather amusing episode.

London still had pea-soup fogs in the 1930s; the last really bad one was in 1952, which stopped the traffic for hours and caused many deaths. Since that time there have been very strict regulations about burning smokeless fuel, so now a pea-souper is quite rare. When this particular fog was at its worst, during the afternoon my phone rang and the agitated voice of Van Wyck, an agent with whom I had done some business, said: 'I'm in an awful situation at Queen's Hall. I have Stravinsky and Dushkin here [Dushkin was a famous Russian violinist] rehearsing for their concert tonight. The hall is full of fog and we can hardly see a thing. The student I got to turn pages for Stravinsky has been thrown out by the maestro, who is in a terrible rage. Do you think you could come over and help?' I said I would do what I could and groped my way round to the hall. The two performers were crouched in a corner of the platform and Van Wyck took me over and introduced me. Stravinsky just looked at me and snorted. Dushkin gave me a warm smile. They were to give the English première of the *Duo Concertante* that evening – that was if any audience was able to appear. I went over to the piano and at once realized that this was to be a very horrible experience. Propped up on the piano was a very thick mass of music manuscript sheets, which at first appeared to be quite blank. Peering closer, however, I could just discern some faint pencilled outlines of ghostly note shapes on the staves. I was about to run for it when Stravinsky came over to the piano, pushed me down on the chair which had been vacated by the evicted page-turner, and said, in a loud voice:

'Commençons!' Dushkin hadn't even picked up his fiddle before the maestro was well into the first page. From what I could see of the ghostly shapes through the fog, the manuscript appeared to be a series of shorthand symbols, which conveyed everything to the composer, but nothing to anyone else! I managed the first turn all right because a few scattered notes appeared at the bottom of the page which I recognized, but at the bottom of the second page I was quite lost; the maestro seized the sheet and flung it into the air with the most awful grunts and hisses. We finally got through the work with me getting about every other page right, and by then the floor was littered with the sheets Stravinsky had thrown in the air! As the last note sounded, the composer jumped up and went straight off without saying a word to either Dushkin or me. Van Wyck appeared from the artist's room and I said I did not think I could stand the strain of the concert under those conditions, at which he nearly wept and implored me to give it a try. I felt I couldn't leave him in the lurch, so I turned up in the evening and by then, the fog had cleared a little and a small audience had assembled. If only the piece had been available for me in some form to look at, things would have been a lot easier, but only the violin part was written down, most of the piano part being still in the maestro's head. We got through with only a dozen sheets lying on the platform, but he never said one word of thanks or even acknowledged my presence the whole of the evening. Dushkin could not have been more charming and knew just what I was thinking.

What an experience! I can never hear the *Duo* today without recalling that macabre scene in my mind's eye. The amazing thing was that I had intended to go to the concert anyway in order to ask Stravinsky about the bars in the score of his *Apollon musagète* ballet mentioned earlier, but I hadn't the courage to reveal my identity after the horrors of the evening! Some thirty years later, however, when I met him in the United States I confessed to the whole thing, but he had only a hazy recollection of the whole affair, for which I was really thankful.

About the time of the Stravinsky adventure I was doing the music for a few films in the Elstree Studios, just to keep body and soul together. I made no money out of the Boyd Neel Orchestra, as it only just kept alive by my ploughing back anything that I might possibly have claimed as my fee, so I had to scrape up work elsewhere wherever I could. Elstree was busy in those days and Albert Coates was conducting a film of *I Pagliacci* with Richard Tauber, for which I had to train the chorus

and soloists and take some of the rehearsals. This was a great experience and there were many occasions when Tauber ascended the
podium and Coates and I sat and watched. Tauber could have been a
fine conductor, but he always had trouble in concentrating on anything.
He was a prankster and spoke always of 'my friend, Schnappertipuppi,'
who was everywhere, and who decided everything. 'Where is Schnappertipuppi?' was his constant cry. 'He should be here by now. I asked
him to bring my cigarettes. Please look behind the tuba, will you? He
likes it there,' and so on. I think that he came eventually to believe
Schnappertipuppi really existed. He was a charming man and a magnificent artist. Nobody has sung Mozart as well during my lifetime.

Richard Tauber was great fun, but so was Albert Coates. For me,
having grown up with his Wagner at Covent Garden, working with him
was a great privilege. He never lost the foreign accent of his half-
Russian parentage and had endless stories of Nikisch, the great German
conductor with whom he had studied. He always referred to Glinka as
'ze Rooshian Beethoven.'

I used to watch them shooting various films while I was at the
studios, and it was a strange world for me. I was appalled at the utter
boredom of the proceedings, with the endless waits between takes.
When one saw the finished film spliced together, one could hardly
believe the result. Since seeing the way film actors have to work, I can't
say they are overpaid for such soul-destroying drudgery. It is certainly
true that a film is made by a director. It seems to me that the actors have
little to do with the final result. They merely do exactly as they are told
and I don't believe there is such a thing as 'film acting.' I have seen
someone who seemed to be a half-wit in the studio appear on the
screen as quite a passable actor.

My only appearance on the screen was in a film called *Dreaming
Lips*, believe it or not, which had Elisabeth Bergner and Raymond
Massey as its stars. It was directed by Bergner's husband, Paul Czinner,
and William Walton had been asked to provide the score. As the hero,
so-styled, was a concert violinist, there were many scenes needing
musical treatment. The finale of the film was a concert in Queen's Hall,
at which Massey had to play the Beethoven *Violin Concerto* with
Bergner sitting in the audience. Walton wrote a good score with the
Beethoven as its thematic basis, the four drum taps which begin the
work coming in very useful for dramatic effects throughout. We recorded
the whole film score including the first movement of the Beethoven in

a recording studio where we could see the various shots for synchronization. As far as I can remember, Antonio Brosa played the concerto for the sound track.

All the music for the film was synchronized in the studios except for the Queen's Hall concert portion, which had to be done with soloist, orchestra and audience visible. A wonderful scale reproduction of portions of the hall had been built in the studio and an audience of some thousand supers was seated. The music of the concerto, which had already been recorded, had to be played back through loudspeakers, and soloist, conductor, and orchestra had to make the correct movements to fit. For some strange reason nobody had thought of finding out if Massey was able to imitate a violinist or not. Someone had been detailed to coach him, and we all imagined he was ready for it. Came the entry of the soloist. I gave him a big cue – and he just stood there and looked at me. As we were not on microphone, I yelled, 'Play!' but by that time the solo had gone by several bars. One more attempt was made, with disastrous results. Massey said: 'To hell with this thing,' flung the violin on the floor, and rushed from the set. 'Cut,' yelled Czinner and pandemonium broke loose. 'Thirty minutes' break,' screamed Czinner. Then the awful truth was revealed – that Massey was tone-deaf! Just why it was left until this stage of the shooting to discover this fact I never found out, but if the film was to be finished, Massey had to be able to imitate a violinist in performance. It was as simple as that. A stand-in, maybe? It would take weeks to find a double with the requisite musical ear. Imagine the cost – a symphony orchestra and a thousand supers, with minutes ticking away. Something drastic had to be done, at once.

The British orchestral player is nothing if not resourceful, and two of the boys in the violin section volunteered to solve the impasse. If Massey stood to attention, with his arms held firmly at his sides, one of the players would crouch to his right with a bow and the other would crouch to his left holding the violin from below. All Massey had to do was to keep his chin firmly on the chin rest. The camera would be trained over his left shoulder and the audience (including Bergner) could be seen ecstatically listening to the concerto. The trouble was that the supers had to sit and watch this three-headed monster on the platform and preserve a look of unutterable bliss! Every now and then someone gave way and burst out laughing, ruining the take. But the scene was finally completed and I defy anyone seeing the film to notice anything peculiar whatsoever. What a nightmare for all of us and what an ingenious solution! I think there should have been credits for the two players. The bowing and fingering were perfect as seen on the screen.

The success of the Boyd Neel Orchestra made my name known as a conductor and I began getting invitations from orchestras everywhere. I remember a concert with the Eastbourne Municipal Orchestra which, in those far-off days was an excellent group engaged on an eleven-months' contract and large enough to perform the average symphonic repertoire. What a shame it no longer exists! At a concert I did with them Myra Hess played the Schumann *Concerto*, and when I made the first big downbeat at the lead into the finale, I ran my baton right into the middle finger of my left hand. The baton broke off and was sticking out. I realized what had happened, but as there was no bleeding, I didn't worry too much. I finished the concerto and as we came off Myra said: 'I saw what happened and it nearly made me sick.' We took our calls and I went out to the dressing room, pulled the remains of the stick out and, of course, out came a great deal of blood. It was now the intermission and I was able to staunch the flow and go back and complete the concert. It healed eventually and I forgot all about it. Twenty years later a small lump appeared on the spot where the baton had penetrated. It got steadily larger and following the old adage from hospital days that 'anything growing comes out whatever it may be,' I had it removed. The job was very thoroughly done, which was the correct procedure, and luckily it turned out to be of a benign nature. The resulting scar, however, gave me a limitation in the movement of the joint which sadly put paid to my piano playing, and to the very modest attempts at playing the viola and clarinet that I had previously indulged in.

About this time also, I conducted a concert of Bach's two-harpsichord *Concerto in C Minor*, played by Alice Ehlers and her star pupil – Greta Kraus. This was one of Greta's first public appearances, and she was very, very nervous. I little thought then that one day I should have such a happy association with her in Toronto many years later!

I was having my Sunday morning 'lie-in' about this time when the phone went at 9:30 a.m. and a worried voice, which I recognized as that of Beecham's secretary, said: 'Can you come down to Covent Garden at once and conduct Sir Thomas' concert this afternoon, as he has hurt his foot and cannot appear?' I said: 'O.K.,' and arrived at the Garden at

With Raymond Massey
in his role as a famous violinist in the film *Dreaming Lips*
(Trafalgar Films, London)

With Szigeti in rehearsal, London, 1937

Richard Tauber with Boyd Neel
at a costume concert at Queen's Hall

about 10:15 and found the London Philharmonic waiting patiently on the stage for Sir Thomas to appear. I found it was to be a Mozart program, two C Major symphonies, the *Magic Flute* overture, and a piano concerto, the, in those days, very seldom played *B Flat* (K. 456), with Lili Kraus as soloist. The *Jupiter*, of course, I knew, but I wasn't so sure about the *Linz*, so I asked if we could substitute the *C Major No. 34* (K. 338), which I knew well. The piano concerto I didn't know at all. We rehearsed for a couple of hours and that was it! Actually the concert went off pretty well, but what an ordeal! I discovered that Beecham had asked for me especially as he had admired my Mozart performances, so I was very flattered.

At the beginning of 1939 the orchestra made its first trip abroad. The British Council had asked us to do a tour of Portugal under its auspices, so we found ourselves outward bound from Tilbury, feeling that this was the beginning of an international career for us all. The concerts were well organized and the orchestra made a great impression. We played, first, three concerts in Lisbon, then one in Coimbra, the old capital, and finally three in Oporto. The tour was a tremendous success, and we made a lot of good friends. Suggia, the great Portuguese cellist, whose portrait by Augustus John hangs in the Tate Gallery in London, and who had been a great supporter of the orchestra since its inception, was a wonderful help to us on this trip. The programs were mostly of British music, and we played works by Britten, Delius, Howells, and Elgar.

The Coimbra concert, however, nearly ended in disaster. We played a matinee performance in a theatre where a circus was performing in the evenings. The scene had been set up on the stage and just behind it were all the animals which belonged to the circus. These included elephants, horses, lions, tigers, alligators in tanks, and even snakes in large boxes. Hens in large numbers clucked around – I presume they were there to provide eggs for the pythons to eat. It was the oddest collection of circus beasts I have ever seen. The owners were German, and though we did our best to persuade them to put at least some of the larger animals outside the theatre while the concert was going on, they would not hear of the suggestion. 'The animals would catch cold; they are very valuable, etc.'

There was nothing to be done but to go through with it to the bitter end, and how bitter was that end! At the rehearsal all seemed fairly quiet. One of the snakes – a large python – was having its throat painted at intervals, as it was suffering, apparently, from a 'bronchial cold,' according to the man who looked after it. The proceeding consisted in gripping the snake by the throat, forcing its jaws open, and putting a stick in to keep them apart. The snake then lashed about in its box, making much noise, while the inflamed throat was painted with a long brush. This performance took place about every half-hour. Each time the snake had its throat painted, the other animals protested sympathetically in their various ways. The alligators were the noisiest, and lashed with their tails. To make matters worse, when we arrived for rehearsal I imagined that all this clutter would be removed before the performance; then I heard to my horror that the animals were to stay there, as there was nowhere else to put them. There were two alligators in a shallow box, which required buckets of hot water to be thrown over them from time to time in order to keep them warm.

Well, the concert began. I felt I had the advantage over the players as I was facing backstage, and if any monster suddenly appeared I would be the first to see it and could make my escape over the footlights. The players kept looking nervously over their shoulders. All went well for half an hour, but when we began the Britten *Variations* all hell broke loose, the lions roared, the alligators thumped their tails, and the hens cackled! We struggled on for about five minutes, but finally I had to stop conducting and turned to the audience to apologize. By that time the circus attendants had been summoned, and some sort of order was restored. We started again, and with some interruptions managed to finish the concert. We did, however, leave out several pieces.

There is no doubt that string players find such a climate as that of Portugal most sympathetic to their technique. The strange fact we observed was that the instruments never seemed to go out of tune in that climate. It was probably the result of the very equable temperature.

A few weeks later we had one of our very rare travel mishaps; in fact, I cannot recollect another occasion when we were not on time for any concert anywhere in the world. We were due to play at Taunton in Somerset, and snow fell the whole day. I had gone the previous night to stay with a doctor friend nearby at Sherborne, and we were to drive over the following evening and meet the orchestra at Taunton. We managed to get across, although it was snowing very hard. When we reached Taunton there was no sign of the others and the concert was due to start in half an hour. The station had told me that there was an indefinite delay on the main line. The audience assembled, and I went on to the platform and explained the situation. Nearly an hour went by and some of the audience left. At last one or two wild figures were seen running through the snow, having had neither food nor drink for about seven hours; the boys went on and played as they were; as far as I can recall, the playing was not too bad.

The great event of 1939 was the London Music Festival, to which we were asked to contribute two concerts. On successive evenings one could hear concerts conducted by Beecham, Toscanini, and Bruno Walter. Kreisler, Szigeti, the Lener Quartet, and the Hungarian Quartet all played again and again. Even Edinburgh has never equalled it for sheer musical splendour. We gave one concert in the Queen's Hall and one in Hertford House (the Wallace Collection). For the Queen's Hall concert we were to have had Ethel Bartlett and Rae Robertson as our soloists, but Ethel Bartlett was ill so the program had to be altered slightly. For Hertford House we had Szigeti. The setting was perfect, with the *Laughing Cavalier* smiling down at the audience from the wall behind the orchestra. This was the occasion when, on entering the room to conduct, I slipped on the highly polished floor and went absolutely flat on my back with a resounding crack. A more dramatic entry has seldom been made by any artist. The audience was too surprised to laugh, and the whole episode passed off in complete silence, as though it had all been part of the show!

Later that year we took part in a stage performance of Debussy's *The Blessed Damozel.* Maggie Teyte sang at this concert. I had long admired her from the audience and was one of her ardent fans in the opera house. There will never again be a Mélisande to compare with her. She proved to be one of the easiest people to work with (great artists usually are), and the Debussy work went very well.

Just after this, Queen Charlotte's Hospital, London's famous maternity institution, gave a concert in the Queen's Hall in aid of its rebuilding fund and asked me to take part. The idea was to give the whole thing in the costume of Queen Charlotte's time and play contemporary music of that period. I got hold of Richard Tauber, with whom I had been making the film of *I Pagliacci,* and asked him to sing. He was delighted and suggested we ask a young Australian who had just arrived in England and who, besides being the Australian Ladies Golf Champion, was also a very fine singer. This was Joan Hammond, who was to make such a big name later. The platform was beautifully arranged, with two candles at each orchestra desk and, as a background, the actual portrait of

Queen Charlotte by Gainsborough, looking magnificent in its special lighting. Our costumes had been used in a film about Mozart and were authentic down to the last stitch. Richard Tauber and Joan Hammond sang duets from Mozart operas. In the old days at Munich Tauber had given some superb performances at the opera there, but after Lehár had written *You Are My Heart's Delight* especially for him the course of his career changed completely. He was a good friend and a wonderful artist. We finished the program with the *Farewell Symphony* of Haydn performed, as at its first performance, with each player getting up at the end, blowing out his candle, and creeping off the platform, much to the amusement of everyone. This must have been one of the very few occasions when it had been performed in this fashion since the original performance under Haydn. The concert caused quite a sensation at the time, and large photos appeared in all the papers. We little thought then that it was to be the last time we should ever play in our beloved Queen's Hall.

10

Through the War

That summer was full of rumours and counter-rumours. There was no tour abroad, but we were extremely busy in England. September 3 came as a shock. The Munich 'agreement,' the year before, had been a prolonged strain; this time it all seemed to happen very quickly. We had a very full season ahead of us and the orchestra was becoming very celebrated. Overnight we lost all our work, including a tour with Fritz Kreisler as our soloist. Every concert was cancelled. The players were still very young and so all belonged to the earliest call-up groups. We were stunned and had no idea what to do. In a few months all the players were in the forces, girls as well, and I was faced with literal starvation, as my whole means of livelihood had gone. It was terrible to think of the work of years wiped out in one fell swoop.

The first thing I did was to take the whole of our, by then, very valuable music library down to the country, where it was stored in a loft over a barn for the duration of the war. Unfortunately, I kept a lot of my valuable scores and research material in London, as I felt I might want them, and anyway they were in my home, whereas the orchestral material had been kept elsewhere.

Obviously there was only one thing for me to do – back to medicine; and back to medicine it was for the next six years, first helping a friend in the West End with his practice, and then, on being called up, working on artificial limbs, which I did for the rest of the war. This meant Roehampton Hospital and meeting Douglas Bader, who used to come and have his legs adjusted from time to time. It also meant that I was only half an hour from London, and when Myra Hess organized her National Gallery Concerts (which many servicemen will remember), she would call me up to do a Bach or Mozart concert with her during my lunch hour. These were strange days and wonderful audiences, especially when the bombardment began. I well remember one day doing the Bach *F Minor* with Myra and bomb *obbligato*!

The wartime audience was certainly a new phenomenon, and when later we were able to get together as an orchestra to play to the Services and workers in factories we had some extraordinary experiences. The authorities came to the decision that the concerts were essential for morale, and I was asked seriously to take up the arranging of concerts and the giving of talks to service personnel. With a small orchestra of my own I visited hundreds of camps and ships all over the British Isles, playing for institutions such as the Entertainment National Service Association (ENSA) and the Arts Council, both products of the war, although the latter was then known as the Council for the Encouragement of Music and the Arts (CEMA). One fortnight was spent in the dead of a very severe winter up at Scapa in the Orkneys, where we played to thousands of sailors, twice daily, in an enormous cinema. Although the orchestra bore the name of Boyd Neel, it was a very scratch affair with none, or very few, of our original members in it. Every now and then, however, those of the boys who were in the various Service orchestras would get to London, and we would all find time for a very ad hoc and hurriedly arranged concert. Such a concert took place in June 1943, when we celebrated our tenth anniversary and Benjamin Britten wrote us a superb birthday present with a separate part for each of the eighteen players. This was the *Prelude and Fugue*, which has the dedication on the score. We actually managed to rehearse it and play it at the Wigmore Hall, where it had a great success.

At one of my early 1940 wartime concerts, I conducted the première of Britten's *Les Illuminations* with the Swiss soprano Sophie Wyss, to whom it is dedicated. I have always thought these Rimbaud settings are one of Britten's finest achievements.

By this point in the war I was working at various hospitals in the south of England, because in 1940 I lost my home in London with a direct hit. I happened, luckily, to be down visiting my mother in the country, but actually had the car out ready to return to London. She persuaded me to stay another night and go back in the morning. She told me afterwards she had suddenly felt a strange premonition. When I got back to London the next morning, the street was roped off, and I could see a vast hole where the house had stood. The police wouldn't let me near it as they said there were two unexploded bombs from the same stick farther down the street. I finally persuaded them, and for three days I dug with shovel and pickaxe in that crater, helped by Tom Taylor, the producer of the Boyd Neel Memoirs radio program, who was in the RAF and had been billeted with my mother. He had been moved to London and had called around to see me. When all he saw was a huge crater, he imagined that I must be somewhere at the bottom of it. While he was trying to take it all in, I appeared with my car. So Tom also set to work with pick and shovel, and we got some of my precious manuscripts out of the mess, but a large number were lost forever. My piano had disappeared entirely. Some days later I located it three streets away, upside-down on a lawn without its legs, and I was actually able to have it repaired successfully.

At some time in 1942, when I was at Roehampton Hospital, the BBC called and asked me to go up there as soon as I could get away. I went up the next day and was ushered into a top-secret room, which I had never known existed. One of the music staff was there and some other people I didn't know. I was told this was a very confidential matter, and I was not to discuss it outside. I was vastly intrigued at being made a James Bond character all of a sudden. On the table was a tiny packet which contained a microfilm and a message from, believe it or not, Arthur Honegger in France. The packet had been dropped by parachute, exactly where I never discovered, and it contained a request that someone, preferably Boyd Neel, should broadcast the score on the microfilm, as the composer hoped it would give encouragement to occupied countries. The microfilm was blown up and developed and it turned out to be what we all know today as Honegger's *Second Symphony*. It is for strings and single trumpet, the trumpet chorale at the end of the work indicating the message of hope. Of course, I said I would do it and did, with an ad hoc orchestra. In a week's time, another message from Honegger arrived by parachute. He had heard his symphony – reception was perfect – and he hoped it had given courage to all who needed it. Imagine my delight at all this, and imagine how the people of the occupied territories must have felt (and these included my own relatives in the Channel Islands, the only part of the United Kingdom occupied by the Germans)!

About this time I remember crossing swords in the press with Ernest Newman, the famous critic, over something he had written about conductors treating certain works as showpieces for their own glorification. I replied as follows:

Sir: Mr. Ernest Newman, in his article last Sunday, castigates conductors for giving their own readings of musical works. Surely any musical *performance from that of a Toscanini down to that of the humblest ballad singer, is an individual reading of some sort? It cannot be otherwise in an art such as music, where performance always has to be through the agency of some performer? Even the composer himself, when also the performer, gives his own reading of his own work, which, as Mr. Newman probably knows from his own experience, is not always a very happy solution owing to deficient technique in many cases.*

Even the most objective of all performances, i.e., 'reading the score by the fireside,' is bound to be a 'rendering' of a sort, no two readers 'thinking' the music in exactly the same way. It would seem that Mr. Newman has ignored the fundamental difference between music and the other arts.

Newman came back with:

A letter such as that of Mr. Boyd Neel in The Sunday Times *a couple of weeks ago simply had to be written, of course. It has, in fact, been written me, in one form or another by several correspondents, whom I must ask to be content with this omnibus reply. It is impossible to write on any subject without a number of people rushing to tell you, with the air of bringing the latest message straight from Sinai, something so obvious that it must have occurred to everyone who has given the smallest attention to that subject. Here, for instance, is Mr. Boyd Neel, informing me that 'any musical performance' must of necessity be 'an individual' reading of some sort. To which I can only ejaculate, with King Marke, 'Mir Dies Tristan, mir?' This to me? This is to one who has dwelt again and again on the personal equation in art; has not only drawn attention to the investigations of some German scholars into the psychical 'blood-groups,' so to speak, into which humanity can be divided; not only pointed out, with Wolfflin, that ten artists painting the same landscape at the same time will unconsciously produce ten dif-*

ferent 'readings' of it; not only argued that this individual equation is further complicated by a racial or cultural equation – I shall never forget standing behind a young Japanese who was copying the famous Corot in the Louvre and watching him all unconsciously translate it into his own national idiom – but has coined the term 'temporal equation,' to describe the difficulty each later epoch of even the same civilization has in seeing the art of an earlier period as that period itself saw it. All these and other factors complicate the problem of aesthetic judgement enormously: and I myself have been racking my poor brains over that problem for a good many years. And now the wise ones of this world advance on me in serried ranks with the novel information that 'any musical performance is an 'individual' reading of some sort!'

I thought I had made it clear enough what I meant in my previous article when I said of a certain type of conductor that 'we do not want "his" Beethoven, "his" Mozart, "his" Wagner, and all the rest of that naive quackery.' I can respect and admire a performance even when I feel, as was the case with Toscanini's noble performance of the Elgar Variations *in Queen's Hall a few years ago, that something or other in the conductor's mental make-up has given a very English work a faintly foreign flavour. Even when the 'reading' is, beyond question, hopelessly wrong, as when a French conductor and a French orchestra essay the* Gerontius *prelude, I feel no resentment, because I recognize that they have done their honest best according to their personal and national lights. What does move me to wrath is the attempt of some mountebank or other to impress me with what he would call 'his' Beethoven, let us say, by starting the main theme of* Leonora No.3 *in an almost inaudible pianissimo in order to bowl a simple-minded audience over with his following* crescendo *and* fortissimo. *(Mr. Boyd Neel seems to have missed completely the significance of the inverted commas in which I enclosed each 'his' in my article of April 19.) I could multiply examples by the hundred, tapering down from calculated quackery to mere feebleness of intellect.*

No, I have no grievance against any artist merely because he sees a great work through his own eyes instead of mine. But I have no hesitation in saying that, thanks to the gullibility of the public, there is more bluff, more mountebankery, more charlatanism to be found in present-day conducting than in all the other species of musical performance put together. The sort of conductor I have no use for, is the one who imagines that what really matters at a concert is not Beethoven, but the effect he can make with Beethoven. Give me Allah, and you can keep the whole Mappin Terrace of his prophets.

And I had one last shot with:

Sir: May I reply to Mr. Newman via your columns? I find myself almost entirely in agreement with him, although I would plead that I am not quite the simpleton he would make me out to be; I have been his faithful disciple ever since he took his famous holiday, through the days when he craved utter objectivity and tried to become a 'sensitized plate,' up to the present time. I know he had pondered this eternal problem many times. But the point behind my remarks was that, as every performance is, of necessity, an 'individual' one, all that the poor listener can do is to decide which artist appears to give the nearest approach to the performance intended by the composer, and to stick to him. Whether this is the performance intended by the composer who can say, except the composer himself, if he is still alive? And, as I pointed out, it must very often be a living composer's opinion of someone else's performance that must guide us, as his own can often be far from the ideal. Many people preferred Richter's and Ronald's Elgar to Elgar's Elgar.

Where does the dividing line between true artist and mountebank occur? Mr. Newman cites the opening of the Leonora No.3 allegro *as a place where the mountebank starts in an almost inaudible* pianissimo *in order to secure a greater effect in the following* crescendo. *But why should this brand him? All dynamics are relative. There is no empirical* piano *or* forte. *The passage in question is marked* pp. *How soft was the* pianissimo *intended by Beethoven at this point? Surely a very 'special'* pianissimo, *because ten bars previously he had written* fff, *which I can only recall him doing in one other place in his works. The contrast had to be violent. I don't see why anyone should be a 'mountebank' because he happens to have had the perception to realize this.*

Now all this was really an attack by Newman on Furtwängler, whom he detested. I was no special champion of Furtwängler, but I always felt Newman was very unfair to him, so I couldn't resist taking up the cudgels. Although Furtwängler's name was never mentioned, everyone knew what it was all about.

POST OFFICE

No. 0220 OFFICE STAMP

TELEGRAM

Prefix. Time handed in. Office of Origin and Service Instruc.

41

From

To

141 1.15 DAVENTRY LE 74

PRIORITY BOYD NEEL BRITISH BROADCASTING CORPORATION

LANGHAM PLACE LONDON W 1

= FOOL RIMSKY KORSAKOFF BE BLOWED DONT YOU KNOW YOUR

ROSSINI FOR THE PASSAGE YOU QUOTE TODAY IS AN ACTUAL

QUOTATION FROM HIM AND QUITE IN KEEPING WITH THE SUBJECT

AND QUITE UNLIKE THE PASSAGE YOU PLAYED FROM RINSKY

APOLOGISE OR LIBEL ACTION WILL FOLLOW IN FURY NOT ONLY

POST OFFICE

No.

0220 OFFICE STAMP

TELEGRAM

Prefix. Time handed in. Office of Origin and Service Instructions. Words

98

From

WITH YOU BUT ALSO OTHER BLOCKHEADS WHO DONT

KNOW ROSSINI WHEN THEY HEAR IT =

WILLIAM WALTON ++++++

A telegram from William Walton to Boyd Neel, April 19th 1942

The Boyd Neel Orchestra in rehearsal and in performance, 1948

11

International Overtures

The war ended and members of the orchestra gradually trickled back. (Three never came back.)

I felt I really couldn't change professions again – I had done it three times already in my life – but those orchestra members who did come back insisted, so reluctantly I did it for the *fourth* time and started to get things going again. It didn't really take long to pick up the pieces. The BBC started its Third Programme and this gave us much work. The British Council began to arrange tours.

A departure from my usual line was a couple of London seasons conducting with the D'Oyly Carte Opera Company. I loved this, and my affection for these wonderful Gilbert and Sullivan works has never diminished through the years. I started with *Yeoman of the Guard*, and we were at Sadler's Wells Theatre, which at that time was being directed by Tyrone Guthrie and Joan Cross. Half-way through the Trio in the first act, the lights went out. We sat in the dark for about ten minutes and on they came again. The three singers who were sitting on the bench just in front of the Bloody Tower leapt to their feet and went back to their positions for the Trio. I shouted 'From the top' and we were off again with hardly any disruption of the performance!

The company was very strong in those days and people like Martyn Green and Darrell Fancourt were great stars in their way. Besides *Yeoman*, I conducted *Patience*, *Mikado*, and *Iolanthe* during the two seasons. I spent two happy years with the company, and was also given

Rigoletto, Hansel and Gretel, La Bohème, Il Tabarro and *Gianni Schicchi*, and *Madame Butterfly*. Reluctantly I had to leave after two years, as the Boyd Neel Orchestra started to undertake some very long tours which meant my being out of the country for months on end.

One of the first things we did after the war was to give a series of concerts in the Chelsea Town Hall. These were for the first few years a great success, and it was here that we formed a famous team for the *Brandenburgs*, which we recorded about this time. We had Dennis Brain on first horn, Norman del Mar on second, Leon Goossens on first oboe, and Lady Barbirolli (Evelyn Rothwell) on second. Archie Camden was bassoon and George Eskdale did his astounding trumpet in *No. 2*, in which our flute was Gareth Morris. Kathleen Long did the *No. 5* on the piano, which, maybe, was a mistake, but the virtuosity of this team of stars produced some performances which the critic of the *Observer* said 'were as near perfection as one is likely to get on this earth.' So successful were the *Brandenburgs* that we toured them all around the UK, doing two-night stands in all the major centres – three concertos on each night. We then played them at Glyndebourne on consecutive Sundays during the Festival. And this became an annual event.

Early in 1946 we made our first trip abroad after the war, a visit to Paris for the British Council. We played in the Salle Gaveau and in the hall of the Conservatoire. The program consisted mostly of English music, with the Britten works again proving the most popular of all. We found the historic hall in the Conservatoire one of the best we had ever played in, as far as acoustics went. We also gave a broadcast from Radio Paris while we were there. This was the first time the orchestra had ever visited the French capital, which it saw during the most perfect week of winter weather I can ever remember. The sun was so warm that we could sit in the Tuileries without coats on, although it was the first week in January.

Back in London I received a phone call from Dr Roth of Boosey and Hawkes asking me to go round to his office to see something which he thought would interest me. I went straight over (I only lived a few minutes away) and found him with an enormous manuscript on his desk. He told me it had just arrived from Germany and was the latest work of Richard Strauss' Indian summer – *Metamorphosen*. I asked at once if I could give the première, but Roth said that it would be given that very week in Zürich by Paul Sacher, who had commissioned the work. I was very disappointed, especially when I had had a look at the score and realized that here we had a unique masterpiece, and I put it at once into my next Chelsea series and gave the first English performance a few months after the Zürich one. It quickly became part of our repertoire and we played it a great deal in many centres.

During our season of concerts at Chelsea in the summer of 1946 my friend John Denison of the British Council rang me up one day and asked me to go and see him. As we had been discussing the possibility of the orchestra visiting France again in the near future, I gathered it was connected with this, but when I arrived at John's office he introduced a shy little man, with a quiet speaking voice and large spectacles, as 'Dan O'Connor from New Zealand.'

O'Connor said: 'I've been to all your Chelsea concerts and the orchestra seems to have a spirit about it that is unique. It also plays interesting things that the larger orchestras don't tackle. I think it would go well in Australia and New Zealand. How about it? The Council are keen and are willing to help, and I think I can bring it off.'

I was, of course, so overcome at this that I couldn't answer for a moment. Australia and New Zealand! Just what I had dreamed about ever since we began going abroad, but had always imagined was quite beyond being even a possibility, owing to the distances involved. I finally managed to murmur something about it being just what I had longed to do for ages, and 'Dan,' as he was soon to become, said: 'Right, now let's go ahead. When can you leave? The best time would be to arrive there about the beginning of April next year and reckon on a six-months' tour, including travel.' I said: 'How on earth are you going to get twenty people to Australia in six months' time, when even single people have been waiting as long as a year for a passage?' The shipping position was in its chaotic post-war condition, and priorities still held fifty per cent of passages. Dan agreed that it was going to be a problem, but the Council might be able to wield some influence. Denison agreed to put the wheels in motion, and the great scheme had begun.

After Dan left, Denison explained the Council's part in the proceedings. He said that hitherto the Council had worked only in foreign countries, and never within the Empire. Recently it had been decided to start an Empire Division and to begin with Australia. Sir Angus Gillan had made an exploratory journey out there, and the Council was about to send its first representative. This turned out to be Charles Wilmot, who was just about to leave for Australia, and the Council was anxious that the first artists it sent out under its auspices should be something rather out of the ordinary. Apparently Dan had approached the Council just as it was considering the possibility, and so all parties were pleased. The project could never (so we then thought) be a commercial proposition on its own, and therefore the Council had agreed that it would pay, as its share, the fares of the party to and from Australia. In other words, it would deliver the orchestra to Dan in Sydney and would take it back again at the end of the tour, but the responsibility of the trip while the tour was on would be his alone.

Now, such a thing would have daunted many ordinary men, but Dan was no ordinary man, and he was willing to take the risk of having twenty people on his hands at the other end of the earth, and of being responsible for them until such time as he could get them back to England. In ordinary times this might not have seemed such a formidable proposition, but with shipping as it was, it was a real problem. I went to see our secretary and we had a long discussion. We came to the conclusion that it was going to be very difficult to have the players idle for six weeks while travelling out, and six weeks travelling back, as they would not be getting paid during that time. The contract with Dan provided for a weekly salary, starting from the date of the first concert. The more we thought about it the more hopeless it seemed. In the morning Paddy, our secretary, rang to say that the British Council could get no satisfaction from the shipping authorities, and it looked as though the whole thing was off. We didn't know then the reaction of O'Connor when the call to battle sounded, as it often did in subsequent days.

Dan wasn't in the least disheartened, although we had also told him of our particular worry concerning the orchestra during travel. Actually it was this fact that eventually gave him the idea of *flying* the whole party! Such a thing had never been known before. To transport an entire orchestra and its instruments half-way round the world seemed fantastic in those days. The recognized route from London to Australia at that time was flying *east* via Karachi and Singapore; it took about a week, although one or two fast planes were taking only two and a half days. This short journey solved our problem and also meant that we could go on working up until the last minute. But again came disappointment. We could only fly in twos or threes over a period of four weeks or so, which didn't help at all, as we all had to work together until the day of leaving, so it looked as though the last hope had gone. But Dan had a friend in a tourist agency who said: 'Why not fly the *other* way round?'

This genius then made inquiries, and found that in the planes going to and across the USA seats were reasonably easy to get; also, the new service from San Francisco to Sydney was never very fully booked. So it was all fixed in a few hours. We were to leave London on 30th of March and arrive in Sydney on the 9th of April, with our opening night on the 16th. This would give a week's rehearsal and time to acclimatize ourselves.

Members of the orchestra began to get very excited at the prospect of the tour. One or two of them got qualms about being away from home so long. Even Fred Grinke was in two minds whether to come or not, and I had to point out what a pity it would be to miss the chance of making his name in Australia, which, of course, he eventually did. His personal success was one of the outstanding things of the trip. It was just at this time that Beecham made him an offer to lead his newly formed orchestra, later known as the Royal Philharmonic. I think every orchestra of any sort in the British Isles had, at one time or another, tried to get him as leader, but he would never consider it, and said he always regarded the BN as *his* orchestra, and it would remain so until he gave up orchestral playing entirely. Apart from playing in the RAF Symphony Orchestra during the war, he never played in any other than the BN and it became his orchestra just as much as mine. We both felt that it was his creation to a great extent, which, of course, it was, and you can't lead a combination for ten years without impressing your style and personality on it very strongly. The understanding we had of each other's musical feeling in the end was quite extraordinary. A glance or a wink meant everything, and no more was required. Fred had that vigorous and commanding style of playing so essential to good leadership, and his bow was always alive and ready to bounce. I hope we avoided that dreary heavy style of 'on the string' playing one hears all too often. I think the mental approach is as important as anything. The rest follows automatically.

The date for our departure was upon us very quickly. Paddy was up until all hours of the night working on the Australian arrangements, and the constant short tours we had to do kept upsetting her plans. Actually, she didn't come on one or two of the tours just at this time. The winter of 1946–7 was a nightmare for travellers, and some of the journeys will never be forgotten by any of us. We had planned to keep two weeks clear before leaving. Unfortunately, the Dutch radio could only fit me in during that time, and were anxious for me to pay a return visit. I agreed to go – it was always a trip I loved doing – and I remember well going to Marlborough to play three *Brandenburgs* and having to dash to Swindon immediately after the concert so as to catch a train which got me to London in time for the Harwich boat train.

On returning to London from Holland I had only a few days to get things together, and to do the hundred and one jobs that had to be done. We had our worries. Double-basses were a new problem for airlines, and we had two with us. After trying to get them into the baggage compartment of the Dakota to Shannon, it was decided to treat them as passengers, and so the front seats on either side of the cabin were removed, and the two basses rested there for the rest of the journey and in every subsequent plane.

We flew in cloud all the way to Dublin. At Dublin airport there were many press reporters and photographers as the news had spread that this, in some ways historic, journey had started. We then flew on to Shannon where we were told that our plane had been delayed in Paris and would not arrive at Shannon until the following day, so we were all taken to an hotel about thirty miles away for the night. The bus passed through Limerick and our hotel turned out to be at Killaloe (a strange coincidence, for I had brought Trollope's *Phineas Finn* to read on the flight and Finn came from Killaloe). Our plane left Shannon the following day at 1:00 p.m. Besides our party were one or two French people, a rabbi, and two Roman Catholic priests. I have seldom flown in any part of the world without a member of the clergy being among the passengers! We had an excellent crossing and landed at Gander, Newfoundland, twelve hours later. The snow was three feet deep but the waiting room at Gander was an impressive sight; enormous, very brightly lit, and the seats all covered with brilliant red leather. The sudden transition from the black, cold night of the skies to the land and light and warmth was an extraordinary sensation. We took off again for New York at about 9:30 p.m. and touched down at La Guardia at 3:00 a.m., having been flying for eighteen hours, so we were just about 'all in.' Meeting us were Fred Grinke's family, who had come all the way from Winnipeg to see him. We spent the following day in New York and were due to leave that evening for San Francisco. It was good to walk down Fifth Avenue again – it was twenty-one years since I was last there as a medical student. I was delighted to see a lot of our records in a Fifth Avenue shop window. They were all discs that were unobtainable at home and it was good to know that *someone* was enjoying them. After breakfast I rang up Maggie Teyte, who I knew was still in New

York, and she had quite a surprise, as she had imagined I was travelling the other way round. She said she had a charity concert at the Plaza Hotel that afternoon. 'Couldn't the orchestra play, and we could do some of our old things together?' I told her it was a wonderful idea, but what about the orchestral parts? A mere detail; but it would have been fun.

We took off that night at 10:30 p.m. When dawn broke we were presented with a spectacle I shall never forget. We were right over the Rockies. As far as we could see in every direction were snow-capped peaks all rose-tinted with the dawn; some of the peaks beneath us were fourteen thousand feet in height, and yet appeared as mere hills. It was breathtaking. We were roused from our contemplation of these wonders by the hostess producing an excellent breakfast. Afterwards the captain came in and showed us the Grand Canyon miles below. At that height you could see everything at once, and could follow the course of the Colorado River for hundreds of miles. The baked brown colour of the Colorado desert was very marked after the white of the Rockies. Presently the country became greener and we crossed the last range of hills before arriving at the west coast, landing some minutes later at Los Angeles. By now everyone was feeling pretty tired; but on we went to San Francisco where we went straight to bed. We had two days there and were able to see a lot of the city. We discovered that the reception clerk at our hotel was a Boyd Neel fan and he was thrilled to meet all the orchestra. I autographed some records for him.

We took off from Oakland airport in a comfortable Skymaster DC 4 – our first contact with Australian Air Services, who were to become such old friends before the end of the tour. The flight to Honolulu was then one of the longest non-stop civil runs in the world, about twenty-two hundred miles. Sunrise was beautiful, and after a good breakfast, the island of Oahu, on which is the city of Honolulu, was sighted. I have a memory of green pastures and volcanic mountains, of golden beaches and lines of white surf, and then of finding ourselves standing outside a Nissen hut in an atmosphere completely different from that of the previous night. The shock of the sudden transition of climates when travelling long distances by air is very real.

Honolulu! What romance I had always connected with the name! I had imagined moonlit beaches, soft voices, and distant guitars. The reality is, at first, rather a shock. You want, of course, to see the famous Waikiki beach and surf riding, so you take a tram down a long, straight road which might be anywhere and arrive at the beach, which has been spoiled by over-commercialization: ice-cream bars jostle souvenir shops and big hotels. The actual beach is really a very small stretch of sand, but the natives are there, surf-riding all right, and it is a grand sight. If you take a walk through the fine park for about a mile you will find the Honolulu of story books. Here are the sandy beaches with the palm trees waving overhead and the surf lapping the shore.

Our next landing was at Canton Island, just south of the equator, and hundreds of miles from anywhere. Before the war it was a deserted strip of coral, but during hostilities it was made into an air staging post. I believe the highest point on the island is six feet above sea level, and from the air it looks like a dime in the ocean. As we had just crossed 'the line' we were given beautiful certificates from King Neptune by the captain. The visit to this unbelievably isolated coral reef was most interesting.

One of our fellow travellers was none other than that superb singer Ninon Vallin. She was making her first flight and was going to sing in Australia and New Zealand. She soon became one of the party, and the journey was made much less tedious for us in listening to her anecdotes and reminiscences of operas and concerts. I had long been one of her most fervent admirers, and her stories of Fauré, Debussy, and Charpentier, all of whom she knew very well, were engrossing. I was shocked to see what a poor audience she had when we heard her in Sydney the following week. She sang with great artistry and her Fauré songs especially were perfect.

We reached Fiji about lunch time. Everything was very green, reminiscent of the English Lake District. A sight I shall never forget was of a crowd of natives playing rugby football – in that great heat! It was intensely hot and humid. We were greeted by a chief in a native village who took us into his lovely cool hut, then showed us schoolchildren sitting out under the trees having their lessons. The magnificent heads of hair of some of the men are a feature of Fiji.

We took off at about 9:00 p.m. and were due at Sydney the following morning. Up until now we had had the most wonderful weather with hardly a bump all the way. Soon after take-off we ran into a patch of bad weather, and afterwards I caught my first glimpse of Australia.

I think, in a way, this was the most exciting moment of the whole trip. We struck the coast just south of Brisbane, and then proceeded south to Sydney. We circled the city and harbour about four times – the most perfect introduction to Sydney. The layout of the whole place was so impressive I felt I knew my way around when we finally landed. It was a perfect morning, real Sydney weather; Charles Wilmot and Dan were there to meet us, Wilmot as cheerful as usual but Dan slightly subdued. Wilmot drove me to our hotel and en route told me that Dan was worried about the tour. The advance booking was to open the following day and he was not particularly optimistic, but Charles himself was quite sure everything would go well. It seems strange now, looking back on it, that there could have been any doubts as to the outcome, and later, during some of the greatest triumphs, Dan and I would recall those first few days of anxiety.

We all stayed at an hotel standing up on Cremorne Point on the north side of the harbour, with a view of the whole of the harbour below the bridge spread out beneath the balcony. To get there we had to drive across the famous bridge. One is certainly awed by its sheer size in spite of having seen the Golden Gate and Oakland bridges previously. One of the delights of Sydney is having to travel by one of the numerous ferries, and to reach the city from our hotel we had to take the ferry every day. The return journey across the still water on a moonlight night after a concert remains unforgettable.

I soon found that after my first day in Australia that the tour was to be a real test of physical endurance. I think my iron constitution really stood me in good stead. There was a clause in our contracts that we were to attend as many social functions as possible. Later in the tour, the rule was slightly relaxed as far as the orchestra was concerned, but I, of course, always had to attend everything. It usually meant a speech for me and endless introductions. This was by far the most tiring part of the tour; the concerts alone would have been child's play. In every town and city we visited we were given a civic reception by the mayor, and in all capital cities there were parties given by the respective governors, not to mention the endless parties and receptions given by the societies, clubs, unions, guilds, colleges, and universities! Never, I'm sure, has a party of people been entertained and welcomed as we were wherever we went. It started as soon as we arrived. Some press men had already interviewed us at the airport, and we had been photographed there, but Dan informed me that we were to meet the press officially at a tea party that afternoon. I longed for sleep but duty called.

Now, I had been warned about the Australian press, and told to weigh every word I uttered very carefully, but I found the Sydney reporters very easy and moderate in their questions. This may have lulled me into a sense of false security, because later I was not so fortunate. After the first of many press conferences Dan whisked me to a commercial broadcasting station, where he, Paddy, and I all said little bits into the microphone and felt very stupid.

During the tour, the first visit I made in every town we played in was to the local radio station, where I was interviewed in front of the microphone. In Sydney, as it was our starting-off place, the Australian Broadcasting Corporation asked me to give a talk over a nation-wide hook-up to introduce myself and the orchestra, and to explain the why and wherefore of our visit. This proved to be a great success, and my early experience of talking at the microphone stood me in good stead. I received hundreds of letters from all over the Commonwealth, and I felt at once that we had come to play to friends.

Charles Moses, the director of the Australian Broadcasting Corporation, proved to be a likeable fellow, good-natured and boyish, and made me feel at home immediately. It was tragic to find how much they had to depend on gramophone recordings for their programs owing to the lack of enough local artists of sufficient talent. This seemed strange to me when I thought of all the fine Australian musicians (especially singers) whom I had known at home. I discussed this with many people during our stay in the country, because I felt that there was something fundamentally wrong somewhere. I discovered that as soon as Australian artists showed any signs of talent their one object was to go to England as soon as possible, which most of them did, and never came back. Everywhere I went I had the same wail from the people: 'Why can't we get something going out here? They go to England because there is no work for them here.' 'But,' I used to say, 'of course there is no work for them here for the simple reason that they all go away.' It was a vicious circle, and it will be broken some day. While we were there things were already moving in the right direction, anyway in the orchestral world. Sydney had formed its new Symphony Orchestra, which was lavishly subsidized. As I left, they had engaged Eugene Goossens to come as permanent conductor, so that in a few years' time there would be a really first-rate orchestra in Sydney.

Our plans had allowed for a week's rehearsal and acclimatization in Sydney before our first concert, and this arrangement was extremely wise. We all felt the need of time to think a little, and to get used to the climate. When we arrived it was the beginning of their 'winter.' Having just arrived from the famous winter of 1946–7 in England, we could not help smiling when the Australians thought it was getting 'chilly.' The weather during our entire stay in Sydney was what we would describe at home as a glorious summer. How we sun-starved Britons revelled in the long hours of bright sunshine every day, and how wonderful to feel the warm breeze on our faces and limbs when we went out! Sydney air is like no other. When you step outside, you have the feeling that your whole body is clothed in some delightful soft warm wool.

The orchestra at this time consisted of:

1st Violins

Frederick Grinke
Violet Palmer
Breta Graham
Vivien Dixon
Matty Bosch
Alfred de Reyghere

2nd Violins

Kathleen Sturdy
Sylvia Cleaver
Joyce Juler
Brian Fairfax

Cellos

Peter Beavan
Phyllis Woodward
Paul Ward

Violas

Max Gilbert
Mollie Panter
Samuel Rosenheim

Basses

Charles Gray
Julian Hemingway

Of these, Gilbert and Rosenheim had actually played at the very first concert in 1933, and several others had joined for the second and third concerts, so we still had a nucleus of the old originals, even after the war. The story of Vivien Dixon was rather amusing. She had joined us about six months before we left England, having just arrived from New Zealand, where she had spent the previous eight years, although actually English-born. No sooner had she joined us than she found herself on the way back to New Zealand! Her family were still there, her father being the director of the Conservatory in Nelson.

For our opening program we had chosen: *Concerto Grosso No. 1 in G* of Handel; *Divertimento in D* (K.136) of Mozart; *Variations on a Theme of Frank Bridge* by Benjamin Britten; *Two Aquarelles* and *Air and Dance* of Delius and *Serenade, Op. 22* of Dvořák. We thought that this was a good representative start to a season. Our Handel concerti were already known through the records, the Mozart had always been considered one of our 'star turns,' the Britten was, of course, written for us, and had not been heard in Australia before. This program proved so popular that we opened with it in every city during the tour, later omitting the Delius, and sometimes substituting the Tchaikovsky *Serenade* for the Dvořák. I had never heard the orchestra play better than they did at the rehearsals, and I realized that the form was going to be good, but could they keep it up for four months, playing nearly every day and travelling long distances in between? As it turned out they stood it wonderfully, and I think we only had one member missing on two occasions – a remarkable record.

We not only had to rehearse our opening program, but also all the works we were to play in the next few weeks. In regard to this a crisis occurred. Owing to travel by air we were very limited as to weight of baggage and it was quite impossible to bring everything by plane, especially the music, which weighs a lot. We were each allowed sixty-six pounds of luggage, not much for a six-months' trip, and the unfortunate players had to include their instruments in that amount, so you can imagine how many clothes the wretched cellists and basses were left with, when the weight of the instruments had been allowed for. I was more fortunate, but made up for it by putting a lot of music in my luggage. We decided to take the music for our first six programs with us in the plane, each person taking one work, and I myself taking four, as I had no instrument. In this way we knew we were safe for a couple of weeks, should the remainder, which had been sent by sea, not arrive on time. When we got to Sydney we heard that the ship with the music had arrived at Melbourne and would leave shortly. We heaved a sigh of relief, little knowing that there was the usual dock strike on at Sydney, and no ships were being unloaded. I had wondered why there were so many ships lying out in the harbour at buoys. When the ship finally arrived we had the infuriating experience of seeing her drop anchor about a hundred yards from our hotel. Every day we passed within ten feet of her stern (and our music) as we crossed in the ferry, and time was getting on. Finally she was docked the day before we had to have the music; Dan's cousin, Arthur Tracey, was a great help to us all through the tour and went down himself and took it out of the hold, defying customs officials and strike pickets; otherwise we should never have had it on time.

But to return to our opening concert. On the day the booking opened

Dan had a face as long as a runway and of a kind of ashen colour. His pessimism knew no bounds: there had been no queue when the booking opened; only a few seats had gone; the tour was a failure; we might as well go home. This, mark you, when the box office had only been open a few hours! But we got to know our Dan in later days. However, on the opening night, the Town Hall was quite well filled, about two-thirds of the seats being sold. It is an enormous hall and holds close on three thousand people when full. I was worried about the acoustics, as I always am. How few halls in the world are really suitable for music! I had carefully thought out my tempi in relation to the resonance period. The orchestra knew what I had told them so often – *not* to take any notice of the acoustics, but play their own performance always.

It is useless to try and fight a hall. Never let it take charge of you. Play your dynamics with always the same weight. If the hall helps you, so much the better, but if it doesn't – well, you can't do anything about it, apart from adjusting tempo, which is the job of the conductor. All quick movements have to be a shade slower in a very resonant hall, but this does *not* mean that the converse is also true, and that all slow movements have to be slightly quicker in a dead hall. This is a point not often realized. On the whole I think we were amazingly lucky on this tour and struck very few really bad halls.

For our first night in Sydney we were all especially keyed up and determined to do well. The dreaded Neville Cardus, critic of the *Sydney Morning Herald* and terror of all artists in Australia, was to be there. Cardus had come out to Australia for the *Manchester Guardian* to cover the Test matches just before the war and had stayed there. He had always been known in England as a brilliant writer on both music and cricket, and had now established himself as the oracle of music in Australia. 'What Cardus said' was taken very seriously and argued heatedly by all and sundry. Such a following had he that even people not in the slightest bit interested in music would always read him, and thousands listened to his Sunday evening broadcasts on music. He was extolled, reviled, lauded to the skies, and execrated. But he was scrupulously fair and only praised those who deserved it. Everyone was unanimous on that point. I found later how much he had done to set some sort of standard and probably Australians had much more to thank him for than they then realized.

12

A Great Success !

The night of the first concert was drawing near. The atmosphere in Sydney is always very humid, and I had never before conducted in such a climate. Before we had played ten minutes of our first performance I was perspiring as I had never done before, and so it continued to the end of the evening. I am not a conductor who makes much gesture, although very tense in myself, and, of course, the nervous tension of the occasion did not make matters any better.

The Britten *Variations* went splendidly and at the interval I felt we had almost 'made it.' The applause was very good, and I was recalled half a dozen times. At the close of the evening we knew we had been successful, and the ovation was quite thrilling. In the dressing room that night the first of the many delightful people we were to get to know came to introduce themselves, and many old London friends who were now in Sydney came round, among them Max Oldaker, who, since I had known him as a student at the Academy and later with the D'Oyly Carte, had become the matinée idol of Australia. He was appearing in a version of *Fledermaus* at one of the Sydney theatres, but had been out of the show for some weeks owing to illness. It was good, too, to see Lauri Kennedy, who had given up cello playing and had been running an hotel in Sydney. He spoke of returning to the music world. Fred Hartley was another familiar face; he was now more or less settled in Australia, doing broadcast work. After the concert we all repaired to the Australia Hotel and found Dan in almost cheerful mood. I think we all felt it had gone well, but just how well?

The first half of the concert had been broadcast by the ABC and the first inkling that I had that we were making an impression was the face of the control man, whom I could see through a window to the left of the platform. He was evidently very shaken one way or another, and kept opening his mouth and keeping it open for long periods, until a turn of pages in the score would cause him to shut it again. He certainly wasn't yawning! At the close he seemed very excited and muttered something about 'never having heard anything like it before.' We were to hear this same remark many times during the next few months.

The next morning we were front-page news and we knew we had won. Those who hadn't been to the concert had listened to the broadcast, and everyone was talking about it. Cardus gave an ecstatic notice in the *Herald*; in fact I think it was Cardus who shook the public more than the orchestra, because everyone said the same thing: 'What has come over our Neville?' He had never been known to write in such terms before. The other papers were equally excited, and the opinion was general – that here was something the like of which had never been heard in Australia before.

The things that seemed to have impressed most were: (a) the volume of the tone from so few players; (b) the extraordinary fact that a whole evening of strings, far from proving monotonous, was an exciting experience; (c) the precision of the ensemble; (d) the fact that the players seemed to be enjoying themselves; (e) the Britten *Variations*, which was a tremendous success everywhere we played it, most places asking for a repeat performance; (f) the tone of the violas. This last was commented on time and again during the tour. Apparently the local viola tone was different, but I never had a chance to hear any. The fact that the players appeared to enjoy themselves was mentioned many times later. We couldn't make this out at first, but we gathered that Australian players apparently took life very seriously, and never smiled when playing. Every bar of our repertoire had by now got some joke attached to it, and I'm afraid we could never resist a smile at each other as the various laughs we had had came to our minds. I often wonder if we didn't laugh rather too much during a performance, but I think it kept the atmosphere fresh and everyone happy. It was most gratifying to find how the members of the orchestra themselves had impressed the public. I think I can say that each individual member had a great personal success on this trip. Soon they all had their particular fans. Fred, of course, was regarded as outstanding, even before he had played a concerto, and all were agreed that he was the orchestral leader *in excelsis*. His vitality stimulated the whole band.

The next day Dan was a different man. There had been a queue for booking in the morning, and it looked as though the second concert would be sold out. I think I can rightly say that after the opening night, there can hardly have been a hundred seats empty during the next four months!

As Dan had forecast, the second concert was sold out. What a difference when I came on for the second concert! The audience was jammed tight behind the orchestra on the platform, and right up to the organ at the back. Fred and Max played the Mozart *Sinfonia Concertante*, for which we borrowed a few wind players from the local orchestra. Our old friend Horace Green, whom we had all known in the BBC Orchestra at home, was first oboe, and it was good to see and hear him again. Besides the Mozart, we did a Handel *Concerto Grosso*, the *A Major Op.6, No.11*, which Fred always enjoyed playing, owing to the elaborate solo part; the little *E Flat Symphony* of Abel, one of our special favourites, and the Tchaikovsky *Serenade*, of which Cardus said: 'the lavishments of the performance are perhaps not capable of accurate description. So long have we starved for tones so warm, so eloquent, so vivacious and alluring by turn, so vibrant with true string tension, so insinuating with true string colour and curve of melody, that probably the immediate effect of it all on our consciousness might be likened to sudden and greedy eating and drinking after considerable enforced and marooned abstinence.' The ovation we received in the hall was something we had forgotten could ever happen with an audience. All this had a good effect on us, for after the last disastrous Chelsea season when we were deserted and just left to sink by the London musical public and after the tragic last tour of the *Brandenburgs*, we had all indeed begun to wonder whether there was any point in going on, at any rate in England. What was the good of putting all that work into trying to achieve good performances when it was so often ignored by a public, which, we were always being told, had become so music-minded during the war and had so increased in its appreciation of good music? It made me very angry to hear this cry repeated everywhere parrot-fashion, when I knew it simply wasn't true when you came down to brass tacks. It may have been *apparently* true, but surely even a simpleton could see that, merely because the Albert Hall was always full when the Tchaikovsky *B Flat Piano Concerto* was played (to frenzied applause, however indifferent the performance) one could not say that the vast English public had suddenly become music-minded. Yet it was on this, apparently, that these optimists based their enthusiasm.

In the first place, the mere fact that the people went to the Albert Hall showed that there was no discrimination or even awareness of what an orchestra sounded like, because what they heard in that ghastly mausoleum was certainly not an orchestra, but merely a confused jumble of meaningless sounds. The fact that the Albert Hall was absolutely packed for the 'five works' was a tragic sign of the times. There was no nucleus of very enlightened and discriminating people in London, probably a few thousand who attended all the interesting musical events and took an all-embracing interest in the art. They were the backbone, but they alone, alas, were not enough to keep our institutions going in a permanently secure way.

Such, in my view, was the position when we left for the Australian tour, and it was our experiences on the tour which gave us new hope for the future and made me realize that the optimists who maintained that England had suddenly become music-minded were only wrong in assuming that it was a *fait accompli.* The Australian response, it dawned on me, was an example of what might be at home, too, *if we could only get at them.* In Australia *everyone* came to the concerts. There was none of your 'upper ten' or your 'nucleus of true music lovers.' It was the sort of audience I had always dreamed about, but never thought possible. Every chambermaid and waiter in the hotel in which we stayed came to the concerts whenever they had a night or afternoon off. There was no talk of 'highbrow' or that ghastly word 'classical.' They just came and enjoyed the music, and they had no prejudices and listened to Britten and Bartók as they listened to Mozart and Handel. They took it as it came and *loved* it. They packed the hall night after night, and from the amazing letters which we received in hundreds, many seemed to have undergone a kind of spiritual conversion. These people had been starved of music. The ABC agreed with me that it was *not* the usual subscription audiences that went to the Symphony Concerts.

Originally six concerts had been announced in Sydney, but so great was the success that extra ones had to be arranged at once. The first two were given in the Town Hall, but after that Dan moved to the Conservatorium of Music, which was smaller, but we had the advantage of the most perfect surroundings. It is situated on a hill overlooking the harbour, surrounded by the most beautiful gardens. One is at once reminded of Glyndebourne. Strolling through the gardens in the interval, with a perfect view in the distance, is indeed a joy. And it is only a few minutes' walk from the centre of the city. Originally the building was the stable of Government House. I think Dan would have had all the concerts in the Town Hall if he'd known the success it was to be, but he had booked the other hall so had to use it.

I think we played seventeen times in Sydney altogether and hardly repeated a single item! This is, I imagine, a pretty good record for any orchestra. And we hadn't brought anything like all our repertoire with us. Some of the works which had the greatest success were: *all* the Britten compositions – the *Variations, Simple Symphony, Prelude and Fugue*, and *Les Illuminations*, especially the last – the Shostakovitch *Prelude and Scherzo*, Elgar's *Serenade* and *Introduction and Allegro*, the *Serenade* of Dag Wiren, the *Serenades* of Dvořák and Tchaikovsky, and Mozart's *Sinfonia Concertante*, Finzi's *Dies Natalis*, St. *Paul's Suite* of Holst, John Ireland's *Concertino*, Larsson's *Little Serenade*, the Honegger *Symphony*, the Leueu *Adagio*, Strauss' *Metamorphosen*, the *Serenade* of Wolf-Ferrari, the *Divertimento* of Bartók, and the *Grosse Fuge* of Beethoven. All these had outstanding success. We also played much Mozart, Handel, and Bach, as well as Italian classics, which always formed the nucleus of our programs. Besides concerts in the city, we played at some of the suburban halls for local music clubs. I remember especially a superb modern hall at Rockdale near Botany Bay, and a flourishing music club whose officers were almost entirely doctors or dentists. Everywhere we went in Australia and New Zealand there were a great many doctors and medical students in the audience. In fact the medical students at the universities were far keener than the music students themselves! It was always a medical student who 'wrote up' the concert in the university magazine.

In each of the big cities we played in the university at lunch-time concerts. These concerts were to me the most inspiring concerts we did. There is no audience quite like a student audience *as long as you have it on your side*. But woe betide the artist who falls foul of it! The vice-chancellor at Sydney was a jovial fellow called Roberts, an historian and an expert on Central European affairs. After an excellent lunch with him we played to the packed-out lecture theatre which I believe was built to hold eight hundred, but which, on this occasion, held twelve hundred. (The Lord Chamberlain in England would have had a fit if he had seen the gangways!) The applause was not ordinary applause; it was like thunder. Fred played the Bach *E Major Concerto* quite beautifully and we did the Britten *Simple Symphony* to finish up with. The audience roared and stamped for more. I knew, however, that lectures were due to start at 2:00 p.m. so refrained from any extras. Roberts got up and announced that the 2 p.m. lecture would be cancelled for all subjects and the concert would go on! Never have I heard such a tornado of whistling, shouting, and stamping as that which ensued. Apparently this had never been known to happen before, and it was front-page news the next day. I love this sort of audience – it reminded me of my lectures to the troops during the war, and the sensation of the quick, eager young minds so ready to respond to one's slightest innuendo is most stimulating.

It was in Sydney, too, that Dan started his idea of downtown lunchtime concerts which were to prove such an astounding success, eventually leading to one of the biggest traffic jams Melbourne had ever known. Dan's scheme was to have one concert from 12.10 to 12.50, empty the hall quickly and have another concert from 1.10 to 1.50. The great thing was the emptying of the hall in quick time. It is no easy task to get three thousand people out of a hall when three thousand others are waiting to come in! I had witnessed amazing scenes at the National Gallery in London during the war-time lunch-hour concerts, but the audience there was always the audience you would have *expected* to find, whereas in Australia everyone went, and it was not long before we were known wherever we appeared. Tram drivers would shout out as they passed: 'Doing the Britten tonight?' or 'Play the old Tchaikovksy again, please!' The old man who worked the engine on the ferry used to discuss Shostakovitch on our way home at night.

Many were the good friends we made while in Sydney. After each concert, people flocked round and invited the members of the orchestra to their homes. Picnic parties in cars and boats were very popular, and we all had our first experience of an Australian barbecue – chops roasted over a fire out in the bush, and how good they tasted!

One night, after the usual crowd had left the artists' room, a shy-looking man edged his way through the doorway and asked if he could have a word with me. He introduced himself as Neville Cardus and asked me if I could lunch with him one day. I said I would be delighted, and he withdrew in just as frightened a manner as he had entered. Surely this could not be the dreaded Cardus of legend, who had had his name brought up in parliament in Canberra with a query as to whether, owing to the virulence of his writing, he was a desirable person to have in the country! But it *was* he, and that meeting marked the beginning of a good friendship. Many were the talks we had in later days over a bottle of excellent Australian wine at his favourite restaurant. I found him to be an utterly sincere person with very high standards in everything worth anything. He told me of how despairing he had been over the music in Australia when he had first come out, and how he had criticized fearlessly and said exactly what he thought, with the result that he was feared and detested in some quarters; but, as I already knew, he was revered and looked upon as a *white hope* in really musical circles. This had been the fearless and outspoken criticism they had been waiting for. Standards had sunk very low, and through the war years there had been no contact with the outside world for comparisons. He attacked the local musicians for complacency and smugness. He fought a lone battle and gradually began to prevail. He started broadcast talks on music, which, again, were hated by some and popular with others, but the fact was indisputable that they *did* have an effect on the public taste, and all praise should go to the ABC authorities, who kept them going in the face of criticism. I am sure that the Australian public have to thank Cardus for much more than they realize. He had a great deal to do in preparing the ground for our tour, which, he felt, had come just at the right time, and I was convinced that it was partly the fact that everyone 'read Cardus' that accounted for that incredible audience of all types. First, the cricket fans read his music articles, and became interested, and then gradually all sections of the public were drawn under his spell. It will give some idea of how potent his influence had become, when I found later that even people in New Zealand read Cardus avidly.

Our initial five weeks in Sydney were drawing to a close, but the audiences showed no signs of diminishing. I believe we could have played in that city alone for six months. However, it was Dan's intention to return for a couple of farewell concerts before we left for New Zealand later in June.

Melbourne was the next city on our list. After our five weeks in Sydney and the frequent broadcasts, requests were pouring in from all over the continent for us to visit different centres. It was unfortunate that we were not able to go to Brisbane and Perth on this tour, but a combination of circumstances made it impossible. We were booked for Melbourne, and off we flew. (We had only one journey in an Australian train, and one journey in a New Zealand ship; otherwise the entire tour was either by air or by bus.)

When we reached Spring Street and I had my first view down Collins Street, I saw at once what a beautiful city Melbourne is. I think one feels 'at home' immediately. Sydney seemed in some ways more the American type of city, while Melbourne approximated more to the British. By the time we arrived, news of the Sydney success had gone round and the hall was sold out immediately. What an ovation we had on opening night! We repeated the Sydney program, and the press was just as ecstatic. I met Sir Bernard Heinze, director of the Melbourne Conservatoire for many years, who had done so much in raising the standard of musical appreciation in the country. The governor of Victoria gave us a warm welcome at Government House, where the whole orchestra was entertained at a party. Again, the furore created by our visit necessitated many extra concerts being put on, and the original six soon became fifteen! This was even more astonishing than the success in Sydney because *all* our Melbourne concerts were held in the Town Hall with a three thousand capacity. The idea of playing regularly to three thousand people was something we could never get used to. When we thought of our excitement at home if we got five hundred into a hall, it all seemed unreal. We broke every record for the Melbourne Town Hall except for that of Gracie Fields. Such a thing had never been heard before – an orchestra playing *serious* music getting such audiences! A jazz band perhaps, or a singer – but an orchestra, and a small one at that, consisting of only string players playing Britten and Bartók – it just wasn't true.

In Melbourne, as in Sydney, the work which caused the greatest sensation was Britten's *Les Illuminations*. I was anxious to do this piece in Australia, but the soprano part, which is very exacting, requires all the best qualities of both a dramatic and a lyrical voice for its perfect interpretation, as well as an intelligence above the ordinary. Very few singers are able to tackle it. Soon after arriving in Sydney Dan brought along Peggy Knibb, a very handsome girl, who had only sung in New Zealand, apart from her native country. We had a run through the Britten and I could see at once that we had the right singer. She knew the fiendishly difficult music inside out, and I made sure she would have the great success which she undoubtedly did. Everyone was astonished at a local girl of such excellence being so little known, and I am glad to think that it was through us that she became properly appreciated. I had never heard the work better sung, and as we did it more and more during the tour, she improved with every performance. Later on, she sang French and German songs with us, as well as Finzi's *Dies Natalis*, but the Britten remained her best performance.

While in Melbourne I did a great number of broadcasts of all kinds, even appearing in a variety show. The members of the Melbourne Orchestra were very kind and gave our orchestra a magnificent lunch party. Our hosts attended every concert and were amongst our most ardent followers. One day while I was sitting in the lounge of the hotel after a matinée concert an elderly lady came across and introduced herself as Mrs Patterson, the youngest sister of Nellie Melba. She had been to all the concerts and enjoyed them very much. She invited me to her home – an invitation I was unable to accept as we were leaving the following day. She also spoke of her son Gerald Patterson, who had won the Wimbledon Tennis Championships twenty-five years previously. I remember him playing his winning final – I believe it was the first year the championships were played at the new grounds. I shall never forget his cannon-ball service, which caused a sensation. The name of Melba is still much revered in Australia and there is no doubt that, as the first great internationally known Australian artist, she did put the Commonwealth on the musical map.

It was at the Town Hall corner of Collins Street that there occurred unprecedented scenes on the occasion of two lunch-hour concerts. A queue began forming early in the morning for the first concert, and, long before the doors opened, the queue for the second concert had also started to form, with the result that the crowds overflowed into the road, and when the moment came for opening there were well over six thousand people waiting and only three thousand could get in for each session! By this time the traffic had been brought almost to a standstill and the police had to be brought in. Such a scene had never been witnessed in Melbourne before. It was at one of these concerts that a photographer took a flashlight photograph. I was so angry I completely forgot what piece we were playing, and the orchestra finished the last few bars somehow by themselves, because in my fury I stopped beating! The audience also made deprecatory noises.

While in Melbourne we had an invitation to visit Geelong Grammar

School – the Eton of Australia. We found the children in Australia and New Zealand, on the whole, a better audience than we had found those in Britain. The attention and quiet while they were listening were extraordinary and they seemed very alert. At the close of every concert a boy or a girl always made a short speech of thanks, and I was astonished at their aplomb. While we were there the headmaster asked me if I would come back in August and judge their end-of-term inter-house music competitions – an annual event which was always very hotly contested. This I am glad to say I was able to do.

Hitherto we had played only in the big centres, but Dan was making an experiment by visiting places in the Outback, which rarely, if ever, had concerts. This idea arose from the Australian Council for the Encouragement of Music and the Arts which had branches in various towns and organized concerts and art exhibitions as our CEMA had done at home. We heard that people had been intensely suspicious of CEMA and suspected it of being, of all things, a Communist organization.

Another trip in the country was to Ballarat. We set off from Melbourne by bus for Ballarat, the old gold-rush town and scene of the Eureka Stockade. We played in a hall which had to be seen to be believed. It seemed on facing the hall from the platform that there were two halls, the further one being higher than the nearer, and the two communicating through an opening. I was told by my host, a doctor, that the hall had been built after a long and acrimonious battle between the two halves of the town, which were divided by a river, as to which side it should be built on. The discussion was amicably settled – King Solomon fashion – by the hall being built *over* the river, so that each half of the town had half of the hall! You can imagine the atmosphere of the hall when the evening mists commenced to rise from the water below! The next day we moved on to Bendigo, another gold-mining town, where the mines were still working.

From Bendigo we set out for the most interesting drive of our Australian visit – to Griffith in New South Wales, which meant a drive of over three hundred miles all in one day in a very hard-seated and crowded bus, which only just held us and our instruments. The drive was mostly along tracks in the bush, far away from populated parts. We drove across completely flat country nearly all day, past many great sheep stations. It was a mystery to me what the sheep found to graze on in that sun-baked country where there was little green grass. I wondered how many miles of wire there are in Australian fences. As we drove through the bush, wonderfully coloured parrots flew all round us, and the biggest thrill of all – we saw many kangaroos in their wild natural state. I just happened to look at our speedometer while one of the kangaroos was racing beside us, and it registered 45 m.p.h. The creature seemed to enjoy the fun for a while and then, suddenly tiring, made a superb jump over a fence and hopped away into the bush.

Griffith was an interesting place. Twenty-five years before, there was no town there at all. Then a vast irrigation scheme was begun for that area, and what had been arid land became fertile and wonderful fruit-growing country. Many Italians settled there and one heard Italian spoken in the streets. The vineyards here are very fine, and we visited two of the large wineries with the inevitable result! In Griffith a remark-able woman called Mrs Blumer had not only organized all the concerts, but had started an art school and a dramatic society and still managed to run her own home entirely alone. What these cultural activities mean to a community living four hundred miles from its nearest city can well be imagined. I was amazed when two people from Griffith later turned up in Sydney to hear our farewell concert.

From Griffith we moved to the town with the delightful name of Wagga Wagga. It is a beautiful place, rather like Leamington Spa or Cheltenham. Here we had a most wonderful audience, some of whom had come a hundred miles. We were up the next morning at 3:30 a.m. in order to get back to Melbourne in time for a rehearsal. That night we played Schönberg's *Verklärte Nacht*, and a new work by the American David Diamond. While in Melbourne Dan had a wire from the Zinc Corporation mine in Broken Hill saying they would fly us from any-where in Australia and back if we would go and play for them. This town in the south-western corner of New South Wales consists of four great mines which supply the world with a large proportion of its lead and zinc. Everyone working for the mines was entitled to a bonus above their wages according to the price of lead in the world market, and while we were there rumour had it that the lowest-paid workers in the town were making seventeen pounds, ten shillings a week – an extraordinary amount by contemporary British standards. The concert was given in the town hall to an enthusiastic audience. At a supper party afterwards I was introduced to Paddy O'Neill, the uncrowned King of Broken Hill, a hard-bitten old Irish miner who had been there since 1893 and had become the acknowledged leader of all the miners. There was no Arbitration Court at Broken Hill in those days; if there was a dispute Paddy settled it, and there had not been a strike in the town since 1919.

From here we flew to Adelaide where, before landing, the pilot flew us round the city to enable us to see its superb lay-out – the central square mile, the green belt of parks, and the residential areas outside that again. The inhabitants had given the man whose vision made it all possible – Colonel Light – a fine memorial, which depicts him gazing down with satisfaction on his noble creation. I loved Adelaide, its people, its climate, and the atmosphere of ease and culture. At the Conservatoire of Music I met the director, Professor Davies, brother of the English composer Walford Davies. He was then eighty-two and full of life, but alas, he was to die before I left Australia. The Music Chair at Adelaide was the first to be founded in Australia – about seventy years before. Melbourne had had one for many years, and Sydney was electing its first music professor while I was there.

On the way back to Sydney we called at Canberra for one concert. This trip made news. We travelled in two planes and the weather was fine. I was in the second plane, which must have been about fifty miles behind the other. When we were about fifteen minutes from landing, we were told to strap ourselves in and hold our instruments in our arms because the plane ahead had had some trouble with air pockets. The warning came just in time, for the next moment we felt exactly as if we were going over a waterfall. It was a dreadful feeling. The hostess fell flat on the floor. After a few more large bumps we landed safely and found Charles Wilmot looking rather anxious. He told us that the first plane had dropped a thousand feet in an air pocket, and no one was prepared. Everyone was flung in all directions, a typewriter in a rack had fallen through a double-bass, and the other bass was also smashed. Several people were injured, but not seriously. All, however, had suffered severe shock. The pilot said that in all his years of flying he had never known anything like it. We, in the second plane, had evidently entered the same turbulent patch, but had been warned, and it was therefore not nearly such a terrifying experience. Apparently Canberra is famous for this. It is surrounded by hills and the air currents coming off these make the approach always very bumpy. The trouble was that we naturally had a concert that night. It was quite impossible to use the double-basses; in fact Charles and Julian were rather doubtful whether they could ever be repaired properly, but luckily we managed to borrow two rather ancient instruments locally and made do with those.

Our concert in the evening was attended by the entire diplomatic corps and all the ministers of the federal government. The Governor-General, Mr McKell, who had succeeded the Duke of Gloucester, came with his family. His appointment had caused quite an uproar in Australia because it was the first time a former party politician had been given the position, which is, of course, non-political. After the concert there was a big reception where we met the entire diplomatic corps and government. The following day I was offered a lift by car to Sydney, and I was glad of the chance because we were leaving Australia in a few days' time, and I had hardly seen any of it from the ground. It was also good to be back in Sydney again and I was fortunate in getting a flat high up over the harbour. The magical hour in Sydney is dusk with all the twinkling lights. There seemed to be more neon lights there than anywhere else in the world except perhaps San Francisco. To eyes starved of light for so many years during the war the effect was overwhelming.

The last week in Sydney was one round of parties, receptions, and farewell broadcasts, press interviews ('What had I thought of Australian audiences?' *ad nauseam*!), not to mention several concerts and bidding goodbye to friends. The last night was unforgettable; the town hall packed to suffocation and everyone out to enjoy themselves and give us the biggest ovation of our lives. As each member of the orchestra went on he was greeted with frantic applause, and it was some time before we could get the audience calm enough to begin. Peggy again sang Finzi's lovely work. It is interesting to note, though, that *Dies Natalis* did not make the same sensation as *Les Illuminations*. There is something in Britten's music that takes an audience by the throat. I have never known it to fail.

So ended the Australian visit, which had broken all records for concerts in that country and which had turned out to be one of the greatest popular and financial successes in the history of Australian music. Dan and I could not help smiling when we thought of that morning three months previously, when he had sat in his office with a long face and more or less persuaded himself that the whole thing would be a tragic flop!

Our quest was only half over; we had fresh fields to conquer. At 5:00 a.m. on the morning after the Sydney farewell we took off in a flying boat from Rose Bay in Sydney Harbour to fly to New Zealand. It wasn't worth going to bed, and Charles Wilmot and I had turned over and over in our minds how we could get some official support in London for the orchestra, which had so obviously become a potent weapon of cultural propaganda. It would be criminal for the orchestra to go home and possibly disintegrate for lack of support. Various schemes were discussed, and I left at 3:30 a.m. to catch the plane!

I hadn't heard very much at that time about the treacherous crossing of the Tasman Sea. I knew that quite often people were held up for some days, but we had an excellent crossing of eight and a half hours, the only unpleasantness being the fact that the heating apparatus ceased to function, and we flew at ten thousand feet most of the way. Without oxygen and with the intense cold it was difficult to move about without getting short of breath, and people began to look rather blue. Thick ice formed on the windows, and your breath froze into small crystals in front of you as you exhaled! All the same, it is much more pleasant coming down through cloud over the sea than over the mountains, and the last hundred miles or so we flew just over the waves, which was delightful. Looking at the map, one is apt to think that Australia and New Zealand are next-door neighbours. I was surprised to learn that very few Australians ever visit New Zealand.

Geologists tell us that Australia is the oldest part of the earth's surface and New Zealand is the newest. This is exactly how it strikes the ordinary man flying rapidly from one country to the other – Australia, with its venerable gum trees and mellow colouring, New Zealand with its vivid greens and bright flowers. Our first impression of a New Zealand hotel was not inspiring. As in Australia, it was well-nigh impossible to get used to the bars closing at six o'clock. I saw many more drunken people around in both countries than I ever saw at home and was convinced that it cannot have a good effect. 'It gets the men home early' is a point put forward in its favour, but surely one of the good things about British life is the fact that, *after* his supper, a man can take his wife round to the pub, where they can spend an evening with their friends. This kind of social life was entirely absent in Australia and New Zealand, nor were there any cafés open late in the evening where one could meet friends and have a chat over coffee. There was just nowhere to go and nothing to do after seven o'clock, with the consequence that there is a dire lack of that vital social intercourse so valuable for the exchange of ideas between chance acquaintances. It is very hard to meet new people if you are a young person alone, living in digs, and doing a job during the day. In Britain you can always drop round to the 'local,' and meet twenty people in as many minutes. I have heard more stimulating conversation in pubs than in any university common room. Perhaps that is the fundamental difference? Whereas in Britain the pub is regarded primarily as a social meeting place, in Australia or New Zealand it was looked upon solely as a place to drink in, from which women were banned.

One homelike touch occurred almost as soon as we arrived – all the lights went out for half an hour. Another thing to get accustomed to was the fact of having to have your meal punctually at the stated time, or not having it at all. It was no country for the dreamer or the habitually unpunctual, and yet, strangely enough, we found audiences turning up late and concerts had to be held up more in New Zealand than anywhere else. At one concert in Wellington so bad was it that no more than half the audience was seated at the advertised time. Strange in a people so accustomed to 'now or never' in matters of food and drink.

Another thing that the less hardy visitor needed to be warned about was the prevalent idea that everyone wanted to wake up at 6:45 a.m. This may suit a certain portion of the population, but for the unfortunate artist who works until 10:30 p.m. and who never gets to bed until after midnight, when all the social aftermath of a concert finally disperses, it is sheer unadulterated cruelty.

In Auckland, whose harbour reminded one very much of Sydney, there was the usual civic reception at the town hall. Dan's home and headquarters were in Auckland, and we started there. A few minutes after my arrival at the hotel my phone rang and I heard a familiar voice at the other end: 'Hello, Boyd, so glad to hear you! You're just in time for my concert tonight; party afterwards at our hotel.' It was Eugene Goossens, who, on his way to take up his new appointment in Sydney, had found his ship in Auckland for a few days and had been asked to conduct the newly formed National Symphony Orchestra of New Zealand. I had heard with great interest of the formation of this orchestra, the first fully permanent organization of its kind in New Zealand, and it had only been in existence a few months. I was frankly astonished at the standard of the orchestra, and knew that if it could be kept together it would have a big future. Eugene was delighted with it, and appeared to be in his best form. I also ran into Warwick Braithwaite, who was born in Dunedin, and had returned to his homeland from Britain to conduct the new orchestra.

At our first Auckland concert, exactly the same thing occurred as in Sydney: town hall was not quite full, terrific enthusiasm, ecstatic press, and all further concerts immediately booked out. Many of the concerts both there and in Australia were broadcast in part, and we found that these were eagerly listened to all over the country, especially in the isolated districts, from which we had many moving letters. In general New Zealanders are much more reserved than Australians, and one found one didn't make friends as quickly, but when the shyness barrier was broken down they proved to be just as warm as their neighbours. There was far more travelling to be done in New Zealand because of the smaller population of the cities, and consequently fewer concerts possible in each. I did a large number of broadcast talks while there, or rather I recorded them for future use. Professor Shelley, the director of broadcasting, was a striking looking man with a leonine head. I believe he was an expert on Shakespeare, and was a professor of history before taking his present post. In New Zealand there is both government and commercial broadcasting, but the commercial stations are also controlled by the government.

While in Auckland I was able to see something of the coast running north up the peninsula. I found an old friend who used to be a neighbour at home, living there in a charming little house he had bought when he retired. It was an earthly paradise and stood on a high cliff, below which was a sandy beach, private to the house. Out to sea were green islands, to either side sandy bays, with one or two farms dotted about on the slopes behind them. You could see about thirty miles in any direction. It was supposed to be winter, but we sat outside all day and got quite sunburnt. We never saw a soul all day, and he told me he had only once ever seen anyone else on the beach in two years. How strange is the distribution of population over the world. Here was a 'land fit for heroes,' yet hardly a soul lived there.

We played roughly the same programs as we opened with in Australia, with, of course, always one or very often two English compositions. A young New Zealander, Douglas Lilburn, had sent me a charming little work called *Diversions*, and I was very glad to have been able to play it in Wellington and Christchurch, where it had a great success. His name was not unknown to me, and I knew he had studied with Vaughan

Williams at the Royal College. This was the only useful composition among the hundreds submitted during our tour. At least ninety per cent were ballads for voice and piano. Perhaps their composer thought I *sang* a few items during a concert?

After our Auckland concerts we flew down to Wellington, and I had my first taste of the wonders of the New Zealand scenery. Mount Egmont was stunning as we passed it, the great snow-capped cone bathed in sunshine. Its brother volcano nearby, Ruapehu, had recently been erupting. It is a great thrill the first time one does the flight down between the two huge mountains. We were to do the journey many times during the next month and each time the great peaks appeared in different lights and colours. At Wellington I stayed at Government House with my old friends the Freybergs. Bernard Freyberg, after a brilliant career in both wars, had been made governor-general of the country of his birth about two years before our visit, and was proving one of the most popular that New Zealand had ever had. I had known Lady Freyberg for many years in London. The Freybergs did much to give the concerts in Wellington a great send-off, attending every one, even the school's concert. Peter Fraser, the Prime Minister, came to the first concert and was so delighted he immediately organized a great party in our honour at Parliament buildings at which a whole troupe of Maori dancers entertained us with their fascinating songs and ritual. Both Fraser and Nash, the finance minister, were the hosts, but could never be at the party simultaneously, owing to one having to be in the House all the time in case there was a division! They only had a majority of four, but as the party was in the same building they could take it in turns to be host. There were seven hundred guests at this function. The concerts had caused just as much of a sensation here as elsewhere, and queues formed at 4:00 a.m. whenever booking opened.

After Wellington we visited the South Island, playing at Christchurch, Dunedin, and Invercargill. We had three days' holiday up in the mountains at Queenstown during this time, enjoying the endless variety of scenery in this extraordinary country. I don't think there are many more beautiful places in the world. The return journey through North Island included, as well as return visits to Wellington and Auckland, concerts in provincial towns such as Hamilton, Palmerston North, Napier, and Hastings.

The return to England was to be by sea, and the party split up into various ships. I returned via Australia in order to keep my appointment at Geelong Grammar School, where I adjudicated their annual music competitions. So ended our trip round the world. That it made history there is no doubt, and the orchestra obviously created a profound impression in Australia and New Zealand. Nobody knew how it would go or even whether such a vast, in those days, undertaking was feasible at all. It prepared the way for the visit of the Old Vic Company which followed us the next year.

Arrival of the Boyd Neel Orchestra in Broken Hill, Australia

13

A Guide to Music

On our return from Australia I again got a call from Dr Roth, and I
wondered if another work had arrived from Strauss. This time I was in
for a pleasant surprise for I walked into Roth's office to find Strauss
himself sitting by the desk with a score on his lap. He told me that he
had heard reports that we had 'made very well the *Metamorphosen*' and
wished to thank me. I was so overcome that I couldn't think of anything
to say. This was his last visit to London before his death in 1949. It is
said that, when asked why he suddenly produced all those instrumental
works during the war after a life of writing enormous operas, he replied:
'It's quite simple – all the great opera theatres have been destroyed and
one can't play cards all the time.'

The first Edinburgh Festival had just finished when we got back from
Australia in September 1947, and we were immediately engaged for the
second one in 1948. But in the spring of 1948, we were asked to go to
Portugal again. By now, we had accumulated a vast repertoire of works
no one else ever played, but signs were to appear on the horizon that
our long period of being alone in the field was coming to an end.

For our second tour of Portugal we played only in Lisbon and Oporto.
No crocodiles this time – and we had a faithful public which remembered us from ten years previously. This time we played the Bliss *Music
for Strings*, which had always gone down well abroad. This is a very
brilliant piece and, although extremely difficult, is well worth the work
it requires.

The Edinburgh Festival of 1948 was exciting. Everything was new and no one in that lovely city had, as yet, got into a groove. But how we had to work! We gave *ten* concerts in eleven days, many including large and complex works. How thankful we were that we had this huge repertoire which could be brought out and polished up for an occasion such as this. We did among other works: *Music for Strings, Celeste and Percussion* by Bartók; Schönberg's *Verklärte Nacht*; the Honegger *Second Symphony*; Benjamin Britten's *Variations on a Theme of Frank Bridge*; Michael Tippett's *Concerto for Double String Orchestra*; Darius Milhaud's *Concertino de Printemps*, and Chausson's *Poème de l'amour et de la mer* with Maggie Teyte – this last a never-to-be-forgotten experience. Then there was the *Metamorphosen*; Rawsthorne's first *Piano Concerto*; Stravinsky's *Apollon musagète*; and the Britten and Dvorák *Serenades*. We also included many shorter eighteenth-century works. Not bad for ten days? The Rawsthorne is a good piece and much better in its original form without the fuller orchestration which was added later. The Chausson *Poème* was one of Maggie Teyte's greatest performances, and I did it with her many times during those years. The Tippett *Concerto for Double String Orchestra* is fiendishly difficult to perform well, but is rewarding and has a very beautiful slow movement.

This 1948 Edinburgh Festival was a good one. Cortot played, and Piatigorsky, Menuhin, Kentner, Schnabel, Michelangeli, Furtwängler, Boult, Gui, Barbirolli, Münch, and van Beinum were all heard during the three weeks. Kathleen Ferrier sang with Gerald Moore, and Segovia gave a recital. What a galaxy! Maggie Teyte also sang with Gerald Moore and I think her recital, for me anyway, was the highlight of the whole Festival.

It was about this time that Malcolm Sargent had to give up the Robert Mayer Children's Concerts as he had become too busy to devote enough time to the famous series. Sir Robert Mayer asked me if I would take them over. I had already done some for him before the war and had enjoyed them enormously, so I accepted gladly. These concerts, which have become such a vital part of English musical life, were some of the most delightful I ever took part in, and I did them for about six years. The Queen Mother (or Queen as she then was) used to bring her two daughters nearly every Saturday morning and they were among our most ardent supporters. They often came around afterwards and discussed the program, and would ask me to include some favourite piece of theirs in future concerts. When her daughter became Queen, the Queen Mother started taking her grandchildren to the concerts. The interesting thing about these concerts, from a conductor's point of view, was to work with a committee of children, who helped run the concerts and chose a lot of the music. They published their own little magazine which contained program notes on what was to be performed. A splendid idea! We had all the great English orchestras in turn, and many famous soloists were asked if they would come and perform for the children. This was a happy undertaking for me during those years. I often meet people today who came to my concerts as children and who say how much it helped them in their appreciation of music.

In 1950 we were off again on tour, this time to Italy. We played right down as far as Reggio, and then went across to Sicily and played in Palermo, Messina, and Catania. How different it looked from when I had last been there during the war! We nearly always played in the local opera house, and the beauty of those old auditoriums, not to mention the usually wonderful acoustics, was a constant inspiration.

Other tours took us to Germany, France, Switzerland, and Scandinavia. When we got to Helsinki, I began to wonder whether there was any chance of meeting Sibelius. I had heard some fearsome stories of him kicking reporters and unwanted visitors down the steps of his porch, and knew he lived the life of a near-recluse. There was a reception after our concert, and I was talking to a very distinguished-looking Finnish lady who spoke excellent English. I told her of my hopes of meeting the grand old man, and she said, if I would be ready at ten the next morning, she thought she could arrange it. I was astonished and overjoyed, and dared to ask how she could accomplish this feat. 'Well,' she said, 'You see I happen to be his eldest daughter.'

Sure enough, the next morning we drove to the north of the city for an hour, and we might have been driving up any highway in Ontario in winter time. The scenery was identical. We turned off to a lake, frozen, of course, and the snow became very deep. At the end of the lake was a long, low log house. My guide warned me that one could speak to Sibelius about anything except his own music, and, if I mentioned that, he would disappear for the rest of the day! When we arrived he came out to welcome us and couldn't have been more charming. He was a huge man, as big as Chaliapin. He spoke no English and I no Finnish. We conversed in a strange mixture of French and German. He said he had heard our Helsinki concert on the radio, and had very much enjoyed the Elgar and Vaughan Williams works. He asked me how his

friend 'Voggen William' was, and then discussed music of a most contemporary kind. I was astonished how he had kept up with the latest
trends. Apparently he listened a great deal to a very good radio on
which he could get most of the European stations. We had brandy,
coffee, and cigars all the morning. Then we had a walk in the forest
along tracks he had made in the snow, followed by a gargantuan smör-
gasbord, followed by more coffee, cognac, and cigars throughout the
afternoon. A red-letter day!

The Eighth Symphony was supposed to be about finished, but no one
dared ask. A great friend of his told me that all Sibelius would say was
that he was engaged on a 'great work.' His daughter told me that he
shut himself away all day and worked at 'something,' but they never
dared ask what! Everyone thought that, at his death, several masterpieces would be found, but there was apparently nothing. When I met a
relative later on, he spoke about 'the great tragedy.' I think that what
happened was that Sibelius felt he just couldn't, after 1926, produce
anything up to his very high standards and fell into a kind of apathetic
despair. After *Tapiola*, nothing. But into that amazing piece he put
everything, and, having seen his home and its surroundings, I can enjoy
the work far more than I used to; it contains the essence of the Finnish
countryside in every bar. That visit to Finland was one of the most
enjoyable we ever made, and as I left Sibelius, he gave me an autographed score of his *Sixth Symphony*, which is now in the music library
of the University of Toronto.

Berlin was also interesting. The first visit we made was long before
the Wall had even been thought of, but the second visit was made after
it was built, and I was determined to go to East Berlin and see one of
Felsenstein's world-famous productions at the Komische Oper. I was
told it was difficult to get there, and almost impossible to get back
again. I thought I would try anyway, so I got into the subway and came
out on the east side, showing my passport at the top of the escalator,
and there I was! Coming back was no harder, and I did this three times
in one week, seeing, among other things, Felsenstein's marvellous production of Janáček's *Cunning Little Vixen*.

The festivals in Aix-en-Provence were also exciting, and we used to
play on the steps of that great church St Jean de Male, where the
acoustics were superb, just as they were on the steps of Strasbourg
Cathedral, where we also played around that time.

Every year when we performed in Paris, Nadia Boulanger and Georges

Enesco came to the concert and sometimes they even took part in our music-making. Enesco did an orchestral version of his *String Octet* which was most effective, and Nadia Boulanger did a superb performance of Stravinsky's *Mass*. She used to come to London every year and work with the orchestra, which she loved, and they loved her. We played also in the social centre of the Peugeot factory at Montbeliard for the workers in the automobile factory. Can you see many other car manufacturers giving such a concert for their employees? But, after all, why not? The tragedy is that the taste of the average man is vastly underrated. When we played to the miners at Broken Hill, New South Wales, or at Uranium City, Saskatchewan, or at Yellowknife, North West Territories, the response was invariably fantastic.

We often went across and played in Belfast, Northern Ireland. The joke of this concert always came at the end. The boat for Liverpool left about 10:30 p.m. and the last work would be started around 9:45 p.m. When we reached the last movement, my secretary would signal to me from the wings as to whether we had to hurry or not. The orchestra loved this, and once a Tchaikovsky finale went very much faster than I have ever heard it before or since! Sometimes they would hold the boat for us for ten minutes or so; we got to know all the crews very well.

In 1946, while with the Sadler's Wells Opera, I had had a very heavy week at Bristol ending with a *Bohème* matinée and a *Butterfly* evening on the Saturday. *Bohème* went splendidly, and *Butterfly* with Joan Cross likewise, until the final scene, when I blacked out completely. I can't remember finishing the opera at all, but apparently did so, because nobody made any comment. I found myself in my dressing room, changing, and felt all right but, of course, very frightened. I kept quiet about all this, but naturally began to worry as to what could have been the cause. It is on such occasions that having medical knowledge is a great drawback: one immediately begins to imagine the worst. I decided to do nothing, and await developments, if any. For some weeks nothing occurred and I began to forget the episode, putting it down to great fatigue and nervous strain.

My trouble seemed to get no better and a neurologist friend confessed that he was stumped and that, as he could find nothing wrong organically, a psychiatrist seemed to be the only solution. But I was adamant; I had seen too many disastrous results in my own practice. The solution came quite unexpectedly, and dramatically. I was asked to give a lecture in Cardiff to a music society and decided to drive down

Maggie Teyte with Boyd Neel at the Edinburgh Festival in 1951

Talking over the score of the sixth *Brandenburg Concerto* with soloists
(left to right) Francis Baines, Boris Rickelman, Rosemary Green, and
Kenneth Essex, Birmingham, England

The Festival of Britain at Bath, 1951. 'Wigs'

In East Berlin, Unter den Linden

Boyd Neel and his mother, Ruby Neel, at her cottage in England

and call in to see my mother, who lived near Henley, on the way back. It turned out to be a dreadful day, with torrents of rain so bad I had to keep stopping as the road became completely invisible at times. When I got to the hotel at Cardiff, I stepped out of the car and blacked out just as I had done at Bristol during the opera six years previously. In a flash I knew the cause of my troubles – my eyes.

When I returned to London I saw an eye doctor, who gave me some spectacles, and, from that moment, I never had another attack. No history of any eye trouble all my life, and I was always considered to have splendid eyesight – or I would never have got into the navy. I had been to see a specialist at Moorfields hospital a year or so before, and found what I knew, that one eye had some astigmatism, but not enough to require correction, though it very nearly ruined my career at the time. Later in my life it was my eyes once more which let me down; but that's another story!

Working so much for the BBC in post-war years, I found that apparently I had certain talents which I never suspected. I was asked to give a talk on some subject (I think on changing professions) and it went over rather well. The result was that in the years after the war I became equally well known to the public as a broadcaster of what the BBC calls 'the spoken word.' I found myself giving regular talks, mostly about music, but sometimes of a general nature as well. I was a regular contributor to Music Magazine and Children's Hour, where I attained the laureate of being known as 'Uncle Boyd,' and I did commentaries of all kinds as a sort of classical disc-jockey. All this culminated in having my own program on the air for quite a long time. It was known as 'Boyd Neel's Music Club' and it was not just a Third Programme series, but an hour a week on what was then known as the National Programme in, as radio people say, prime time. At that time the BBC had three major programs, the National, the Home Service, and the Third Programme.

The Chief of the National Programme at that time was an extremely cultured man called Tom Chalmers, and it was his idea that I should work out something geared to 'the man in the street.' After some weeks, I came up with an idea which he liked and we started work. I had a good budget, and we decided that, as a start, the series should confine itself to the regions near London but would, of course, be heard everywhere. In a thirteen-week series, we would select a number of places which the club would visit. I would first make personal trips to these centres, contact the local dignitaries, and tell them of the scheme, asking for their co-operation. We would choose places like Hornsey, Greenwich, Whitechapel, and some towns within easy reach of London. I tried to find out all the musical associations of the places in history. For instance, Greenwich was the place to which the royal party is supposed to have gone on its river picnic, accompanied by musicians performing Handel's *Water Music* on another barge.

In researching each location for a visit by 'Boyd Neel's Music Club,' I tried to find out if any well-known composers were born or had lived there, and if certain works were composed or performed there. It is surprising what a lot of interesting material came to light. I also asked the people who lived in the various communities to suggest program material. Those whose suggestions were accepted would come on to the platform at the broadcast concert, and give their reasons for their choice, and announce the work. A famous orchestra performed at each concert, and I did the announcing and conducting. This was an experiment which had never been tried before (hardly any TV then) and it brought musicians hitherto only *heard* on radio into direct contact with the listening public. The Music Club ran for a year, and was so successful that other BBC producers began to take an interest in the idea. They asked me what I thought of a similar series, done, this time in the studio, and called *The Plain Man's Guide to Music*. This would consist of talks by the conductor on various aspects of orchestral music and listeners would be encouraged to write their queries.

My work with the Boyd Neel Orchestra had increased to such an extent that I felt I could not take on the whole burden of this new series, so I decided to share it with two other colleagues. We therefore invited Adrian Boult and John Barbirolli to take part, and they entered into the spirit of the thing and did a splendid job. I think *The Plain Man's Guide to Music* was a good idea, but with the coming of TV, all these things had to give way to such innovations as the Bernstein approach to the Plain Man, with its added glamour of full-colour presentation of a conductor, orchestra, and audience on the screen. I was never any good on TV. I can talk for hours to a microphone, but when confronted with cameras and those dreadful lights, I just dry up. In the early days of BBC TV at Alexandra Palace, I was asked to do *Peter and the Wolf*, and had to conduct and speak the narration myself. This was very difficult because I was often breathless for a moment or two after some strenuous music, and immediately had to talk and appear calm. I suppose today it would all be videotaped and these problems would never arise.

In 1951 we returned to Edinburgh, but this time it was not quite such a marathon as in 1948; we gave only six concerts on consecutive days, which was bad enough, but could just be survived. I see, on looking through the programs, that we did the *Symphony* of Jean Françaix – a delightful piece that seems to have slipped into oblivion.

We performed Stravinsky's *Concerto in E Flat, Dumbarton Oaks, 1938*, and for this we had Dennis Brain and Norman del Mar, horns, plus other winds. (Incidentally, the following year we actually gave a concert at Dumbarton Oaks, the Washington DC home of Mrs Robert Woods Bliss, the commissioner of that famous piece.)

Another work we played that year, a great favourite of ours, was Vivaldi's *The Four Seasons*. The *Prelude and Scherzo* of Shostakovitch was also one of the Edinburgh pieces. This wears extremely well and was always in our repertoire. The Stravinsky *Concerto in D for String Orchestra* was quite a novelty and was at that time not very much played. It has since become quite popular, but I feel that unless you have seen the score you miss many of its subtleties.

Also performing at the Usher Hall during our two weeks at the Edinburgh Festival in 1951 was the New York Philharmonic with Leonard Bernstein. Their manager was, at that time, the legendary Arthur Judson. After one week of our concerts, he came round and introduced himself, inviting me to lunch. He told me he had wandered into the Free-mason's Hall several mornings during the week to hear us play and he had been very impressed. He had some of our recordings, but he said they gave a very sketchy idea of the astonishing sound which the eighteen players produced. He said he wanted the United States to hear this unique ensemble, and that he would arrange a tour of Canada and the United States for the following autumn, through his Columbia Artists Agency. The contract arrived very soon, and we were all set to leave in October of 1952. I little knew at that time how this tour was to change the whole of the rest of my life.

14

Settling in Toronto

We flew first to Gander in Newfoundland, and played four concerts in St John's. They told us that we were the first 'live' professional orchestra they had ever heard in Newfoundland, which had only just joined Canada three years previously as the tenth province. The hospitality was boundless and we were charmed and delighted with everything. There was, of course, no decent hall in St John's in those days, and we played in something called the Pitt Hall, which was suspended in space from the top of a cliff over the city. It is astonishing to visit St John's these days and marvel at its quick development in thirty years. I did not have the pleasure of meeting the famous Joey Smallwood on that occasion, but, some years later, we met in London and he told me of the impact the orchestra had made during that visit.

From St John's we flew to Halifax and worked our way by bus through New Brunswick to Quebec and Ontario, playing everywhere. We never played in Toronto – why, I have no idea – but we had concerts in Barrie, Oakville, and Oshawa. I stayed in Toronto with an old friend who supervised all our recordings at Decca in London for many years and who was, at that time, a music producer for the Canadian Broadcasting Corporation: later, when I came to Toronto, Terence Gibbs was in the control room for many of my broadcasts. While I was in Toronto, I had a call from Edward Johnson, who had just retired from the Metropolitan Opera in New York after many years as its general manager, and had come back to his home town, Guelph, in his native Canada. He was now chairman of the board which looked after the Royal Conservatory for the University of Toronto. So confused has been the history of music at the University of Toronto, that I feel this might be a good place to attempt to sort it all out.

The Royal Conservatory had its origins in the Toronto Conservatory of Music founded in 1886. In 1897, it moved to a new building on College Street, becoming a private trust in 1910, and Dr Vogt becoming principal in 1913. So much for the Conservatory.

The University of Toronto had been offering a degree in music since 1844, but no faculty of music was established until 1918 with Dr Vogt as dean. This was the first connection between the University and the Conservatory. This was also, incidentally, the point from which all the subsequent trouble took root. In 1921, the Ontario Legislature passed an act whereby the trusteeship of the Conservatory passed into the orbit of the university, and this meant that the appointing of Conservatory trustees devolved on the university, which was thus able to control the policy of the Conservatory. The trustees were all members of the Board of Governors of the university, but operated as a separate organization. This was the board of which Edward Johnson was the chairman in 1952. In 1926, Sir Ernest MacMillan had become head of the two institutions and was both dean of the Faculty of Music and principal of the Conservatory, which had not yet attained its regal prefix. In 1943, MacMillan retained only the university position, and a new principal was elected to the Conservatory owing to the growth of the institution.

In 1947 the Conservatory was awarded the 'Royal' in its title in honour of its Diamond Jubilee, which occurred that year. MacMillan resigned as dean in 1952, just about the time that I arrived in Canada with the orchestra. The resignation sparked off a crisis as to who should succeed him. Dr Ettore Mazzoleni had been made principal in 1945, and seemed to be the obvious successor to the dean's position. This, however, was not at all the idea of a large faction headed by Edward Johnson, and a bitter struggle developed which split the Conservatory from top to bottom.

Why, you may well ask, was the Conservatory so interested in who became dean of the Faculty? The reason was the crazy set-up which had been foisted on to the institution. As the Faculty had grown, no one knew where to house it. What more convenient place than the Conservatory building on College Street? This building was already too small for the Conservatory by itself, so it can be imagined what horrors of overcrowding were created. Added to this, nobody really knew how much the running of the building was Conservatory business and how much University. Whom did the pianos belong to? Who paid for the heating? Who paid for the electricity? And, above all, who was in charge of the building? Chaos and anarchy reigned and the whole institution very nearly collapsed. This was the situation when Edward Johnson took me out to lunch and asked me if I fancied the post of dean, as it was very urgent that they should have someone as soon as possible if the place was to survive. I laughed when he asked me and reminded him that I had a famous orchestra, which had four years of engagements lined up ahead of it, and the subject was dropped. After our meeting in Toronto, we continued on our tour travelling by bus through much of the United States, ending up in New York at the town hall, where we received a great ovation. Our next American tour was already being discussed.

I arrived back in London at the beginning of December, having gone back to Canada on my way, to conduct some CBC concerts, and give some talks on the radio. I had only been back a week when one morning the phone rang, and a voice said: 'This is Edward Johnson. I'm at the Park Lane Hotel. Could you have dinner with me tonight?' I had accepted before it dawned on me what it all meant. I did think it rather peculiar, as I had seen him only a few weeks previously in Toronto. Then I began to realize that he had been sent over to see me. I was right. He came straight to the point. 'After you left we had a meeting of the board at which it was unanimously decided that I should go over and see you to tell you that you are the man we want in Toronto, and to persuade you to accept the job. We feel that, as you have had a much wider scope of action in your life than the average musician, you would be admirably suited to undertake the task of saving the Conservatory from collapse, and maybe put it back on the road to growth and expansion.' I was completely taken aback at this frightening affirmation of faith in my abilities as an administrator, especially as I had never done any work of that nature. To say that I was flattered would be an understatement. I replied in terms similar to those I had used in Toronto – the orchestra, the years of engagements ahead, etc. He was ready for this, and asked me to go over to Toronto for two weeks, when I would be given the keys of the place and left alone to find out what I wished. This appealed to me as I had been very taken with what I had seen of the University while I was there.

As it happened, I could not go for four months owing to work in Europe, but in April of 1953, I arrived in Toronto and set about finding out things in detail. I had for some time been toying with the idea of one day, if ever I was free, taking a university job of some nature. When one had been 'on the road' for years – the airport, the concert hall, the hotel, year in and year out, the same pieces, about ten of them, which one is forced to play over and over again so that the hall will not be quite empty – no time to learn anything new properly; in fact no time to think about music! – one wonders what the future holds. But this is the life of the average touring musician, and most musicians have to tour because you cannot play in the same city over and over again for very long or your career will wither or die. When you consider a group like the Boyd Neel Orchestra, touring was its life-blood, as it is for similar groups today. I know there are such groups today who hardly tour at all, but spend most of their lives in a recording studio, seldom making contact with the public. These groups are nothing like the Boyd Neel Orchestra in its greatest days, when it had the same personnel for years at a time and was always playing 'live' to the public all over the world. Some of today's groups have perhaps fifty names on their roster of players, of which only about twenty are ever playing at any one time, and then never the same twenty. How can a real ensemble be created in this way? This sort of thing demonstrates how 'commercial' music has become.

But to get back to the invitation to Toronto. When I arrived, I was installed in the Park Plaza Hotel, whence I issued forth on my tours of inspection. The first thing that struck me as quite wrong was the fact that the Faculty of Music, the Royal Conservatory, the Opera School, and other music student activities were all housed in a building which was nothing like large enough for chamber music; there was no hall where an orchestra could play, and certainly no theatre where the Opera School could perform.

I met the principal of the Conservatory, Dr Ettore Mazzoleni, for a few minutes and then the director of the Faculty of Music, Dr Arnold Walter, who had a room on the second floor of the Conservatory. There was a library (so-called) with a few hundred books and scores, plus some old and terribly scratchy records. For some reason, Sir Ernest MacMillan, whom I had understood to have resigned, was still installed in an office on the ground floor and when I asked Johnson where a new dean would work, he indicated some room with his finger. I

watched the students at work and heard some fine talent. I was naturally very interested in the orchestra and was told that it hardly existed at
this time. Apparently, at the end of the war there had been a huge
inflow of discharged 'veterans' from the forces, and the orchestra had
suddenly become large and excellent. Alas, all these ex-service men
had now passed out of the school and the remnant was pathetic indeed.
I then asked how it was there were so few students of orchestral
instruments and found to my astonishment that ninety per cent of the
students learned only the piano! The piano appeared to be the national
instrument. I had never come across anything quite like it. If you were
said to be 'learning music,' it meant you were learning the piano. There
was no other music. This meant that the staff of the Royal Conservatory
consisted almost entirely of piano teachers. How this farcical situation
had arisen I had no idea. It appeared that if you were a teacher of *any*
instrument (or voice), you did not, as in most cities, put a plate on your
front door and wait for students. No, you *had* to teach at the Conservatory or not at all. This was held to be the perfect way of 'maintaining
standards': whereas it only had the effect of keeping many fine teachers
away from the city who might otherwise have come there. The teachers
who were there also taught Faculty students, and the performance side
of the Faculty of Music was confused in the extreme. There was, of
course, at that time no performance degree; in fact that only came into
being about fifteen years later. The bulk of the Faculty students were
doing the Music Education course which had recently been set up in
consultation with the Education Department of the Ontario Government. This was naturally the correct thing to start with, and its effect on
school music in the province could be noted even at that early time,
and I was astonished at the standard of many school orchestras which I
heard.

Except for the director, Dr Walter, the Faculty were housed in two
crumbling old houses next to the Conservatory building. Musicology
had been added and the Graduate School had begun to take shape; but
everybody suffered from one all-embracing handicap – lack of space. I
well remember thinking, during my inspection weeks, that if I ever did
take the job my first aim would be to get a new building and separate
the Faculty of the University of Toronto from the Conservatory. They
had, after all, little in common with one another. This may sound
strange, but the Royal Conservatory of Music and its thirteen branches
around the city dwelt chiefly with the average amateur or dilettante

type of student who was, more often than not, of very tender years. As a preparatory school for the Faculty, it was, of course, of great value.

While in Toronto, I met the president of the University, Sidney Smith, a bluff hail-fellow-well-met type with whom I got along very well. He acknowledged that he was tone-deaf, but knew very well the value of music as a discipline on any campus. I also met the entire board at a large luncheon at the Hunt Club. Subtle hints were constantly dropped in my ear and I was given the royal treatment everywhere. Finally, I decided to come for a trial period of two academic years – eight months of each year. The remaining four months I would continue my musical activities around the world as before.

On returning to England I told the orchestra that they would be having more guest conductors than usual during the next two years and that, if I didn't like the Toronto job, I would be coming back to them full time. There was, of course, a certain amount of consternation but, on the whole, they seemed to think it was quite a good idea. Anthony Collins had just returned from Hollywood after many years, and he agreed to take some of the concerts, as did Charles Groves and others who had worked with the orchestra from time to time. Charles Gregory was a tower of strength as manager, having had years of experience with the London Philharmonic Orchestra in the same capacity. Charles was Beecham's first horn, right from the start of the London Philharmonic Orchestra, and knew the orchestral business through and through.

I had the summer of 1953 to prepare for my transatlantic move, and I went over for the autumn semester in Toronto, but had arranged to return to England for November and December to get things finally cleared up and do many concerts which had been left outstanding. I finally set sail in the *Queen Mary* on December 29th with several members of my family and many boxes of *lares* and *penates* in the hold.

My first task was to try to create an atmosphere in which the staff and students could work happily. A long period of bitter internecine war had weakened the structure and brought the whole thing to the verge of bankruptcy. This last I discovered in the most alarming way. As soon as I arrived I had to have some money to get things for my new home, so I asked for an advance of salary. The business administrator took me to the bank and disappeared into the manager's office. I sat for nearly an hour outside. Finally he reappeared and beckoned me in. The manager was profoundly apologetic and said he had been explaining to my companion that it would be quite impossible to grant any more credit to the Conservatory as funds were not available until various debts had been settled, and a new set of collaterals arranged. I was horrified and kicked myself for not having looked into the finances in more detail. I was ready to pack and return to England, but first I went to the president and told him of the situation. All hell then broke loose. I kept out of it as much as I could, but was soon drawn into the fray. I said that unless I was given an advance of salary (dollars were impossible to get in the UK at that time) and an office to work in, I would go straight back to England. The president was astounded that I had not been given an office. I told him that I had been given a chair and a table out in the corridor which ran past MacMillan's old office. MacMillan had walked out of the building a few weeks previous to my arrival with the portrait of himself which hung in the hall under his arm. Johnson had immediately moved into his office, and was there when I arrived. Just what he was supposed to be doing there I never discovered, as he had no administrative position as board chairman. There he was, however, and he never even acknowledged my presence in the corridor as he went in and out! The Marx Brothers could not have done better.

This incredible situation was maintained for a few weeks until I informed the president of what was going on. He at once told Johnson to leave the building and not to show his face again; then gave orders for a complete renovation and refurnishing of the (my) office. It therefore took me some weeks even to install myself in the building of which I was supposed to be the head. During this time I never set eyes on either the principal of the Conservatory or the director of the Faculty of Music, so I called a meeting of the three of us when I, at last, had an office of my own. They both appeared and sat at the table with their backs to each other. By the end of the first hour the angle of incidence had decreased to 45° and, by the end of the meeting, we were all facing the table! Having gained their confidence, I suggested that the three of us should meet every Wednesday morning, a custom which we kept up for some ten years.

Having gained the grudging collaboration of my chief colleagues, I turned my attention to the staff, or rather they turned their attention to me! I had made a speech outlining what I would consider the ideal size of a music school such as we had, and suggested that five hundred students instead of eighty-five hundred would be a more viable number. All hell broke loose again, and I was summoned (yes, that's the word) to 'appear' before a meeting of the teachers and explain my speech. I shall never forget that afternoon – rows and rows of the fiercest-looking people I had ever seen faced me. I sat alone on a raised dais, rather like Joan of Arc at her trial. My cross-examiners were a leading violin professor of some international reputation, and a theory professor who, I believe, was a church organist. The attack was bitter and direct. What business had I to come here and tell them what I considered to be an adequate-sized school, and would I please make a public apology at once or things would be made very unpleasant for me. I refused to do anything of the kind and walked out. When I got back to my office, the president phoned to know if I was all right. I asked him why, and he said he had been attacked by a man in his office, who had threatened violence to both of us. From his description I recognized one of my cross-examiners. I told him about the meeting. The president was seething with rage, as he had just heard of the money crisis, and the affair of my office. We met for a drink at the York Club and, I must say, had the best laugh I had had since I came to Canada. That night I had a phone call at 2:00 a.m. from an anonymous teacher who used more obscene language than even I, brought up in the navy, had ever heard, and told me to go back to England as soon as possible. Years later, I recognized the voice with a shock and quite by chance. It belonged to one of the best-known piano teachers in the city! She kept up the attacks for some years afterwards.

Looking back, I can hardly believe that it had all happened (and there was much more which I have not told). If you witnessed such things in a play or film you would think how grossly exaggerated they were.

So the field of battle was marked out and the opposing forces drawn up in their various formations. My job, for the first few years, was to try and keep the peace long enough to get the place on an even financial keel so that we could progress towards new premises where everyone could do their work properly. As to the reorganization of the Conservatory, that would have to wait; and, of course, it never can happen until the one vital element is corrected – that is, that no teacher in the school is on salary. This has always been, and still is, the chief cause of all the troubles. Why is this? Because there are far too many teachers, and salaries for all would mean a gigantic budget of ridiculous proportions. All the teachers work on a commission basis which leads to needless acrimony arising from accusations of 'stealing' pupils. Why are there so many teachers? I don't think anybody quite knows, or has ever known. A music school of near to ten thousand students, as it was then, is, of course, a farce. A music school which has to balance its budget is an abomination in these enlightened days of education, but the Conservatory has never had any subsidy from anywhere except that which it has created for itself. This has been done by organizing a vast examination system which extends right across Canada, and even into the United States. This had developed into a huge business, the profits of which have saved the school from bankruptcy many times. The other lifeline has been a legacy. The Frederick Harris Music publishing company was left by its founder to the Conservatory many years ago. Since the Harris Company is the sole publisher of examination grade books, the whole thing is, as they say, 'tied up.'

By the end of my second year I had achieved what might be called an armed truce. People at least spoke to each other again, and so everyone was probably wondering by now what all the fuss had been about. Basically, it was the resistance of the old hard core of the Conservatory staff against any sort of change, and that meant the establishment of a real Faculty of Music in the University, which would be a full-time music school with a salaried staff and a manageable number of five hundred students. The Conservatory knew very well that it could never, in its present form, compete with such an organization. But why compete at all? Gradually it realized that its function was not a university one, but a pre-university one of great value, although it still pretended, even up to a few years ago, that it was the former, and used to hold 'Convocations' in the University Convocation Hall at which diplomas (its own) were presented, and caps and gowns were worn. It was all rather pathetic and pretentious, and I'm glad to note that all such nonsense was eventually dropped.

As my second year drew to a close, I went to see the president and told him my contract would be running out shortly. He asked me if I wanted to go on, and I said I had become intrigued with the place, and saw that the Faculty of Music could grow, if it were given a chance, into something quite formidable. I told him I had been working on all the influential people I could meet on the subject of a music building for the campus, without which we could never achieve much. I went to call on every member of the Board of Governors one by one, and put my case as strongly as I could. The response was quite wonderful, but it was to be another seven years before the first brick was laid. Anyway, I decided to give it all another two years' trial, and asked the president if I could have another contract or letter to that effect. He asked me why we should bother? 'Just stay here as long as you like. We love having you with us,' were his actual words, and for *seventeen* years I was just 'there.' The university could have fired me whenever it chose, and I could have walked out whenever I wished. Surely this must have been unique in university history? And what a wonderful arrangement of trust and friendship!

Gradually I found myself being drawn more and more into the Canadian scene. Soon after I took up the position of dean at the Royal Conservatory of Music in 1953, several of the local string players called to ask me if it would be possible to form in Toronto an ensemble like the Boyd Neel Orchestra in England. There was fine material available as far as players were concerned, and the city had had no such group for some years. There were many reasons for establishing such an orchestra: to absorb the finest talent graduating from the Royal Conservatory and other Canadian music schools; to bring to the smaller centres of Canada some of the music which might otherwise never be heard performed there; the establishment of a regular series of concerts on the campus, together with a talk to the students and faculty on the content of each program. Finally, although there are many full symphony orchestras in Canada, there have hitherto been no small orchestras of a permanent nature like the Hart House Orchestra – thirteen players – sometimes augmented to eighteen when performing in large cities. The enormous repertoire unearthed in recent years for this kind of orchestra and played by groups in other countries like the Boyd Neel Orchestra in England, the Stuttgart Chamber Orchestra, and the Virtuosi di Roma, has been almost completely neglected here. The need for presenting this great music of the past three centuries to audiences, both large and small, seemed all too apparent.

At about the same time, the president of the Women's Musical Club, which still gives Toronto one of its best concert series, asked me if I would give the club an orchestral concert next season with an ad hoc orchestra. I was pondering this offer when Columbia Artists Community Concerts phoned from New York and asked me if I had a Canadian ensemble that could tour the following season.

All these more or less simultaneous happenings were the sparks leading to the formation of a chamber orchestra which, as yet, had no name. This was a real challenge and we felt the orchestra should first have an 'official' name. Many were suggested and, while the discussion was under way, a group of students from the university approached me and asked whether I would consider giving a few concerts in the Great Hall at the University of Toronto's Hart House during the ensuing academic year. These were to be free and held on Sunday evenings. Here was the obvious name for the orchestra, and it would also carry on the tradition of the Hart House String Quartet, which had made an international reputation in the 1920s and 30s. The Massey family played a leading role in the development of this quartet.

The Hart House Orchestra made its debut in a concert for the Women's Musical Club on November 25, 1954. Columbia Artists sent up a representative, a tour for the following year was immediately booked, and the Sunday evening concerts were started at Hart House. It was an auspicious start and the Hart House concerts became one of the most popular series Toronto has ever had.

In 1958, the Canadian government sent the orchestra to the Brussels World Fair, with Glenn Gould as soloist, to play on Dominion Day. Concerts were also given in various Belgian and Dutch cities.

Tours of Canada were started under the auspices of the Canada Council. These tours covered, over a period of several years, pretty well the whole country from St John's to Vancouver, and from Windsor to Yellowknife and Uranium City. No other Canadian ensemble has covered so many thousand miles.

This was the pattern for about seven years – Hart House Sunday evenings (broadcast sometimes by the CBC or CFRB), two thirteen-week series on CKEY, and an annual tour of various regions of Canada. So popular did the Sunday night concerts become that a crisis arose which almost wrecked the series. The outside public began to attend in ever greater numbers until, on a famous Bach evening, the line-up stretched right across the campus. Unfortunately, many in the line-up were students who had bought series tickets and who never got into the concert at all. The next day, the president sent for me and said he thought the whole thing had got out of hand, and that we must bear in mind that the concerts were given by the students for the students. He suggested that we devise some means of keeping the public out.

It must be remembered that in those days, nothing whatever took place in Toronto on a Sunday night unless admission was free, and we knew we had been breaking the law when admission had to be charged to the public. We had got round the difficulty by selling tickets in advance so that no money was taken at the door. This worked for a while, but the Lord's Day Alliance raised a first-class rumpus at the fact that the minds of our students were being polluted by listening to Bach and Mozart on Sunday instead of sitting at home watching television. This developed into a famous landmark in Toronto history, because it led to the changing of the law in Ontario.

All this, of course, was the most fantastic publicity for the concerts, and the applications for tickets became a flood. We realized, however, that the original purpose of the concerts had been by now completely forgotten, and that they had become something that their originators had never intended. This state of affairs had also caused me intense embarrassment as a working musician, because I had always given my services for the concerts, regarding them as part of my job as Dean of Music, and part of my obligation to the students, when they were now, in fact, ordinary public concerts, which could just as well have been held at Massey Hall or the Eaton Auditorium.

Ridiculous situations began to arise. For instance, I can remember giving a Saturday night concert in Weston (a twenty-minute drive from Hart House) to a large public audience that had paid for admission and, of course, we all performed as professional musicians and received our usual fees. The next evening we played at Hart House to, for all I knew, some of the same people who had heard us the night before, and I received no fee at all. The concerts had led me into an anomalous position as far as my professional status was concerned. There was only one solution, and that was to return to the original idea of the concerts as private affairs for *bona fide* students who would be admitted free. So the concerts had to withdraw into their shell as private affairs, much to the fury of the public, which had been getting such a good bargain.

The concerts went on for some years until I retired as dean from the university. I was quite willing to continue (as a professional, of course!) but the powers-that-be decided to end what had been an exciting seventeen years of music-making. The repertoire we covered in that time was enormous; and towards the end, we were doing concert performances of Handel operas and sometimes Schubert and Vivaldi choral works with the Faculty Choir. The orchestra made only three records, not counting the CBC recordings of concerts given at Expo in

1967, when we played a whole week of Canadian music. We commissioned several Canadian works during the orchestra's existence, and others were dedicated to us.

The orchestra was invited to play at the Aldeburgh Festival by Benjamin Britten in 1966. We gave two concerts including *Les Illuminations* with Heather Harper. We also played in Brussels, Scandinavia, and London on our way home. The London *Daily Telegraph* headed its notice with:

COMPETITORS OUTSHONE BY CANADIAN STRINGS

It seems curious that the only London appearance by Canada's Hart House Chamber Orchestra in the course of its European tour should take place, not in one of the major concert halls, but in the Commonwealth Institute.

It takes considerable attraction to fill this capacious but rather unfriendly theatre and Boyd Neel, the orchestra's conductor, must have been disappointed that his players should draw so little attention in a city by no means over-endowed with top-class chamber groups.

The Hart House Orchestra is the Canadian successor of the old Boyd Neel Orchestra. Dr. Neel founded it when he went to Toronto in 1953 and he has built it into a unit that can fairly stand comparison with its famous predecessor.

From the point of view of performance, last night's concert was a complete success. All the works were for the strings and there is no doubt that in this department the orchestra is many a mile ahead of its English competitors.

The apparent ability of any of the sixteen players to take a prominent solo line was very noticeable. So, too, was the rich full-blooded tone which the orchestra achieved in tutti *passages with no looseness of ensemble and only the slightest tendency to deviate in intonation.*

15

Music at Stratford

In the last chapter I wrote about the formation and growth of the Hart
House Orchestra. In this chapter I will be writing about music at Stratford, which is not really connected with the Hart House Orchestra. The
idea of adding music to the season of plays at the Stratford Festival in
Ontario, some hundred miles west of Toronto, is not of recent origin.
During the first festival in 1953 a series of concerts was given in the
theatre tent. These concerts suffered somewhat from being the poor
relation of the plays. They had little publicity and were swamped by the
flood of glamour which, quite rightly, descended on the plays. The
following year, there was again a suggestion of having music during the
festival, but everything was left until much too late, and nothing happened. However, in these discussions the seeds of the 1955 Music
Festival were sown.

I had worked a great deal with Tyrone Guthrie at Sadler's Wells,
where he had directed that production of *La Bohème* I conducted many
times in the years following the war, and he asked me if I would take
on a season of eleven concerts in the old 'Casino' building later known
as the 'Third Stage.'

Fundamentally, the idea behind the program of music was one of
making the festival more of a 'resting point' than it had been hitherto.
As director, Tyrone Guthrie wanted to make Canadians more 'festival-
minded,' to persuade them to stay and browse around Stratford, absorb-
ing the atmosphere, instead of rushing down to see a play and then

rushing home again immediately afterwards. There would always, of course, be the 'special excursion' by train or bus, for those whose work made it impossible for them to see the plays in any other way, but a festival demands a more specialized type of audience if it is to fulfil itself completely. One of its major delights should be the discussion, at some neighbouring café, of the evening's performance, with a simultaneous speculation on the delights in store on subsequent evenings. This was impossible with the 'there and back' method of going to the Stratford Festival.

When it had been agreed to go in for music in a big way, the first thing to decide was what that way was to be. What kind of music? Where was it to be performed? When were the concerts to be held? How long were they to be? Should the artists be entirely Canadian? Many of these questions solved themselves automatically as plans developed, but in the initial stages there were endless discussions. Eventually it was decided to build the programs around a series of concerts for small orchestra. It was thought that this would provide sufficient variety, while remaining within the limited budget. The first task, then, was to find a small orchestra capable of dealing with so large a program in so short a time. We felt that only an organized body, trained as an ensemble and with some sort of established repertoire, would meet the case. There was no such group available. The solution, therefore, was to form a group and train it throughout the year, giving as many concerts as possible with it during that time. Having had experience in organizing such bodies, I was asked to attempt it. Little did I know what I was letting myself in for.

By this time it was October 1954; we had nine months to bring our group to the required pitch. This should have been easily possible in normal circumstances, but we soon found formidable obstacles appearing in places we had never expected. It is sufficient here to say that it *was* formed despite obstacles both expected and unforeseen, which were surmounted only by the selfless devotion of a few people who were keen enough to want it.

Louis Applebaum was appointed director of music; he had looked after the incidental music for the plays since the festival began in 1953 and it was chiefly his enthusiasm that brought the idea of a music festival to a definite shape. He started work with no office and no staff.

The Festival Concert Hall turned out to be far better acoustically than we had dared to hope. The platform in the round was splendidly effective for the production of Stravinsky's *L'Histoire du Soldat*, but not so effective for seating an orchestra.

The next decision concerned the type of program. A festival scheme can take two forms. There is, first, the festival which celebrates a certain event or composer. You can have a festival to mark, say, the bicentenary of a certain composer. A festival of the latter type is usually held in a place which has been associated with the composer in question, such as Mozart and Salzburg. In the other form of festival, any type or period of music is performed without any special theme or central idea running through it; and we decided that we would build our programs on names. Anyone who has had experience of this kind of thing will tell you what a complex jigsaw puzzle this can be. You decide you will have a violin concerto which will fit very well with certain other pieces in the program. You think Signor X would be just the person to play this. Signor X would be delighted, but can only arrive one hour after the concert has finished, as he will have to fly from Los Angeles where he is playing the night before. You move the violin concerto to the following night to find that, as that concert will be broadcast, you cannot fit it into the available time. You try again. Could Signor X come two weeks later and arrive a day early for rehearsal? Yes, he could. All seems well until it is discovered that the orchestral material for the concerto is not available at the later date, as it is on hire elsewhere. And so it goes on. Telegrams, phone calls, midnight conferences, early-morning planes to New York, and so on. All this would tax a highly trained staff in a fully equipped office. Lou Applebaum dealt with all of this virtually single-handed in a most efficient way. Another complicating factor was that many of the concerts were to be broadcast live. Without the splendid co-operation of the CBC it is doubtful whether there could have been a music festival at all.

The final set of programs formed an interesting group. There was much music which was quite unfamiliar to Canadian audiences and there were many performers of international reputation who took part. One of the things which took as much discussion as anything was *when* to have the concerts. Would the music draw off the play-going public and vice versa? Should the concerts be morning, afternoon, early evening, or late evening? The answer to the first question was established before the festival had even finished: the concurrence of plays and music had *no* effect on the audience attendance at either house.

The opening concert was in the nature of a tribute to Saint Cecilia.

Vaughan Williams visits the Royal Conservatory of Music, Toronto, in 1954.

OPPOSITE

top With Claude Bissell, President of the University of Toronto
(Ken Bell)

bottom Order of Canada, investiture, December 22nd 1972
(John Evans Photography Limited, Ottawa)

The Festival Chorus, which made its debut during the season under its talented conductor, Elmer Iseler, sang Purcell's *Ode to Saint Cecilia* and Benjamin Britten's *Hymn* to the same saint. The Festival commissioned Healey Willan, dean of Canadian composers, to write a short choral work called *Song of Welcome*, with words by Nathaniel Benson, to be performed on the opening night. The orchestra played Honegger's *Symphony No. 2*.

In a review of July 11, 1955 the *New York Times* described the scene of the first concert at Stratford:

The most ambitious professional summer music festival that has yet been undertaken in Canada opened here last night. It is a case of one festival begetting another, for the new project is an extension of the Stratford Shakespearean Drama Festival, which is in its third year.

It is also a case of drama helping music, for it was because of the success of the first two play festivals that the Stratford Shakespearean Festival Foundation of Canada was able to vote $50,000 toward the establishment of a sister art in this friendly and now festival-conscious town of 19,000.

To house the music festival the foundation has taken over the fifty-year-old wooden building that from the outside suggests a cross between a big barn and a Quonset hut. The building which was originally a hockey arena and then, in sequence, a dance hall and a badminton court, is now, in its new guise as a concert hall, painted a pale green. The smell of paint still lingered last night as the first concert began.

Preparations had been hectic right up to the last moment. Louis Applebaum, director of the music festival, said he thought it would be 'touch and go' as to whether everything would be in readiness. But by 8:30 everything was in order, including the great block of ice put in buckets at the back in the hope of bringing down the temperature.

Since almost 1,000 persons crowded into the hall and the night was very hot, the ice could not do much to offset the heat. But the temperature was the only thing about the concert that was not first-class.

In arranging the music festival, Tom Patterson, the over-all planning director, and his associates have taken the same two lines that they took with the drama festival. That is, they have relied on Canadians to provide most of the performers and they had boldly gone to persons with star names to provide leadership and box office appeal.

Boyd Neel, who became noted as founder-director of the Boyd Neel

Orchestra in England, was chosen to play somewhat the same role in the music festival that Tyrone Guthrie played in the drama festival. Since last fall Mr. Neel has developed the Hart House Orchestra into as good a chamber orchestra as any on this continent.

Music of every period was represented in that first year and we played as much Canadian music as would fit into our scheme. Besides the Willan choral work, especially written for the opening concert, other Canadian works which caught the fancy of the audience were the *Two Etudes* by Godfrey Ridout, the *Divertimento* by Oskar Morawetz, which received its first performance anywhere, the *Suite for Harp and Strings* by Harry Somers, and John Weinzweig's *Interlude in the Life of an Artist*. The brilliant harp playing of Marie Iosch in the Somers *Suite* was one of the highlights of the concert. As soon as she touched the harp a string broke. The consequent delay and fuss of repair would have quite unnerved most artists, but she remained calm through it all and went on to an ovation at the close.

Other Canadian artists who had outstanding successes were Lois Marshall in Bach's *Jauchzet Gott in allen Ländern*; Glenn Gould in Beethoven's *Second Piano Concerto* and the *Goldberg Variations* of Bach. The Vivaldi concerto turned out to be one of the outstanding events and, artistically, was certainly one of the most satisfactory. Three eminent Canadian violinists joined forces in his *Concerto for Three Violins*, and finished the concert (with Mr Alexander Schneider) by giving a superb performance of the newly revived *Concerto for Four Violins in B Flat*. This masterpiece is, in my opinion, finer than the well-known work in B minor, which was the only composition of its kind played to any extent during these and previous years. The fact that Bach had admired it sufficiently to reset it for four pianos had always been its chief claim to fame. The B flat work is a far greater and more mature composition, and I hope it will retain its place in the repertoire. The three violinists were Albert Pratz, Noel Brunet, and Eugene Kash. The singers in Handel's *Acis and Galatea* were Elizabeth Benson Guy and Jon Vickers.

The performances of Stravinsky's *L'Histoire du Soldat* were outstanding. Brilliantly played by a small group under the Canadian conductor Paul Scherman, and produced in a most interesting and original way by Douglas Campbell, the famous piece made a profound impression as performed on the Concert Hall stage. This event was especially important from the fact that the superb and unique French mime, Marcel Marceau, took the part of the Devil. William Needles made an outstanding narrator with a glorious resonant delivery. The first part of the evening was taken up with Marceau's own solo recital, which had made him world-famous. I wondered whether the platform in the round would worry him at all, as I had always seen him hitherto on a proscenium stage, but he was able to adapt himself to the conditions without any difficulty.

A work which caused a great deal of interest was the *Concerto for Two Violins* by Mozart, which Isaac Stern and Alexander Schneider played on July 13th. This splendid piece had not been heard in Canada before. Works which had, formerly, been unfamiliar, but which the audience took to its heart, were the *Symphonie Spirituelle* of Hamerik, the *Fugal Concerto* of Holst (with two magnificent soloists in Perry Bauman and Gordon Day), the *Triple Concerto* of Vincent d'Indy, the *Symphony for Strings* by Jean Françaix, and Arthur Benjamin's *Ballade for String Orchestra*.

Among visiting singers were Aksel Schiøtz and Elisabeth Schwarzkopf, both of whom gave memorable *lieder* recitals. Miss Schwarzkopf also sang Mozart's *Exsultate Jubilate* and a Bach cantata with the orchestra. The latter performance, with Perry Bauman and Rowland Pack playing the *obbligati* superbly, was a most memorable one.

At the concert of July 27th the Festival Choir showed what a first-class ensemble it had become under Elmer Iseler, giving a fine display of exquisite music movingly sung. The Choir was joined at this concert by Suzanne Bloch, daughter of the well-known composer, who played on various old instruments and gave a commentary on the music performed.

At the final concert it was decided to combine all the forces once more, and Handel's *Acis and Galatea* was given in the original version without the usual Mozartian trimmings. Lois Marshall and Jon Vickers gave a fine account of the lovely songs and the Choir sang the cheerful choruses with obvious relish. *Acis and Galatea*, like *Hamlet*, is 'full of quotations' and should have more frequent performances than it gets.

The Royal Conservatory of Music in Toronto took advantage of the presence of Elisabeth Schwarzkopf and extended its Summer School activities to Stratford, where a master class in *lieder* was held. This proved to be an unqualified success, about thirty students availing themselves of the wonderful opportunity. The classes were held in the

Concert Hall, and went on far beyond the official hours, so enthusiastic were both teacher and pupils. Miss Schwarzkopf gave unstintingly of her energy and sang a great deal during the classes, which were something the students could never forget. The superb pianist Paul Ulanowsky, who accompanied Miss Schwarzkopf in her recitals, gave a course in the art of accompaniment for the Royal Conservatory students, which proved to be another outstanding event.

There is no doubt that this school program filled a need, and a natural expansion of the idea will, I hope, follow each year. There is a great advantage in holding a school under these conditions. Students, as well as being taught by the world's finest artists, can take the opportunity of watching them work at first hand. Eventually student bodies can be incorporated into performances of large-scale works, as is done in the drama side at Stratford. Classes in all branches of musical study can eventually be held in closest co-operation with such a festival, to everyone's benefit.

Stratford is capable of anything, and there is no reason why, in the future, it should not become as famous as any of the great European festivals.

16

A Faculty of Music

When I finally got things going in Toronto, it took me seven years to get permission to build a new music building, but, finally, after much lobbying in the right quarters, the exciting news came through that we could go ahead.

The planning of the new building took up a great deal of my time for many months, but I had a splendid committee to work with. The architects were wonderfully co-operative and I am afraid we gave them a pretty rough time. It is extraordinary how few people have any idea of what an opera theatre is like. When we got to the details of the orchestra pit, the architects were astounded at the size of the area we asked for. Such a thing was beyond anything they had ever imagined in their wildest dreams. Finally we had to suggest that they go down to Massey Hall and look at the area required for a symphony orchestra on the platform. We explained that many operas require an orchestra the size of a full symphony playing in the pit. I think this gave them the greatest shock of all, but I must say they took it very well.

We invited a cellist to come into the room, followed by a trombone player, and they were both asked to demonstrate how they took up the space of three players owing to movements of bow and slide. And so it went on week after week. The building had to be one hundred percent sound-proof where necessary, and it was, but few people will ever know the trials and torments of this alone.

I knew that my friend and colleague Wilfrid Bain, dean of the great Indiana school at Bloomington, was at the same time building a tower of practice rooms, so I went down to see him and do a little espionage. The problem which baffled our experts was the conduction of sound through the air conditioning system. If the air went through, so did the sound, and there appeared to be no solution. I waited until Bain asked me if I would like to see how the new building was coming along, and then told him of our difficulties. He said they, too, had almost given up in despair, but he thought they had solved it and I was shown what became the famous hexagonal columns which were finally put into all the air registers. The air passed through a 'grove of trees' so to speak, but the sound cannoned itself out against the columns. Simple and obvious, I can hear you saying, but it has been the same with all great inventions.

Construction of the music building at the Toronto university proceeded, much of it pioneer work, as there were not all that many new music buildings connected with universities at that time. Those which did exist members of the committee visited over the months – each of us chose an area of North America and went out to return with boxes filled with pictures, plans, and models. I spent one whole summer vacation visiting many concert halls and opera theatres in Europe. Gradually, this mass of data was sifted and discussed, and the architects absorbed some of our requests which must have appeared, at the time, preposterous.

The building was opened in 1961 and very quickly became world-famous. I spent many hours showing it to people from as far away as Japan, India, and New Zealand. Georg Solti came one day and spent the whole day looking it over. He was especially interested as he was at that time working in England and suffering from the dismal facilities with which the Opera Centre was provided in London. I heard later that he had given people a glowing account of our opera school.

One unexpected visitor was Rostropovich, who was playing the Dvořák *Concerto* with the Toronto Symphony. Somebody phoned my office in the morning of the concert and said that Rostropovich had expressed a wish to see the music building, about which he had heard so much. I said I would be delighted to show him around. About half an hour later another phone call, this time from the cellist himself, asking if he could come and rehearse the Dvořák *Concerto* with our student orchestra. I thought this would be a wonderful lesson for our students, so all classes were cancelled and the stage set up for the rehearsal. The great man arrived, straightway sat down, and off we went. He played the whole work through without stopping and seemed to be enjoying himself enormously, singing along with the music much of the time. The students were wonderful and played better than I had ever heard them. At the end everybody applauded each other, and by that time the word had gone around and the theatre was nearly full, having been quite empty when we began. I naturally expected Rostropovich would leave us and rest before the concert, but to my amazement, he said: 'Now we play it again!' And, sure enough, he played the whole thing, which lasts a good forty minutes, for the second time.

By the end of the repeat performance the theatre was jam-packed with hundreds standing at the back and a line-up waiting at the doors. The news had spread all over the campus, and the work of the university came to a standstill. After embracing everyone on the platform, Rostropovich said: 'Now I take all the cellos down to the rehearsal room,' and down they went to receive a lesson none of them will ever forget. He must have barely had time to change and get to the hall to play the concerto once more with the Symphony at the evening concert. What astounding energy the man had! This kind of incident was the sort of thing which the new music building had made possible. We could certainly never have done it in our old one.

Everyone was astonished at the effectiveness of the sound-proofing in the new music building. You can have a full operatic performance playing in the theatre, two full orchestral or band rehearsals going on underneath the auditorium, a concert in the concert hall, and all the teaching and practising – all of these activities going on simultaneously, and yet, anyone entering the building would think it practically deserted.

The library, with its splendid daylight, all of it indirect, and its excellent listening rooms, proved a great success; when I look at it now, I often think of the tiny room at College Street with its few books and scratchy records. And yet, all that was only twenty years before!

I think one of the most exciting moments of my life was the day I sat, like Ludwig of Bavaria at Bayreuth, alone in the opera theatre, and heard the first sounds of Britten's *Albert Herring* arising from the pit at rehearsal. It was a tense moment, because acoustics are so unpredictable, and I wondered – yes or no? – and it was yes! Of course, some minor adjustments had to be made to the building later, but, on the whole, the acoustics are fine and Toronto has a real opera house, in which the students can learn their craft. The city, alas, still awaits an opera theatre in which the public can hear an opera properly.

17

Taking My Time

During my last years at the university I began to realize that, on retirement, so small would be my pension that any ideas I might have had of taking things a little easier had better be forgotten about. Not that I had ever contemplated 'retiring' in the accepted sense of the word. I could not imagine anything more boring and soul-destroying. Besides, I felt exactly the same at sixty-five as I had felt at the age of twenty-five. The problem was whether to start conducting again, or possibly take some job connected with music or medicine. There was also, of course, always the possibility of taking up something entirely new, but, at sixty-five, this might have been too great a task. It transpired that, when the time came, the decision was more or less made for me, because, as the word began to get around that I was 'free' again, I found that I had more work than I could comfortably cope with.

I was officially on sabbatical leave for my last year, and I had for a long while resolved that, before settling down to anything, I would visit various countries where I had never been before and in which I had always been very interested. I decided, therefore, that I would devote three months to this before thinking about a job of any kind. I had to be quite firm with myself and refused many offers which materialized. I decided to take my time, something which I had never been able to do before, and absorb the atmosphere of the places I visited, which had hitherto been well-nigh impossible on my tours with the orchestra. The problem was finding, preferably, a ship which was visiting all the places

I wished to see. As luck would have it, there was a Norwegian ship which fitted my bill admirably, so, in January 1971, I boarded her at Los Angeles and, after calling at Hawaii, which brought back memories of 1947 and Dan O'Connor, we arrived in Yokohama. I went ashore and took a trip which ended at Kobe, where I picked up the ship again. Tokyo was covered in a thicker cloud of smog than Los Angeles, but the weather out in the country was glorious; clear blue skies and warm sun, although, it being February, I had been expecting severe cold. I thought Tokyo was the most hideous city I had ever seen. Apart from those in the neighbourhood of the Royal Palace, I could not find a building worth looking at. Unfortunately I was unable to hear any orchestra in the flesh, but I heard and saw one on TV which I thought was pretty good. The TV seemed far clearer than ours in Canada and the colour was far, far better. The cheapness of TV sets and hi-fi equipment generally was astonishing. Some people off the boat bought crate-loads of electronic equipment. I met various concert agents, all of whom were very interested in my latest recording, and a return visit in a conducting capacity was suggested.

I then visited the Hakone region and, the weather being so good, the views of Mount Fuji were fantastic. This part of the country I thought very lovely – a mixture of the Scottish Highlands and the Italian lakes. One night it snowed hard for a few hours. When I woke, the sky was clear and the sun just rising over the mountains. I shall never forget the effect of this light on the fresh snow which hung thick on every tree – a scene of the greatest beauty. I had a Japanese bath in the hotel, a huge room with a small swimming pool in the centre, all to myself. It was such fun that I spent hours in it. The hot water gushed out of the hillside (the place was a kind of spa) into a tank, the bottom of which was made of glass and formed the roof of the bathroom. This water was far too hot, in its natural state, to bathe in, but by the time it had been led from the tank down into the bath below, it was sufficiently cooled. One lay in the pool and watched the boiling cauldron above through the glass ceiling. When I returned to the bedroom, a muscular Japanese woman appeared and gave me a massage which nearly dislocated every joint in my body. She ended up by making me lie face downwards, and then proceeded to walk up and down my spine!

The trouble with travelling in Japan, if you are an average-sized Westerner, is that all seats on public vehicles are far too short and narrow, with the consequence that many journeys are fearfully uncomfortable. The average Japanese man or woman is so much smaller than the large-boned and, alas, frequently corpulent traveller from the West, and I found the absence of leg room in buses very trying. I was horrified at the rush-hour crowds in the subways and astonished at the professional 'pushers' on the platform, whose business it is to cram the crowds into the subway cars by manoeuvres never yet conceived by any rugby forward. I don't know how much they are paid but, judging from their muscular condition, they certainly can afford plenty of body-building protein.

I was lucky to visit the famous Kikko shrine on the day of the annual bean-throwing ceremony. Priests come out on the balconies after the ceremonies within, and are joined by well-known actors (why, I never discovered, but apparently simply custom). An enormous crowd gathers below and, at a given signal, the priests and actors proceed to pelt the crowd with fruit and vegetables, mostly beans. The ensuing scramble among the crowd is something to behold. I saw tiny children running off with their arms full of oranges. One Western lady sightseer next to me was hit bang in the face by a very ripe orange, which burst with dire results! Apparently this extraordinary business is of great antiquity. I was privileged to have seen it.

I had a ride on the famous bullet train and one would never have known that it was going at 130 m.p.h. until it passed another train going the other way. Then, there was something like an explosion which was over in seconds! For some reason the seats in the bullet train are much larger than the average, maybe because it was originally devised to carry the international crowds from Tokyo to the Expo 70 site at Osaka. From what I saw of the site, I didn't feel it could have been anything like as impressive as our Montreal counterpart in 1967.

I found Kyoto more interesting than Tokyo, but even there everything seemed to be very Westernized, and one never had the feeling that one was very far away from New York or Toronto. Certainly in the country towns the environment had a very different atmosphere, and one sensed the 'real' Japan.

In Taiwan I felt the same, and I could not get used to enormous posters advertising Western movies which greeted one's eyes on all sides. One of the things about Taiwan which astonished me was the enormous number of shops selling English books and Western recordings at a fantastically low price; I bought the latest edition of *Gray's Anatomy*, which I had been wanting for a long time, and paid $3.00

(US) for it. (Its price in England was seven pounds, ten shillings.) When I opened it, I found out what the catch was; there were no colour pictures, and the text had obviously been photographed in a very crude way from the original. The colour illustrations had come out as a smudge of black. The text was, however, complete, and so worth at least the $3.00. I never discovered who bought all the books and records as the shops appeared to be empty most of the time. The records were probably bad reproductions like the books; I never got the chance to try them out.

In Taiwan it is, above all else, the National Museum one goes to see. The building was quite recent, and was not nearly large enough to house the whole of the fabulous collection which, incidentally, the natives quite openly admitted was stolen! About ten per cent of the whole is on show at any one time, and the rest is stored in caves bored into the hill behind the building. The exhibits are rotated constantly so that, if one lived there, one could probably see it all in a couple of years. No one could possibly estimate its value as most of the treasures are priceless. Its future lies locked with the destiny of Taiwan, and who can guess what that is? One thing that struck me very forcibly in all these Far Eastern countries was the intense pride that the natives had in their own homeland. The guides, the shopkeepers, and the men in the street with whom it was possible to communicate were, one and all, filled with a fierce patriotism. Coming from the West with its lukewarm national feelings, this was a great surprise to me.

When the ship came down the coast of Vietnam there was no sign whatsoever of the war which was then raging a few miles away. We never sighted a warship or a plane in all those hundreds of miles. I was bitterly disappointed that we were not allowed into Cambodia, as I had planned to visit Angkor Wat, while the ship was in Hong Kong. It was my first visit to the Crown Colony, but so much had I read, seen, and heard about it all my life that I felt I already knew it well. But I was not prepared for the forest of skyscrapers which covers the hills from sea-level to their summits. Some of these gleaming white buildings look very precariously perched up on the higher peaks and the overall effect is stupendous. The harbour buzzes with activity. There are so many ferries that they have to line up to get into the dock to discharge their loads. It has rather the feel of Sydney, with a touch of Naples thrown in. I took a car ride through the 'Territories' and was amazed at the vast blocks of apartments the government had built for the Chinese refugees. We drove to the border and saw the huge pipes which come in from China and supply Hong Kong with its fresh water – at a price! The Chinese hold the Colony completely at their mercy should they ever decide to move in, but Hong Kong is valuable to them in many ways and they know it.

Our next port was Bangkok, and here again I found a great deal of Westernization. One was appalled by enormous livid posters, the largest I had ever seen anywhere, at every intersection and traffic circle. At one of these circles there were the remains of the old walled city, which would be still visible today were they not almost completely obscured by the colossal billboards advertising movies. This is strange, because once more I found the natives had a passionate pride in their country, very evident among the ordinary people. The Thais have, of course, a lot to be proud of. They are the only people in this part of the world who have never fallen under the domination of another power. It is all the sadder now to see these signs of encroaching Western influences. Bangkok is quite a horrible city except for one thing – the Royal Palace: this astonishing Oriental Versailles contains within its walls the whole history and atmosphere of the Thai people. It is impossible to describe this celestial Disneyland. It is a place to revisit again and again. I am told that the loss of nearly all the canals, or *klongs* as they are called, had destroyed the atmosphere of this city. Most of them have been filled in to make highways, and one can only imagine what they must have been like. Although the Vietnam war was so near to them, especially since Cambodia and Laos became involved, the Thais appeared not in the least worried or apprehensive.

I saw a very beautiful performance by what corresponds to our National Ballet. This is the government-supported company of dancers which performs in the National Theatre in Bangkok. The theatre is a fine, fairly new building, in design exactly like a Western theatre, but the dancing, of course, is entirely in the Thai national style. The costumes were joyous beyond belief. Not even Bakst in his greatest Diaghilev days ever surpassed them. Before the performance, there was an introduction in the form of a lecture on the national dance given in English with examples danced by members of the company. This was a great help for the foreigners present. Without this, I should have missed most of the complex subtleties of the performances. They told us that the dancers have to commence their training almost in infancy in order to get that amazing looseness of the joints that characterizes this dancing. The hyperextension of the fingers is one of its characteristics, and this is used by all the dancers, male and female. The final ballet, based on a national epic, had choreography of the greatest complexity. In a great dance of the whole company, depicting a battle, there was so much happening on the stage that it was impossible to concentrate on any one group of dancers. The excitement generated by this produced an ovation such as one seldom hears in the West. I cannot think why the big impresarios do not bring this company to the Western centres.

Visiting all these countries in such quick succession gave me an impression of being at some gigantic Expo, and there was a certain unreality about it all, even though I was travelling by sea, with some time to think a little in between stops. What it must be like for the tourist who goes by air I can vaguely imagine from my experiences in the old Boyd Neel Orchestra tours, but then, of course, we were on a 'working tour,' which was not quite the same thing.

Visiting Singapore so soon after Bangkok made me realize how the hundreds of years of Siamese independence preserved Bangkok's individuality. Although the Western influence there is now, alas, beginning to show, with Singapore it had obviously prevailed for a long, long while. One would be hard put not to believe one was in Surbiton or Weybridge when driving through the best residential suburbs. Splendid houses, standing in beautiful gardens full of flowers, can be seen for mile after mile. Being practically on the equator, it has no seasons – just one eternal summer, during which all you can say is that at times it rains more than at others. I was very impressed by Singapore. The construction seen on every side and the rows of luxury hotels which have recently gone up are an indication of the progressive spurt shown by this young and independent state.

We next visited the lovely island of Penang, which bears much resemblance to Ceylon, although the latter has nothing to compare with the wonderful beaches all round the Malaysian island. Ceylon, however, has the more spectacular inland scenery, probably some of the loveliest in the world. I went up to Kandy from Colombo by train – a wonderful journey through glorious scenery. The Tooth Temple was disappointing, I felt, but the trip was worth it for the views from the train. Colombo I remembered from 1947, when our ship had called in there on the way back from Australia.

Our next stop was Bombay and, as the ship was to stay in Indian waters for ten days, I took a train tour to some of the famous cities of this fascinating country. There were enough people to fill one sleeper car, and we had a dining car hitched on, in which we had all our meals. Each night we were shunted into a siding and taken the next day to see the sights of whatever city we were in. This was a most comfortable way to travel and saved endless packing and unpacking. We visited all the famous places, the Taj Mahal and the fort at Agra; a dawn cruise in a tiny rowboat at Benares where we passed along the ghats in complete silence apart from the very quiet paddling of our crew of two. This was extraordinary, the silence, the glassy calm of the river, the ghost-like movements of white-shrouded figures on the banks looking for all the world like moths seeking a resting place, and then the climax of the burning-ghats with the families standing in small groups, absolutely still. The whole thing was utterly unreal and an aesthetic experience of the greatest power, which no theatre or film could ever approach.

We also visited many ghost cities, built by powerful rulers in the fourteenth and fifteenth centuries, and now silent 'ruined choirs' of ancient stone. India fascinated me more than any country I ever visited and I felt I would like to go back and live there for a while some time in the future.

The train returned to Bombay by another route, and we picked up the ship again for an idyllic three days' voyage to the Seychelles Islands. A completely calm sea all the way and the temperature to match. I was in time to see the beautiful Seychelles before they became just another tourist centre. We anchored some way out and went in by motor boat, there being no deep-water harbour. Great activity was going on as parties arrived to build the Sheraton, Hilton, Holiday Inn, etc., which were to make these lovely islands rivals to Hawaii in the tourist business. The jet strip was in the process of construction and I have heard recently that the arrival of the Seychelles into the twentieth century is now an accomplished fact. Where else is left?

Our next call was Mombasa and I left the ship there and arranged to pick her up again in Cape Town six weeks later, which gave me time to see quite a bit of Africa. I started from Nairobi and was astonished at the lovely and prosperous-looking city it had become. If you chat with the local people and ask them when this resurgence came about, they will tell you that it dates from 'When the British moved out!'

I was determined to see as much of the animals as I could while they were still on view because I was sure that, in a little while, it would be much more difficult in the 'new Africa' which is in the process of being created. And, judging from an experience I had, I felt I was not far from the truth in thinking along those lines.

I left Nairobi for Kampala, where I went to get a safari to the source of the Nile in the region of the Murchison Falls. I arrived there just at the time of Amin's coup and found the place very disturbed. I had an introduction to the superintendent of the Makerere Hospital and I found him on the point of going back to England and retirement. He asked me to dinner at his home and during the evening we heard shots at the bottom of the garden. When I expressed surprise and concern he told me that was a common occurrence just then, and that I had come to Uganda at a very bad time and warned me to be 'careful.' I wasn't quite sure what this meant, but anyhow I went to a government tourist office and arranged for a safari of six days.

The driver was to pick me up in the morning. At dawn, a Volkswagen six-seater bus appeared, with two American couples and the driver. We started off up a very fine four-lane motorway and drove for about two hundred miles, then turned off into the bush on to a very narrow road with an appalling surface. After about an hour of this we turned off again on to what was barely a track, a lot of which consisted of loose boulders. Every now and then we came across clearings in the jungle where bales of raw cotton were stacked, having obviously just been picked. Groups of natives stood around these, evidently waiting for some transport to come and remove them. After passing several of these clearings, one of the American women asked the driver to stop at the next one so that she might take a photo. The next clearing had the cotton bales, but not a sign of any pickers. No sooner had we stopped when a horde of about thirty natives rushed out from behind the bales and started attacking the bus, led by a dreadful-looking hooligan with a large stick. I managed to get my window closed and the door locked just in time, but the stupid driver next to me just gaped and made no attempt to close his door. Hands came through the windows and tore the jewellery off the two women; cameras also disappeared. I shouted at the driver to start up and go as quickly as possible, but he seemed paralysed with fear. I remember thinking at the time that he might have been an accomplice and the whole thing a plant, but later I revised my opinion. The stupid man could have got away if he had acted at once, but he left it too late and the leaders of the gang seized him by the legs and started pulling him out. I was in the front next to him, and hung on to his arms, and then there ensued a tug-of-war with the driver as the rope. Finding that they couldn't get him out that way, the leader of the gang leant into the bus and smashed his fist into the driver's face, knocking him out cold. The two women in the back of the bus were by now on the floor trying to keep out of the way of the grasping hands. I suddenly had an idea, while hanging on to the driver with one hand – I put the bus into gear with the other and turned the ignition switch. The bus reared up and for a split second the gang fell back, and I managed to accelerate and just got out of their reach. Then a fantastic chase took place with me steering with one hand and, with the other, holding the unconscious driver. One of the men in the back finally pulled the driver right in and got the door shut, and we drove on with the mob hanging on as well as they could. I knew if we could keep it up for a minute or two they couldn't last out; so it transpired.

Here we were on a track strewn with large stones with an unconscious man, bleeding profusely, deep in the jungle, without any idea where we were. We knew we were going in the right direction, or hoped we were, so we just kept on. In about an hour we came out on a proper road, and, in another hour, came to the camp we had originally been making for. The driver had by now come round and, apart from a gap in his upper teeth, was none the worse for his ordeal.

The camp dispensed first aid to us all, and police were summoned from a nearby settlement. The next day, the driver and two policemen returned to the scene of the fracas and arrested the ringleader, who turned out to have been discharged from prison that very morning of the attack, and was an Obote supporter (Obote was the leader whom Amin had supplanted), and the police said that anyone snooping round and taking photographs would have been under suspicion in that district. Also our driver apparently belonged to an enemy tribe and we, of course, were the wrong colour. A horrible experience indeed, but we stayed out of trouble for the rest of the scheduled time and had a fantastic trip on the Upper Nile in a small boat, getting good close-up photographs of many varieties of animal.

On returning to Kampala we found the city in turmoil and left the following day. I saw my doctor friend before I left and he told me that our experience was quite common in those parts at that time, and he said he hoped we realized how lucky we had been, because the usual story was that the driver got pulled out, the passengers were stripped of everything they wore, and were then driven into the bush and left as a meal for the lions! Apparently this happened all the time, but worse things were to come later.

Having got back to Kenya, I was most anxious to go to Tree Tops or one of the other game reserves. Tree Tops was the easiest to get to from Nairobi, so I made a reservation at once. The plan is that you spend a night at the hotel in Nyeri, where you might be in the heart of the English countryside, and in the afternoon are driven in a bus along country lanes, which might easily have been in Devon or Cornwall. You arrive at a clearing and the rest of the journey has to be on foot with a 'white hunter,' carrying a gun, at each end of the walking party. The Tree Tops Hotel has to be climbed up to on rope ladders which are lowered from above. In front is the large water-hole with several large salt licks placed around it. The first entertainment is a 'tea party' on the roof to which hundreds of baboons arrive as guests. You are warned not to leave loose money or jewellery in your pockets and to hold on to your camera. The baboons sit with you and chatter among themselves. The babies eat as much of the tea as they can get hold of. The baboons, of course, know the exact time of the daily tea party and are never late. They are very entertaining.

The 'hotel' consists of planks set across branches in the trees and there are small cubicles with a bed in each. As dusk falls everyone goes out and sits on benches overlooking the water-hole, which is illuminated with a weird orange light. You are asked not to talk or make any sound and to wear rubber soles. The silence is like nothing one has experienced before. After a while, rustling is heard in the trees and some cracking of twigs. A proud deer comes out of the trees and surveys the hole. He goes back and returns with another deer and three little ones. While his family are drinking, he stands guard, sniffing the air and looking around all the time. The family having finished, they move up to the trees and keep watch while father has his drink, after which the whole family go back into the trees in single file. It was one of the most moving sights I have ever seen. The silence persisted all the time, and every movement the animals made was beautiful and gentle. The dignity of the father deer was something which no sculptor could ever convey.

Following the deer family came a succession of all kinds of other animals, all drinking together and in dead silence. Later a party of rhinos arrived and caused quite a bit of agitation among the others who began to move off, and the silence was broken for the first time. The heavy splashing and breathing of the ungainly beasts was a sad contrast to the perfect manners of the rest. The rhinos were now left alone at the hole. Later, when they had left, came elephants in great numbers, and hundreds of warthogs and hartebeeste prowled beneath all night. At about 2:30 a.m. I went to my cabin to lie down for a bit and dozed off. I woke at 4:30 feeling very peculiar and realized that I had the worst pain I had ever felt in my life. It was in my loin and, of course, I knew at once what it was, having seen a few sufferers in my private practice days. I had, in those days, seen strong men grovelling on the floor asking to be put out of their misery from the pain of renal colic, caused by a kidney stone lodging in the ureter and causing back pressure to the kidney.

Can anyone suggest a worse location than Tree Tops to have an attack of renal colic? You are imprisoned for the night up in the trees, and cannot get out until dawn, when the ladders are lowered again. Wild beasts prowl beneath you all night. There is no resident doctor nor any pain-killer available and all one can do is to endure the agony until morning and then get a car to drive one to Nairobi, which is about a two-hour run. I will never know how I got to Nairobi, as I was only half-conscious most of the way, but I remember finding a doctor who clinched my diagnosis with tests and gave me some pain-killer. I think the stone shifted somewhat because the pain became somewhat less towards evening.

Another complication was that I had booked a flight to Johannesburg that night, which I managed to get on, despite the pain, and I arrived there in a state of semi-collapse. A friend met me and luckily knew of a good urologist, who X-rayed me, and there was the stone stuck halfway down the ureter. However, the passage was not completely blocked, so he felt I didn't require immediate surgery, but I was in two minds as to whether to continue my world tour or to fly home to Toronto in case of a flare-up. I, maybe stupidly, decided to risk it and continued to Durban where I had friends. The pain was by now only spasmodic and I could move about freely.

One of my friends took me to see the head of the Arts Council, who immediately said: 'What are you doing in May?' (It was then March.) I said I had no plans at all as I was in a process of rehabilitation. 'Will you come and do seven *Giselles* for us? We have Merle Park and Donald McCleery coming down from Covent Garden and I need a conductor.' I mentioned that I had done very little ballet, but would enjoy doing some for a change. The whole thing was tied up within a few minutes. I was to go home to Toronto, clear up all the accumulated business there, and fly back to South Africa almost immediately. I never breathed a word about my stone, which had not passed and which might flare up at any moment.

I continued on to Cape Town, which I liked very much, and joined the boat once more. The question was: 'Do I complete the voyage back to the States, or make discretion the better part of valour and fly home?' I was loath to break my original plan of sailing round the world but, on the other hand, knew very well that I was carrying an unexploded bomb in my abdomen which might go off at any minute. I was, by now, only getting sporadic jabs of pain and the thing to do was to drink as much fluid as possible and hope that it might pass. But here again I was in a dilemma. I had discovered some six years before that I suffered from glaucoma in the eyes, for which one has to cut down on all fluids. So I was between the devil and the deep sea. Anyway I started on the trip up the west coast of Africa and we called at Luanda, the capital of Angola. Here was another place I would have been very sorry to have missed. I must say Angola had been just a name on the map to me before this, and when the ship steamed into the great modern harbour, with a background of what looked like lower Manhattan with a touch of Monte Carlo, I was astounded. How little we know of the world, and how small the average person's world is!

From Luanda we moved north to Liberia where I expected to see an enormous number of ships which are registered there, but I think there was one other ship besides us in the rather small harbour at Monrovia, an untidy, rather dirty and dusty city, and after Luanda, somewhat primitive.

The remainder of the ship's run consisted of a call at Dakar in Senegal, and then a direct ten-day crossing to Florida. Did I dare risk being seized with another attack of renal colic in mid-Atlantic? I felt it would be a ridiculous gamble to make, so I flew back to New York and on home after what might very well be called an eventful journey!

I had now only a few weeks to prepare for my return to South Africa for the ballet season, and there was still no sign of the kidney stone. I went to see my doctor and he said I would be crazy to go back until the thing cleared up one way or the other; I was very keen to do *Giselle*, especially with such fine dancers, and so I lay low and silently prayed. My vigil was rewarded and on Good Friday around noon I passed the stone, much to the astonishment of the doctor, who could not see a sign of it in the X-rays.

My readers may begin to think I was a chronic invalid for a great deal of my life, but the truth is that I was always considered a very healthy person, who never had anything wrong with him at all. This was true as far as all my friends and relations knew, but for the last thirty years I had never been without some worry as to my physical condition – worry not due to psychosomatic causes, but to very real organic origins and the inevitable running down of the body, which happens to us all.

Having got rid of my trouble by natural means, I was all set to return to Durban for the ballet season, and I arrived this time in what they regard as their winter. I was met at the airport by Mr Conrad, the Arts Council music chief, who came out on the tarmac with something under his arm, and before we had walked back into the terminal he had made an impassioned appeal to get him and the company out of a hole. It appeared that, alternating with *Giselle*, there were to be performances of *Così fan Tutte* by the opera company. (The government subsidy of the arts in South Africa was amazingly generous, and each province has its own opera and ballet companies.) The conductor of the Mozart opera had apparently left Durban in the middle of rehearsals and they were in a real jam; would I take on the operas *as well?* I said I must have twenty-four hours to consider it, and we escaped through a side door into a waiting cab as the press were all waiting in the concourse to hear of my decision. The thing Mr Conrad had under his arm was a miniature score of *Così*, which he presented to me in the cab. I glanced at it and could see numerous cuts marked. I told him I hadn't looked at the score of *Così* for twenty years, and had never conducted it before, but had my own score at home in Toronto with markings made many years before at Glyndebourne when I was attending Busch's rehearsals. I asked him about rehearsals. Mr Reinhardt from the Deutsche Oper am Rhein at Dusseldorf was already at work with the cast and would direct the production. I was delighted to hear that such a fine director, whose work I had always admired, had been engaged, but how would we be able to fit in rehearsals if I was to do both productions? He seemed to think it would be possible, and he worked cleverly on me, saying that they would be in an impossible situation if I refused and maybe would have to cancel the opera, etc. So I consented to do it, and, of course, with the minimum amount of rehearsal which was available. I had to do the dress rehearsal of *Così* on the afternoon of the day that *Giselle* had its first night, and twice there was a matinée of either the opera or the ballet. Anyway the performances went well and the press was very good, but I wouldn't do it again!

I was asked to stay on for some weeks after the end of the opera-ballet season, and do some concerts with the local orchestra. I don't think I ever worked with such an unhappy crowd of people. They were at loggerheads with the management and with each other. There was no feeling of *esprit de corps* and I had none of my own scores or parts with me as I hadn't been expecting to do anything else after the ballet season. It was, I think, the only time in my life when I did not enjoy making music; to make matters worse, I fractured a bone in my foot and had to walk to the podium with my ankle strapped up, wearing a slipper, and was in great pain throughout the concerts.

I was not sorry to leave the sad country where few people smile and where everyone is anxious about their future.

18

Coda

I imagined that, as I got older, life would gradually slow down, but the opposite is what happened. As people became aware that I was a free-lance once more I began to get requests for my services in many varied activities, such as broadcast talks on subjects connected with music, of which the largest and longest was a 'History of Opera' in forty-eight weekly lectures on CJRT, the FM station of Ryerson Polytechnical Institute. This was a monumental task and needed much research. It was gratifying to find that such was the interest shown by the public in this series that it was twice repeated in its entirety during the last few years.

Besides talking on the air, I adjudicated in international competitions, including the Montreal Concours for violinists and the Van Cliburn for pianists. I conducted in many countries and took rehearsals with the students' orchestra at the Royal Academy of Music in London, the orchestra in which so many of the original Boyd Neel Orchestra members played as students.

On one of my visits to London in recent years, some old Boyd Neel players organized a reunion party of people who had played at any time in the orchestra. No fewer than thirty-two people turned up, some of whom I had not seen for the same number of years; it was an extraordinary, and often moving, experience for me. It showed how the amazing team spirit of the orchestra lived on. During the party, one old member phoned from Wales, another from Scotland, and, best of all, we had a call from Sydney, Australia, which came through at exactly the right moment when everybody had just arrived.

When I returned to Toronto, a friend in the recording business arrived with a phonograph record which he put on without comment. I was astonished when the sound suddenly burst forth from a completely silent background – no hiss or noise at all; the clarity of the instruments was extraordinary. I asked him where these remarkable records were being made and he said: 'About five minutes' walk from here. How would you like to make some?' I replied that I would like to know more about them first, and he told me they were made without any tape intervening between the microphone and the cutting needle. In other words, we were back to the days of the 78s when the vibrations of the microphone went directly to the needle cutting the wax. 'Direct-to-disc' records were a nightmare for the recording artists because, whereas in the old 78 days you could only record for about four minutes at a time, with these you made a whole side of a long-playing record, lasting maybe for twenty minutes. Not only that, but if there was a mistake, you could not just snip it out of the tape in the usual way, but had to go right back to the beginning of the record and do it all over again. So it was possible to make a perfect record for nineteen and a half minutes and then make a mistake, so that you had to start all over again. You can well imagine the effect on the nerves of the poor performer!

I was greatly intrigued and not a little awed by all this, and I found the pioneering spirit, which had so often fired me during my life, beginning to take possession once more. My friend said I could have a chamber orchestra picked for the occasion and there would be a three-hour rehearsal in the morning, followed by a break of an hour, after which we would record from two to five in the afternoon.

I realized that, with this stringent timetable, we would have to play pieces everybody knew. There was also another factor to be considered. At that time, I was almost blind, owing to cataracts in both eyes, and I was awaiting two operations. I had not been able to read for nearly a year, and therefore had to record music which I knew by heart. We started with that good old war horse, *Eine kleine Nachtmusik* of Mozart, which went well, and we got it done without undue nervous strain. The next day we did a Mozart *Divertimento* to go on the other side. Two weeks later, we did the Bach *E Major Violin Concerto* with Steven Staryk, who had to play in a kind of sheep's pen in the centre of the orchestra, and, on the next day, finished that record with three Bach transcriptions. A few months later, we did a record of English music by Thomas Arne, Elgar, and Britten. No sooner had these discs been made than we heard of even newer recording techniques, the products of which would soon come on the market. The whole recording market was in a ferment and nobody seemed to know in what direction it was moving. I realize I am considered a reactionary in these matters, but I still maintain that there has been only one major advance in recording in the last ninety years and that was the start of what became known as 'electric' recording in the late 1920s. There is a record of Mengelberg conducting *Ein Heldenleben* with the New York Philharmonic, made in 1928, which I still think is one of the best orchestral recordings ever made. That record has been broadcast on various occasions without the listeners being told anything about it until they had heard it, and it never fails to cause utter disbelief when its age is disclosed.

I am told of the wonders of stereo, but are they really so wonderful? I still play mono records frequently with the greatest pleasure, but the whole business of making records has become something no musician ever contemplated even twenty years ago. The performer has now taken a back seat in the process, and the recording is today made by a technician, not necessarily always a musician in the accepted sense, but one who has, maybe, learnt his job in a broadcast or film studio. He is a magician of tape manipulation. He can take odd bars of music which he has snipped out of a performance on tape and graft them into another performance, or even rehearsal, of the same piece, but not even necessarily by the same artist! It is a terrifying thought, but there is an instance where that actually happened. A very famous composer was recording a work of his own and could not get it completed in time before flying to some distant engagement. Nothing daunted, the technicians took the missing passage from a performance by another orchestra and another conductor and inserted it into the tape. I do not know how the record is labelled, and I do not think that this sort of thing has often happened, but it shows how careful you have to be.

I myself had a dreadful experience, not of tape-snipping, but of tape-speed alteration. This was with a reissue of a set of *Brandenburg Concertos* which I had made twenty years previously. When I came to play the records, I was horrified to find that every movement of the first three concertos was either much faster or slower than on my original recording, but, believe it or not, *the pitch was the same!* I had always thought that this was impossible, but, on making enquiries, I found that it could be done, though there were very few existing machines capable of doing it. The next question was *why* was it done, because the other record containing the remaining three concertos was an exact replica of the original recording. I immediately demanded that the whole issue be withdrawn at once. At first, the company feigned innocence of the whole affair. I was informed that, if anything was wrong, I had better get the original tapes and let the company have them. When threatened with legal action, they suddenly discovered that the wrong tape had been used in the issue and the correct one had been found, and would be used for all future pressings. But the faulty record is still being sold as my work. It is hard to believe that such things can happen. What protection has an artist against this sort of thing? Once a travesty of a performance has been issued, the damage has been done. How can anybody do a world-wide check to find out if the issue has been withdrawn? What interests me is why a tape with this travesty of my performance on it was ever made in the first place. The whole affair was mysterious and disgraceful. The making of the direct-to-disc records, however, gave me a great deal of pleasure because I felt that they were complete 'performances' with no faking possible, just as were the old 78s. I'm all in favour of 'live' performances being recorded. This is looked at askance by the tape-editing fraternity, because they couldn't then ply their trade with the scissors. I have heard, however, of a recording of an opera which was a montage or collage of eight live performances and sixty rehearsals! So the white-coated brigade had the last laugh.

I am very pessimistic about the future of recording music, unless we can get back to the real performance without gimmicks or faking. The whole world of professional music is now engulfed in electronics of all kinds. The microphone will eventually destroy music as we know it. I used to take many vocal auditions at one time and often the candidates would come on to the platform and look around helplessly. When asked what the trouble was, they would always say they were looking for the microphone and, when told we only wanted to hear them sing, they would retire in confusion. Fortunes are made by 'singers' with absolutely no voice at all. All our criteria have been turned upside-down. The human vocal mechanism may, in not many years from now, atrophy completely through disuse.

Another example of how mechanized music has become is the phenomenon of devices such as synthesizers. Why does a recording of Bach, if played on the instruments for which Bach wrote it with that particular sound quality in his imagination, sell perhaps a few thousand copies, but if the identical notes are played by a synthesizer, it will sell a million? Nobody has been able to tell me why this is, least of all the record makers, who just accept it as 'one of those things' and sit back listening to the merry ringing of the cash registers. There is, however, one work of Bach to which I might offer no objection if I heard it on a synthesizer, and that is his *Art of Fugue*, which he just wrote down, never specifying any particular instruments for its performance; we don't think he ever intended that it be played. People *do* play it, however, and several good arrangements have been made. I now await the synthesizer performance.

So few people write *quick* music any more. Most of it is slow, apparently without joy, and seems to take place in an arid vacuum of disassociated sounds. I can find little to quicken the senses and inspire. There would also appear to be a complete lack of the life-blood of music as we know it – and that is *rhythm*. Our bodies are the most rhythmic things on this planet and react with joy to corresponding stimuli in nature and art with which they can identify. Today, our nervous systems are no longer pleasantly stimulated any more, but gradually become numbed into the utter boredom with which some of the present-day composers have alienated the public.

From the early years of this century, we have been watching a gulf between composers and the public widening slowly, until, it seems to me, we have almost reached the point of no return. The 'new music' is now played to small audiences consisting largely of the composers themselves. Early in the century, the first pieces of the twelve-note composers created a suspicion among the public that all was not well, but soon these pieces seemed to be absorbed into the stream of music as the public knew it, because most of it still inhabited forms with which listeners were familiar. Since 1945, however, a music, fundamentally electronic, and cast in forms which have never yet been clearly defined, has caused the composer-audience gap to widen, almost beyond hope of reconciliation. I put this down fundamentally to the disappearance of *rhythm* as we knew it; of course, by rhythm I do not mean 'oom pah, oom pah,' but the ground swell of great music which one *feels* rather than hears – the Brownian movement of music.

Nobody could accuse me of having been a reactionary during my years in music. I have given as many world premières as most of my peers and commissioned numbers of new works from contemporary composers. But this was during a time when the language of music was still one which I could understand and in which I could always search for, and often find, beauty. I have to confess that much of the language of today sounds completely foreign to me. The happy thing is that there are still composers writing works in the language I was taught to understand and in which I can converse in a musical sense. We must always remember that Schönberg said there were still a lot of good pieces yet to be written in the key of C major.

Boyd Neel Discography
1934–1979

Records are listed chronologically by *date of recording*,
under the following headings:

78 rpm recordings made for the Decca Record Co. Ltd by Boyd Neel conducting the Boyd Neel Orchestra

Composer	Work Title of work	Soloists	Date of recording	Date of issue	Catalogue no.	Matrix no.
Holst	St. Paul's Suite, Op. 29, No. 2		4/10/34	Feb. 1935	F. 5365/6 AmD.20171/2	TB 1605/8
Elgar	Introduction and Allegro for String Quartet and String Orchestra, Op. 47	Louis Willoughby, David Martin, violins Max Gilbert, viola Peter Beavan, cello	13/5/35	Oct. 1935	K 775/6 AmD.25552/3	TA 1800/3
Mozart	Piano Concerto No. 12 in A Major, K.414	Kathleen Long, piano	18/7/35	Sept. 1935	K 772/4 Od. 263751/3 Pol.516685/7 AmD.25529/31	TA 1823/8
Mozart	Piano Concerto No. 14 in E Flat, K.449	Kathleen Long, piano	19/7/35	Nov. 1935	K784/6 Z 209/11 Od.263754/6 Pol. 516670/2 AmD.25532/4	TA 1829/34
Mozart	Divertimento in D Major, K.136		3/10/35	Nov. 1935	K 787/8	TA 1942/4
Mozart	Divertimento in F major, K.138				K 788/9 Pol.516728/30 AmD.25536/8 Od.263501/3	TA 1936/8 TA 1936/8

Composer	Work	Performers	Date	Month	Matrix	Catalogue
Mozart	Serenade No.6 in D Major, K.239 Serenata Notturna	Louis Willoughby, David Martin, violins Max Gilbert, viola John Walton, double bass	3/10/35	Feb. 1936	K 813/4	TA 1939/41
	Andante from Symphony No. 13 in F Major, K.112				K 814 Pol.516731/2 AmD.25623/4	TA 1945
Vaughan Williams	Fantasia on a Theme by Tallis	Louis Willoughby, David Martin, violins Max Gilbert, viola Peter Beavan, cello	29/1/36	Apr. 1936	K 815/6	GA7646/9
Sibelius	Romance in C Major, Op.42		30/1/36	Sept. 1936	K 831 Pol.516705 AmD.25631	GA 7650/1
Castaldi	Tarantella		30/1/36	Matrix rejected — Never issued		GA 7652
	God Save the King		30/1/36	Mar. 1936	M 500	GB 7653
Lotter	Moto Perpetuo coupled with Sistek Slavonic Scherzo rec. 17/9/36		30/1/36	Dec. 1936	K 852	GA 7654
Handel	Concerto Grosso Op. 6 No.1 in G Major	Concertino: Louis Willoughby, David Martin, violins Peter Beavan, cello, Arnold Goldsborough, harpsichord	16/9/36	Nov. 1936	X 119/20	TA 2456/8 TA 2461
Handel	Concerto Grosso Op.6 No.2 in F Major	Concertino as above	16/9/36	Nov. 1936	X 121/2	TA 2462/5
Handel	Concerto Grosso Op.6 No.3 in E Minor	Concertino as above	17/9/36	Nov. 1936	X 123/4	TA 2466/8

Composer	Work Title of work	Soloists	Date of recording	Date of issue	Catalogue no.	Matrix no.
Handel	Concerto in Grosso Op.6 No.4 in A Minor	Concertino as above	17/9/36	Nov. 1936 X 124 only Feb. 1937	X 124/6	TA 2469/72
Sistek	Slavonic Scherzo arr. Lotter coupled with Lotter Moto Perpetuo		17/9/36 30/1/36	Dec. 1936	K 852	TA 2473
Handel	Concerto Grosso Op.6 No.5 in D Major	Concertino as above	15/12/36	Feb. 1937	X 126/9	TA 2705/10
Handel	Concerto Grosso Op.6 No.6 in G Minor	Concertino as above	15/12/36	Feb. 1937	X 129/31	TA 2711/15
Handel	Concerto Grosso Op.6 No.7 in B Flat Major	Concertino as above	18/12/36	Sept. 1938	X 132/3 Z 802/3	TA 2722/3 DTA 2724/5 Retakes
Stravinsky	Apollon Musagètes		17/2/37	June 1937	X 167/70 AmD.25700/3	TA 2836/43
Sibelius	Rakastava, Op.14		1/5/37	July 1937	X 174/5 Z 783/4 AmD.25730/1	TA 3028/31
Dvořák	Serenade for Strings in E Major, Op.22	Concertino: Frederick Grinke, David Martin, violins James Whitehead, cello Arnold Goldsbrough, harpsichord	10/12/37 18/2/38	July 1938	X 214/7	DTA 3419/25 DTA 3418 Retake
Handel	Concerto Grosso Op.6 No.8 in C Minor		18/2/38	Sept. 1938	X 134/5	DTA 2726 Retake DTA 3579/81

Composer	Work	Soloist	Recording date	Release	Matrix	Issue
Handel	Concerto Grosso Op.6 No.9 in F Major	Concertino as above	21/2/38	Sept. 1938	X 136/7	DTA 3582/85
Handel	Concerto Grosso Op.6 No.10 in D Minor	Concertino as above	21/2/38	Dec. 1938	X 138/9	DTA 3586/9
Delius	Two Aquarelles, arr. Fenby		14/7/38 28/10/38	Feb. 1939	X 147	DR 2794 AR 3034
	Air Dance for String Orchestra					
Britten	Variations on a Theme of Frank Bridge, Op.10		15/7/38	Sept. 1938	X 226/8	DR2810/5
J.S. Bach	Symphony No. 2		15/7/38			DR 2816/7
Handel	Concerto Grosso Op.6 No.11 in A Major	Concertino as above	20/10/38	Dec. 1938	X 140/1	AR 3014/7
Handel	Concerto Grosso Op.6 No. 12 in B Minor	Concertino as above	20/10/38	Dec. 1938	X 142/3	AR 3018/21
Grieg	Holberg Suite, Op.40 Cowkeeper's Tune and Country Dance, Op.63 No.2		28/10/38	Dec. 1938	X 144/6 X 146	AR 3028/32 AR 3033
Mozart	Piano Concerto No.25 in C Major, K.503	Kathleen Long	3/11/38 4/11/38	Jan. 1939	X 229/32 Z 790/3	AR 3067/70 AR 3071/4
Lekeu	Adagio for String Orchestra, Op.3		6/3/39	May 1939	X 236/7	AR 3398/400
Bach	Arioso Sinfonio from Cantata No.156, arr. Franko				X 237 C. LBDX11	AR 3401
Britten	Simple Symphony, Op.4		10/3/39	Oct. 1939	X 245/7 X 247	AR 3402/6 AR 3407
J.S. Bach	Fugue in A Minor BWV 947 arr. Nicholson				C.LBDX8	

Composer	Work Title of work	Soloists	Date of recording	Date of issue	Catalogue no.	Matrix no.
J.S. Bach	Six-part Ricercare from the Music Offering BWV 1079 arr. Lenszewski		10/3/39	July 1939	K 903	AR 3408/9
Vaughan Williams	Concerto Accademico D Minor Concerto for Violin and String Orchestra	Frederick Grinke	8/5/39	Aug. 1939	X 248/9	AR 3563/6
Howells	Elegy for Viola, String Quartet and String Orchestra	Max Gilbert, viola	8/5/39	Nov. 1939	M 484/5	DR 3567/9 DR 3570
Liadov	Fuga					
Bridge	Suite for String Orchestra		10/5/39	Oct. 1939	X 250/2	AR 3571/6
J.S. Bach	Symphony in B Flat Major, Op.9 No.3		10/5/39	Aug. 1939	M 486	AR 3577/8
Pergolesi	Concertino No.4 in F Minor, ed. Franko		23/1/40	April 1940	X 148/9	AR 4259/61
Vivaldi	Largo from Concerto in D Minor		24/1/40		X 149 Z 508/9	AR 4267
Respighi	Ancient Airs and Dances, Suite No.3		24/1/40	July 1940	X 256/8	AR 4262/6
Marcello	Allegretto arr. Barbirolli from Cello Sonata in C Major, Op.1, No.5			April 1940	X 258	AR 4268
Ireland	Concertino Pastorale Minuet arr. from a Dowland suite		5/2/40	April 1940	X 253/5 X 255	AR 4285/9 AR 4290

Composer	Title	Soloist	Date	Date	Matrix	Catalogue
Vaughan Williams	The Lark Ascending	Frederick Grinke, violin	9/3/40	May 1940	X 259/60 X 260	AR 4405/7 AR 4408
	Hymn-tune: Prelude, Eventide					
Arensky	variations on a Theme of Tchaikovsky, Op.35a		15/7/40	Sept. 1940	X 261/2	AR 4860/3
Handel	Overture Faramondo arr. Rawlinson		12/8/40	Feb. 1941	K 947	AR 4968/9
Abel	Symphony in E Flat, Op.10 No.3, ed. Carse		12/8/40	Dec. 1940	K 944	AR 4970/1
Grieg	Popular Song, Op.63 No.1		13/8/40	Mar. 1941	K 954 BrzOd.283971	AR 4972/3
Grieg	Two Norwegian Melodies, Op.53		13/8/40	Mar. 1941	K 957 BrzOd.283970	AR 4974/5
Avison	Concerto in E Minor ed. Warlock		6/6/44		K 1177	AR 8573/4
Suk	Serenade for Strings E Flat Major, Op.6		6/7/44		K 1209/11	AR 8563/4
			25/9/44		AmD. Set EDA 66	AR 8571/2 AR 8565/6 Retake
Elgar	Chanson de Nuit and Chanson de Matin, Op.15 arr. W.H. Reed		25/9/44	Jan. 1948	K 1212	AR 8703 AR 8704
Handel	O sleep! Why dost thou leave me? from Semele Care selve from Atalanta	Ada Alsop, soprano		May 1946	K 1164 Lon.T 5275	AR 8986 AR 8987
J.S. Bach	Air from Suite No. 3 in D Major (also issued with Giant Fugue (rec. 4/4/45) on M 625)		16/1/45		M 595	DR 9046 DR 9047
Ireland	The Holy Boy		16/1/45			
J. Strauss	Pizzicato Polka		16/1/45		M 596	DR 9048
Grainger	Londonderry Air		16/1/45			DR 9049

Composer	Work Title of work	Soloists	Date of recording	Date of issue	Catalogue no.	Matrix no.
Grainger	Molly on the Shore Mock Morris		16/1/45	Jan. 1948	K 1215	AR 9050 AR 9051
Grainger	Handel in the Strand		16/1/45		K 1216	AR 9052
Vaughan Williams	Fantasia on Greensleeves				Lon.T5229 Lon.12017 45 rpm 40357	AR 9053
J.S. Bach	Giant Fugue BWV 680 arr. Vaughan Williams and A. Foster coupled with Air from Suite No.3		4/4/45		M 625	DR 9271
Bishop	Home, Sweet Home	Ada Alsop, soprano		Jan. 1948	K 1204	AR 9273
Flotow	The Last Rose of Summer					AR 9274
Grieg	The Hut, Op.18 No.7 From Monte Pincio, Op. 39 No.1 I Wandered One Lovely Summer's Eve, Op.26. No.2	Sophie Schönning, soprano			K 1208	AR 9459/60
Grieg	Two Elegiac Melodies, Op.34	Frederick Grinke, violin	31/5/45	Jan. 1948	K 1217	DR 9461/2
Mozart	Violin Concerto No.5 in A Major, K.219	Frederick Grinke, violin	18/6/45 19/6/45 30/10/45	July 1949	K 1268/71	AR 9507/12
J.S. Bach	Brandenburg Concerto No. 4 in G Major	Frederick Grinke, violin Arthur Cleghorn, Gareth Morris, flutes	18/6/45	Jan. 1948	K 1616/7	AR 9515/8

Composer	Work	Performers	Recorded	Issued	Catalogue	Matrix
J.S. Bach	Brandenburg Concerto No.3 in G Major		21/6/45	Sept. 1947	K 1619	AR 9519/20
Suk	Meditation on St. Wenceslas Chorale, Op.35a		21/6/45		K 1218	AR 9521/2
J.S. Bach	Brandenburg Concerto No. 1 in F Major coupled with Mortify Us through Thy Grace rec. 3/9/45	Frederick Grinke, violin / Leon Goossens, oboe / Dennis Brain, Norman Del Mar, horns	22/6/45 29/10/45	Oct. 1947	K 1514/3 Z 935/7 Amd. set EDA 87	AR 9523/4 AR 9525 retake AR 9526 AR 9778
Elgar	Serenade for Strings in E Minor, Op.20		25/6/45		K 1196/7	AR 9527/30
Mozart	Eine kleine Nachtmusik, K.525		27/6/45		K 1219/20	AR 9531/4
J.S. Bach	Brandenburg Concerto No.6 in B Flat Major		31/10/45	Dec. 1948	AK 1580/1 Lon.T 5666/7 Set LA 221	AR 9776/7 AR 9779/80
Liszt	Malédiction	Franz Osborn, piano	2/11/45		K 1194/5	AR 9463/6
Hamerik	Symphony No.6 in G Major, Op.38 Spirituelle		4/12/45		AK 1420/3 AmD.Set EDA 85	AR 9886/9 AR 9890/3 All takes rejected
J.S. Bach	Brandenburg Concerto No. 5 in D Major	Kathleen Long, piano / Gareth Morris, flute / Frederick Grinke, violin	7/12/45 9/12/47	Sept. 1948	AK 1889/91 Lon.Set LA 191	AR 11885/90
Filtz	Symphony in E Flat Major ed. Carse		19/6/46		K 1680	AR 10401/2

Composer	Work Title of work	Soloists	Date of recording	Date of issue	Catalogue no.	Matrix no.
J.S. Bach	Brandenburg Concerto No.2 in F Major	George Eskdale, trumpet Arthur Cleghorn, flute Frederick Grinke, violin Evelyn Rothwell, oboe	20/6/46	Oct. 1946	K 1550/1 Z 886/7 AmD.Set EDA 27	AR 10403/6
Michael Arne	The Lass with a Delicate Air arr. Lehmann	Ada Alsop, soprano		Oct. 1947	K 1686 Lon.T. 5371	AR 10541
Boyce	Tell me, Lovely Shepherd arr. Poston					AR 10541
J.S. Bach	I Cry to Thee, O Christ Chorale Prelude BWV 639 arr. Hodge			Never issued		AR 10543
Mendelssohn	Woe unto Them O Rest in the Lord from Elijah	Kathleen Ferrier, contralto	3/9/46	Oct. 1946	K 1556 Frequently re-issued and still available	AR 10544 AR 10545
J.S. Bach	Mortify Us through Thy Grace from Cantata No. 22, arr. Hodge. Fill-up on Brandenburg Concerto No. 1 rec. 22/6/45		3/9/46	Oct. 1947	K 1541 Z 957	AR 10546
Haydn	Piano Concerto in D Major	Kathleen Long, piano	19/9/46	Never issued		AR 10646/50
J.S. Bach	O Mensch, bewein'dein' Sünde gross. Chorale Prelude BWV 622 arr. Reger		19/9/46	Never issued		AR 10651
Finzi	Dies Natalis, Op.8	Joan Cross, soprano	29/10/46		K 1645/7	AR 10815/20

Composer	Title	Performer	Date	Issue	Catalogue	Matrix
Leigh	Concertino for Piano and Strings	Kathleen Long, piano	26/11/46	May 1948	K 1832/3 Lon.Set LA 49	AR 10883/5
Byrd	Fantasia ed. Fellowes		27/11/46		K 1833	AR 10886
Tchaikovsky	Two Entr'actes from Hamlet, Op.67		27/11/46	Never issued		AR 10087/8
Boyce	Symphony in B Flat, Op.2 No.1 ed. Lambert		27/11/46	Never issued		AR 10889/90
Boccherini	Cello Concerto in B Flat Major	James Whitehead, cello	12/12/46 13/2/48	Never issued		AR 10948/50 AR 10951/2 Retakes
Geminiani	Concerto Grosso in C Minor, Op.2		8/1/48	Mar. 1949	K 2124 Lon.T 5352	AR 11968/9
Giordani	Air Caro mio ben	Ada Alsop, soprano	17/2/48	Never issued		AR 12024
Handel	Lascia ch'io pianga from Rinaldo	Ada Alsop, soprano	17/2/48	Never issued		AR 12025
J.S. Bach	Bist du bei mir BWV 508 from the Anna Magdalena Notebook	Ada Alsop, soprano	17/2/48	Never issued		AR 12026
	Silent Night O Come All Ye Faithful	Kathleen Ferrier, contralto	6/8/48	Oct. 1948	M 622 Lon.T 5052 Still available on SPA 172	DR 12581 DR 12582
Handel	I Know That My Redeemer Liveth from Messiah	Ada Alsop, soprano		April 1949	K 2137	AR 12342/3

LP recordings made for the Decca Record Co. Ltd by Boyd Neel conducting the Boyd Neel Orchestra

Composer	Work Title of work	Soloists	Date of recording	Date of issue	Catalogue no.	Matrix no.
Holst	St. Paul's Suite coupled with Grace Williams Fantasia on Welsh Nursery Tunes		1/2/49 8/3/49 26/1/50	rejected Feb. 1951	Lon.T.5147/9 Set LA 99 LX 3025 remade Lon.IPS 94	AR 13176/8 AR 13179 AR 13179 ARL 184 DRL 184
	coupled with Britten Frank Bridge Variations (rec. 17/4/52), Warlock Capriol Suite and Serenade, and Ireland Minuet			Sept. 1972 1972	ECS 648 Lon.SDD 2195	EAL 11122/3 EAL 11122/3
Britten	Variations on a Theme of Frank Bridge		16/3/49	Feb. 1950	AK 2307/9 Lon.T. 5149/51 Set LA 100	AR 13309/14
Grieg	Holberg Suite Cowkeeper's Tune and Country Dance		24/1/50	Jan. 1951 May 1951	AX 454/6 LX 3014 Lon.LPS 173	AR 14530/4 AR 14535 DRL 353/4
Handel	Concerto Grosso Op.6. No. 1 in G Major coupled with No.2	Concertino: Maurice Clare, Ernest Scott, violins Bernard Richards, cello Thurston Dart, harpsichord	25/1/50	Feb. 1951 July 1950	LX 3027 Lon.LPS 206	AR 14536/9 DRL 377

Composer	Title	Rec. date	Issue date	Catalogue	Catalogue
Grieg	Two Norwegian Melodies Op.53	25/1/50	Never issued		AR 14544/5
Barber	Adagio for Strings, Op.11 Coupled with pieces by Bloch and Copland on music of the 20th century	26//50	May 1950 July 1951	X 305 LX 3042 Lon.LPS 98	AR 14546/7 DRL 553
Handel	Overture Faramondo arr. Rawlinson	26/1/50	Never issued		AR 14548/9
Handel	Concerto Grosso Op.6 No.2 in F Major coupled with No.1	18/4/50	Feb. 1951 July 1950	LX 3027 Lon.LPS 206	AR 154540/2 DRL 378
Handel	Concerto Grosso Op. 6 No.3 in E Minor coupled with No. 4	18/4/50	Dec. 1950	LX 3024 Lon.LPS 207	AR 18476/8 DRL 476
Handel	Concerto Grosso Op.6 No.4 in A Minor coupled with No.3	18/4/50	May 1951 Dec. 1950	AX 487/8 LX 3024 Lon.LPS 207	AR 14879/82 DRL 468
Handel	Concerto Grosso Op.6 No.5 in D Major coupled with No.6	19/4/51	Dec. 1951	LX 3055 Lon.LPS 396	AR 16068/71 DRL 811
Handel	Concerto Gross Op.6 No.6 in G Minor coupled with No.5	20/4/51	Dec. 1951	LX 3055 Lon.LPS 396	AR 16072/5 DRL 812
Handel	Concerto Grosso Op.6 No.7 in B Flat Minor coupled with No.8	3/12/51	May 1952	LX 3081 Lon.LS 543	AR 16566/9 DRL 1111
Handel	Concerto Grosso Op.6 No.8 in C Minor coupled with No.7	4/1/51	May 1952	LX 3081 Lon.LS 543	AR 16570/3 DRL 1112
Handel	Concerto Grosso Op.6 No.9 in F Major coupled with No.10	16/4/52	Dec. 1952	LX 3099 Lon.LS 585	AR 16578/81 DRL 1199
Handel	Concerto Grosso Op.6 No. 10 in F Minor coupled with No.9	17/4/52	Dec. 1952	LX 3099 Lon.LS 585	AR 17955/8 DRL 1200
Britten	Variations on a Theme of Frank Bridge coupled with Warlock Capriol Suite	17/4/52	July 1953	LXT 2790 Lon.LL 801	AR 17815/20 ARL 1636/7

Composer	Work Title of work	Soloists	Date of recording	Date of issue	Catalogue no.	Matrix no.
	Variations only reissued with Britten Soirées Musicales, Op.9 and Matinées Musicales, Op.24			May 1964	ACL 229	ARL 6241
	coupled with Holst St. Paul's Suite, Warlock Capriol Suite and Serenade, and Ireland Minuet			Sept. 1972 / 1972	ECS 648 / LON.SDD 2195	EAL 11122/3 / EAL 11122/3
Warlock	Capriol Suite for String Orchestra		17/4/52	Dec. 1955	D 71102 (45 rpm)	AR 17821/2
	coupled with Britten Frank Bridge Variations			July 1953	LXT 2790 / Lon.LL801	ARL 1637
	coupled with Warlock Serenade and Ireland Minuet			Feb. 1955	IW 5149 / Lon.LD9170	TRL 341/2
	coupled with Holst St. Paul's Suite Britten Frank Bridge Variations, Warlock Serenade, and Ireland Minuet			May 1969 / Sept. 1972 / 1972	ACL 316 / ECS 648 / Lon.SDD 2195	EAL 11122/3 / EAL 11122/3
Warlock	Serenade for Frederick Delius coupled with Warlock Capriol Suite and Ireland Minuet		17/4/52	Feb. 1955	IW 5149 / Lon.LD 9170	ARL 17823/4 / TRL 341/2
	coupled with Holst St. Paul's Suite, Britten Frank Bridge Variations, Warlock Capriol Suite, and Ireland Minuet			May 1969 / Sept. 1972 / 1972	ACL 316 / ECS 648 / Lon.SDD 2195	ARL 8604/5 / EAL 11122/3 / EAL 11122/3
Handel	Concerto Grosso Op. 6 No. 11 in A Major coupled with No.12		7/7/53	Mar. 1954	LX 3124 / Lon.LS 870	AR 18082/5 / DRL 1772/5

Composer	Work	Recording	Date	Catalogue	Catalogue
Handel	Concerto Grosso Op.6 No.12 in B Minor coupled with No.11	/ /55	Mar. 1954	LX 3124 Lon.IS 870	AR 10567? DRL 1773
Handel	Twelve Concerti Grossi Op6	25/1/50 to 7/7/53	July 1955	LXT 5041/3 Lon.LL 1080/2 set LLA 21 Lon. 5118/20 set A 4311	ARL 2200/5
			Aug. 1970 1972	ECS 550/2 Lon.SDD2187/9	EAL 2200/5
Handel	Water Music Complete	21/7/54	Feb. 1955	LXT 2988 Lon.LL1128 ACL 19	AR 19369/80 ARL 2296/7
			Nov. 1973 1973	Lon.CM9116 ECS 698 Lon.SDD 2191	EAL 2296/7
Handel	Six Concerti Grossi Op.3		July 1954 March 1955	LXT 5020 Lon.LL 1130 Lon.CM 9117	AR 19424/39
			Feb. 1956 Oct. 1969 1972	ECS 509 Lon.SDD 2193	ARL 2300/1 EAL 2300/1
Handel	Overture Alcina Overture Berenice	22/10/54	Feb. 1955 May 1960	IW5147 Lon.ID 9166 CEP 652	AR 19463/4 AR 194675/6 TRL 333/4
	coupled with Handel Water Music and Royal Fireworks Music Suites, and Clarke Trumpet Voluntary		Feb. 1974	ECS 711	EAL 11572
Ireland	Minuet arr. from a Dowland suite coupled with Warlock Capriol Suite and Serenade	22/10/54	Feb. 1955 May 1969	IW 5149 Lon.ID 9170 ACL 316	AR 19467/8 TRL 341/2
	coupled with Holst St. Paul's Suite, Britten Frank Bridge Variations, Warlock Capriol Suite and Serenade		Sept. 1972 1972	ECS 648 Lon.SDD 2195	ARL 8604/5 EAL 11122/3

78 rpm recordings made for the Decca Record Co. Ltd by Boyd Neel conducting the National Symphony Orchestra

Composer	Work Title of work	Soloists	Date of recording	Date of issue	Catalogue no.	Matrix no.
Saint-Saëns	Danse Macabre, Op.40		31/10/44	Jan. 1948	K 1289	AR 8802/3
Wolf-Ferrari	Two Intermezzi from The Jewels of the Madonna		31/10/44	Jan. 1948	K 1290	AR 8804/5
Fauré	Ballade for Piano and Orchestra, Op.19	Kathleen Long, piano	14/11/44	Sept. 1945	K 1130/1	AR 8855/8
Elgar	Bavarian Dances, Op.27 Dream Children, Op.43 No.2		6/12/44	July 1949	K 1295/6 K 1296 Lon.T 5050/1 Set LA 150	AR 8935/7 AR 8938
Mozart	Piano Concerto No.15 in B Flat K.450	Kathleen Long, piano	13/12/44	May 1945	K 1121/3 AmD Set EDA 25	AR 8964/9
Mozart	Overture The Marriage of Figaro Overture Così fan Tutte				K 1297	AR 8970 AR 8971
Thomas	Overture Raymond		6/3/47	July 1947	K 1299	AR 9020 AR 9021 Retake
Suppé	Overture Light Cavalry			Jan. 1948	K 1300 M Lon.Set LA24	AR 9022/3
Saint-Saëns	Amour, viens aider ma faiblesse. Mon coeur s'ouvre à ta voix from Samson et Dalila	Janet Howe, mezzo-soprano	10/1/45	Jan. 1948	K 1200	AR 9030/1

Composer	Title	Performer	Rec. date	Issued	Matrix	AR no.
Tchaikovsky	Adieu Forêts from The Maid of Orleans	Janet Howe, mezzo-soprano		Never issued		
Puccini	Love and Music (Vissi d'arte) from Tosca	Joan Taylor, soprano			K 1201	AR 9032
Gounod	Je veux vivre dans ce rêve from Roméo et Juliette					AR 9033
Puccini	Your tiny hand is frozen from La Bohème	Peter Pears, tenor	12/1/45	Never issued		AR 9034
Gounod	Salut! Demeure chaste et pure from Faust					AR 9035
Gounod	Jewel Song from Faust	Joan Taylor soprano			K 1202	AR 9073
Grieg	Solveig's Song					AR 9074
Mendelssohn	Capriccio Brillante for Piano and Orchestra, Op.22	Moura Lympany, piano		Jan. 1948	K 1191	AR 9206/7
Mozart	Overture Il Seraglio			Jan. 1948	K 1323 Lon.T 5442	AR 9240/1
Mozart	Overture The Impresario coupled with Overture Idomeneo rec. 12/12/45			Jan. 1948	K 1410 Lon.T 5441	AR 9242
Elgar	Concert Overture In the South, Op. 50				K 1381/3	AR 9695/99
Mozart	Piano Concerto No.23 in A Major, K.488	Clifford Curzon, piano	12/12/45	March 1948	K 1394/6 AmD Set EDA 53	AR 9917/22
Mozart	Overture The Magic Flute		12/12/45	July 1949	K 1409 Lon.T 5440	AR 9932/3
Mozart	Overture Idomeneo coupled with Overture The Impresario		12/12/45	Jan. 1948	K 1410 Lon.T 5441	AR 9934

Composer	Work Title of work	Soloists	Date of recording	Date of issue	Catalogue no.	Matrix no.
Mozart	Overture Don Giovanni		12/12/45	— Never issued on 78 rpm —		AR 10946/7
Mozart	Overtures The Marriage of Figaro Il Seraglio The Magic Flute				Lon. LLP 31	ARL.975
	Cosi fan Tutte Idomeneo Don Giovanni The Impresario					ARL.976

Subsequent LP recordings conducted by Boyd Neel

Composer	Work Title of work	Soloists	Date of recording	Date of issue	Catalogue no.	Matrix no.
J.S. Bach	Brandenburg Concerti Nos. 1, 2, and 4	Emmanuel Hurwitz, violin Leon Goossens, oboe Dennis Brain, Norman Del Mar horns Bram Gay, trumpet Geoffrey Gilbert, Phillip Goody, flutes		1956	UNIP 1040	G9-OP-9456/7
J.S. Bach	Brandenburg Concerti Nos. 5, 3 and 6	George Malcolm, harpsichord Geoffrey Gilbert, flute Emmanuel Hurwitz, violin		1956	UNIP 1041	G9-OP-9458/9
					Reissues: Concert Hall 2097/8 Reality Set 50-0439 Olympic Set 8131/2	
				1974		
Mozart	Eine kleine Nachtmusik, K.525			1956	UNIP 1042	H9-OP-25 /1

Composer	Work		Date	Label	Reissues
	Serenata Notturna, K. 239 Divertimento in D Major, K.251				Reissues: K525 — Concert Hall M600 K251 — Concert Hall A2
Dvořák	Serenade for Strings, Op.22		1956	UNLP 1044	H9-OP. 3554/5
Vaughan Williams	Fantasia on Greensleeves Fantasia on a Theme by Tallis				Dvořák Serenade reissued on Concert Hall A3

'Light Music'

Composer	Work		Date	Label	Number
Sibelius	Romance Op.42		1956	UNLP 1038	
Grieg	Two Norwegian Melodies, Op.53				
Bull	Saeterjentens Sondag				
Agrell	Sinfonia in F Major				
Arne	Air and Gigue arr. Rawlinson Dances from Comus				
Handel	Dream Music from Alcina Overture Faramondo				
Freedman	Fantasy and Allegro		Live Concert 20/6/67	CBC Radio Canada 238 Stereo	MS 6948
MacMillan	Notre Seigneur en Pauvre A Saint-Malo beau port de mer				
Surdin	Concerto for Accordion and Strings	Joseph Marcerollo, accordion			MS 6949
Somers	Scherzo for Strings				

Collection

Composer	Work Title of work	Soloists	Date of recording	Date of issue	Catalogue no.	Matrix no.
Arne	Air and Gigue			1969	Canadian Talent Library	
Fauré	Nocturne from Shylock				M 1030 mono	
					S 5030 stereo	
Champagne	Danse Villageoise					
Elgar	Chanson de Nuit Chanson de Matin					
Sibelius	Canzonetta for strings, Op.62a					
MacMillan	A Saint-Malo beau port de mer					
Byrd	Pavan					
Marcello	Allegretto					
J.S. Bach	Sheep May Safely Graze					
Symonds	Pastel for Strings					
Grieg	Cowkeeper's Tune and Country Dance					

Collection

Composer	Title	Performers	Date	Year	Label
Wolf-Ferrari	Intermezzo from School for Fathers		2/10/70		Canadian Talent Library 47-65137 stereo Reissued as 'The Boyd Neel Touch' Citadel CT 6013
Collins	Vanity Fair				
Bizet	Adagietto from L'Arlesienne Suite No.1				
Dela	Adagio Dans Tous les Cantons				
Rimsky-Korsakov	Flight of the Bumble-bee				
Wiren	March from Serenade for Strings, Op.11				
Gibbs	Dusk				
Mendelssohn	Spinning Song from Songs without Words, Op.67 No.4, arr. Burt				
Volkmann	Waltz from Serenade for Strings No.2 in F, Op.63				
Handel	Overtures Alcina Berenice Faramondo			1970	Deutsche Grammophon 2530 015 stereo
Elgar	Serenade for Strings, Op.20				
Holst	Fugal Concerto for Flute, Oboe and String Orchestra, Op.40, No.2	Nicholas Fiore, flute Stanley Wood, oboe			
Elgar	Serenade reissued on 'Music from England			July 1977	2535 259 stereo Musicasette 3335 250

Composer	Work Title of work	Soloists	Date of recording	Date of issue	Catalogue no.	Matrix no.
Vaughan Williams	Fantasia on a Theme by Tallis	CBC Winnipeg String Orchestra	Live concert 1974	1975	CBC Radio Canada SM 281 stereo	
Byrd	Pavan coupled with Leslie Mann Symphony No.1					
Mozart	Eine kleine Nachtmusik, K.525 Divertimento in D Major, K.251		6/6/77 7/6/77	1978	UMB-DD6	
J.S. Bach	O Mensch, bewein' dein' Stünde Gross		22/6/77	1978	UMB-DD9	
	Chorale Prelude BWV 622 arr. Reger					
	Prelude from Partita BWV 1006 arr. Pick-Mangiagalli					
	Six-part Ricercare from the Musical Offering BWV 1079 arr. Neel					
	Violin Concerto in E Major BWV 1042	Steven Staryk, violin	23/6/77			
Elgar	Serenade for Strings, Op.20		17/10/77	1979	ULDD10	
Arne	Air and Gigue					
Britten	Simple Symphony, Op.4		19/10/77			

Index